THE AIA STORY

$\mathcal{M}$ARTHA DALRYMPLE is a former newspaper woman and a long-time consultant to AIA. She has observed the organization's operations both in New York and in the field since its creation in 1946.

THE AIA STORY
Two Decades of International Cooperation

by Martha Dalrymple

American International Association for Economic and Social Development
50 Rockefeller Plaza, New York, New York   10020

TABLE OF CONTENTS

v

INTRODUCTION

The American International Association for Economic and Social Development had an objective that is much simpler than its name.

It was set up to do things that needed to be done but that nobody else was doing, and it was set up to be impermanent. Its whole method of operation was to encourage self-development, to improve living standards, in general to help make life a little better for people in the less fortunate areas of the world, and then to help them do it for themselves.

In 1968, twenty-two years after its incorporation, its work came to an end and it could look back on a good job well done.

In the course of these twenty-two rich and eventful years AIA has turned over nine major programs, including more than sixty separate operating activities, mostly to local governments in Latin America as well as to various private groups, both national and foreign. Also countless thousands of people have been touched, even influenced by a group of dedicated, selfless people who long antedated the Peace Corps.

For all the people involved in these years there has been a kind of magic in the sustained pattern of AIA's life: initiation of a program, involvement of the people most concerned, and eventual delivery to those same people.

Whatever success the Association can claim is due primarily to its philosophy of helping people help themselves.

Everybody who has worked with AIA has a different feeling about what it has meant. To the agronomist it has been the increase in corn production; to the home economist it has been the number of women who have learned how to cook vegetables; to the cattleman the number of heifers that have been inoculated.

1

To Wallace K. Harrison, president of AIA: "The most important thing AIA has done is to make the young people in rural Latin America aware that there is something in it for them, to bring them into the mainstream of their country's life, and to give them a better break than their fathers had."

To John R. Camp, executive vice president, AIA has meant: "A wonderful opportunity to try out some far-out schemes. They haven't all worked, but enough have to prove their worth."

And in tribute to the people with whom he has worked for twenty-two years, he adds: "AIA is made up of people who have been given an opportunity to do a job—not exceptional people or geniuses but people who are dedicated to the ideal of AIA, who have competence in their field of work, who can develop a rapport with others, who have demonstrated patience and understanding yet are persistent enough to see a job done."

And the founder Nelson A. Rockefeller sums up his feeling this way: "In my opinion AIA's staff has, in effect, created a quiet revolution. It has given people the tools—the education, the health, the opportunity—that are essential to achieve a higher standard of living.

"AIA can feel proud of being a pioneer in this field."

It has been impossible to name all who worked with AIA, both staff members and the hundreds of others, government officials, both U.S. and foreign, heads of organizations and private individuals who had more than a little to do with the organization's success. But the omissions do not indicate lack of appreciation for the genuine contribution that they all made to it.

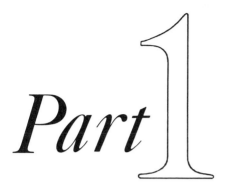

Part 1

HOW IT STARTED

A serious-minded young man stepped off a ship at La Guaira, Venezuela, one spring day in 1937 and started a chain of events that has affected the lives of millions of people.

Nelson Rockefeller had recently been made a member of the board of directors of Creole Petroleum, the Venezuelan subsidiary of Standard Oil of New Jersey. And with typical thoroughness he wanted to see for himself what the company did, where it worked, how it looked in the field.

He was pained—the oil camps were surrounded by wire fences; the people inside seldom got out except to travel to other camps; they spoke no Spanish; and they ate imported delicacies. Just outside the fence there were honky-tonk squatter towns, where people lived in disintegrating shacks, with disease and hunger their constant companions.

Rockefeller returned to New York, expounded his theories to his colleagues on the Creole board, was listened to sympathetically and was even promised some help in his one-man campaign to help the economy of Venezuela. His thesis: American capital must participate in the economic development of the country in which it is invest-

3

ing; if the people of Venezuela could enjoy a rising standard of living and American business firms be identified with that happy event, all would benefit.

In 1939 Rockefeller again visited Venezuela and called on Venezuelan President Eleazar López Contreras in the presidential palace in Caracas and solicitously asked what he thought the country needed for its economic development that U.S. capital might invest in.

Rockefeller was a little nonplussed when López Contreras said he wanted a good modern hotel to attract tourists. He said that the only people who were interested in building a hotel in Caracas were gamblers and López Contreras was not prepared to see his capital turned into a Caribbean Las Vegas. Rockefeller said he would see what he could do.

When he returned to New York, Rockefeller brought together some friends from different walks of life: Wallace K. Harrison, the architect with whom he had worked on Rockefeller Center, the economist Beardsley Ruml, and the banker Joseph Rovensky among others.

War in Europe had broken out and U.S. involvement was approaching ominously closer and closer. It was soon obvious that no U.S. hotel company wanted to venture a project in Venezuela. So Rockefeller decided to do it himself. He asked Robert Bottome, of the renting department of Rockefeller Center, to head up a group and look into the hotel possibilities. Bottome and Edward H. Robbins, also of the renting department, went to Caracas in the summer of 1939 to investigate sites and possible sources of local financing.

The two men came back filled with enthusiasm which infected the always easily infected Rockefeller. As Robbins' wife (who later, after Robbins' wartime death, became Mrs. Allston Boyer and a board member of AIA) put it:

"Nelson would ask us up to his apartment to talk over his plans. We all sat around in a circle while he gave us a solemn indoctrination in the philosophy of hands across the sea, the need to learn Spanish and the great challenge to the private sector of the United States.

"None of us was entirely sure what he meant or what it meant to us, but slowly and surely we were infected with his enthusiasm and not too many weeks later we were on our way to Venezuela to save the country single-handedly."

4

Work got started on organizing the hotel when Bottome and Robbins returned to Venezuela early in 1940, and by March the Compañía Anónima de Fomento Venezolano (Venezuelan Development Company, Inc.) was set up to invest in the hotel company as well as any other development prospects that came along. The hotel corporation was organized a few months later.

One of the first employees in Caracas was Flor P. Brennan, Venezuelan-born, married to an American and a linguist of rare ability. Both she and Mrs. Boyer were destined to have a long career with AIA, and a good part of AIA's success can be attributed to their sound judgment and their quiet but charming way of getting across what they thought was right.

Having listened to Rockefeller's persuasive arguments about the responsibilities of American business for the economic development of foreign countries, the oil companies became investors in both the Fomento and the hotel company.

The Avila hotel (named for the beautiful mountain peak that dominates the city) was designed by Harrison. It was not finished until after Pearl Harbor, so the dream of that golden stream of tourists from the United States did not materialize. Although he was faced with a probable failure Rockefeller felt he had the moral obligation to complete the project. In the long run it paid off handsomely, because for ten years after the war it was the only good hotel in Caracas, and it was the first (and a handsome one) example of modern architecture in Caracas. In effect it was the beginning of the New Venezuela.

In addition to the hotel the Compañía de Fomento was exploring other avenues of development. Most of them centered around food, since that was the crying need in the country at the moment. The production of food was an imperative concern, as was its distribution. If there were no roads, no rails, no waterways, not even mule tracks to get around, any increased production would be useless.

Wartime Coordinator's Office

However, in 1940, before any of these proposals could be pursued the world situation became darker. Rockefeller's little group was meeting again in New York to explore what private groups could do in view of

5

the dislocations caused by the war. Everybody agreed that Europe was a lost cause. It was torn and tattered and it was too late to consider any sort of rational economic development. But Latin America, where Rockefeller's recent experiences had been so vivid, loomed large in the immediate future. The loyalties of the republics of Central and South America, their support, even their neutrality, could in time prove of critical importance to the United States.

The group wrote a document, what Rockefeller called a "little memorandum." Rockefeller and Ruml took it to Harry Hopkins at the White House. Hopkins was impressed, rushed to President Roosevelt with it, and on August 16, 1940, the Office for Coordination of Commercial and Cultural Relations between the American Republics (later, after several name changes, mercifully known as the Office of Inter-American Affairs) was born, with Rockefeller as Coordinator.

The story of the wartime work of the Coordinator's Office is a whole separate story; it has been told many times and will no doubt be told many times again. However, until 1945, when Rockefeller had moved over to the State Department as Assistant Secretary of State for American Republic Affairs, the record of accomplishments was an impressive one. Even though the Office was a wartime agency, it succeeded in promulgating many economic, cultural, sociological, and educational programs which transcended even the immediate and menacing military aspects of life in those days.

One of the significant things it accomplished was to pave the way for easing the postwar letdown. It was inevitable that, as the demands of war vanished, the U.S. would resume its rather degagé attitude toward its southern neighbors and just as inevitable that these neighbors would be disillusioned and even economically hurt. Rockefeller, recognizing that a year-to-year operation, always dependent upon the generosity or mood of a skittish Congress, was not the way to make and *keep* friends, succeeded in getting authorization to set up federal corporations primarily for operations overseas. This device permitted the Office of Inter-American Affairs to commit itself to program operations for more than one fiscal year, in fact some of the corporations could sign contracts for as long as five years. This was an important consideration when the end of the war brought the end of the Office. The corporate device helped to bridge the gap between wartime cooperation with Latin American countries and their complete independence.

In the Department of State, Rockefeller continued his close association with the Latin American countries, shepherding common interests through the Inter-American Conference on Problems of War and Peace at Mexico City from which emerged the Act of Chapultepec, so-called from the stately palace in which the conference met. This document provided that aggression upon one American state by another would be regarded as aggression against all and in effect laid the groundwork for collaboration in many fields in the future. In addition it set forth an Economic Charter of the Americas which recognized the right of peoples to follow . . . "their fundamental economic aspirations . . . to live decently . . . to work and exchange goods productively . . . in peace and security." The delegates agreed that this "aspiration must be given full recognition in . . . a positive economic program . . . through cooperation which will provide for full use of labor, management and capital in the efficient economic development of the agricultural, industrial and other resources of the Western Hemisphere."

From here Rockefeller moved on to San Francisco where the United Nations Charter was hammered out. His role was that of champion of Western Hemisphere interests, with many political alarms and excursions on the side. He pitched into these with enthusiasm but they did not divert him from his single-minded purpose of economic and social development in all underdeveloped countries in Latin America.

Postwar Planning

The day after he resigned as Assistant Secretary of State on August 26, 1945, Rockefeller returned to New York and called together the group, now enlarged to include some wartime colleagues. The nucleus, in addition to Harrison, included John E. Lockwood, prominent New York attorney who had served as Counsel for the Coordinator's Office; Francis A. Jamieson, newspaperman, winner of the Pulitzer prize and head of the information operations of the Office of the Coordinator; Berent Friele, a former A&P executive who had been active in the Brazilian segment of the Office program, and

7

Kenneth J. Kadow, former head of the Department of Horticulture at the University of Delaware and head of the Coordinator's program in agriculture in Brazil.

The goal of their meetings, in Rockefeller's words, was to "see if wartime unity and cooperation with the United States could be translated into peacetime cooperation for economic development and a rising standard of living."

He had little use for members of the U.S. government whose position of diplomatic soothing of postwar problems, particularly with the Russians, seemed to him not the way to get on with the job.

"It disturbed me very much because it seemed to me we had to be leaders, not reconcilers."

Another factor that spurred these meetings to action was Rockefeller's sense of personal responsibility.

"Having been a spearhead for the Administration in Latin America during the war, and having made many speeches about our intentions as a nation to carry on wartime cooperation as a permanent thing, I felt a real personal responsibility."

L to R—Berent Friele, Eduardo Mendoza, Venezuelan Minister of Agriculture, Nelson Rockefeller and Juan Pablo Pérez Alfonso, Venezuelan Minister of Development, conferring in Caracas in 1947.

In view of the fact that there seemed little or no disposition on the part of the new administration or of Congress to carry out a post-war official program of cooperation, Rockefeller felt his position more keenly than ever. Actually the government had already abolished or cut deeply into those departmental budgets set up for cooperation with Latin America.

Rockefeller tells of a conversation he had with a Brazilian journalist "who is a poet and a business man—one of those combinations you find more in Latin America than in the U.S. He told me of the tremendous rise in confidence and hope in Brazil during the war as a result of the association with the U.S. They had gained self-confidence and felt that they had arrived on the world scene. They were looking forward with tremendous enthusiasm.

"Then they were dropped by the U.S. Their new-found confidence disappeared and they felt like lost children. As my friend said these things, tears ran down his face, because this thing was to him a disaster for his country and, being a very sensitive person, he felt it personally.

"This helped to determine me to see whether private effort couldn't make a small start in this direction."

In the family offices on the 56th floor of the RCA Building in Rockefeller Center, the group or segments of it met everyday. Numberless ideas flew around and more questions were asked than were answered. What sort of an organization? What sort of programs? Where to set up in business? Who would do what?

The general consensus finally was to organize a foundation which would have two parts—one non-profit and one profit-making. The profits from the latter would be fed into the former, which theoretically was to perform those functions that could not be put on a paying basis, namely the truly welfare operations, which in this country are largely performed by government.

From the beginning, Lockwood, who never let his emotions interfere with the cool, clear logic of his legal mind, warned Rockefeller that combining the two functions would not work out.

"One of these should be a Sunday company and one should be a weekday company," he insisted. "That is in the historical, puritan,

9

and protestant tradition of this country—make money all week and tend to your eleemosynary operations on Sunday."

It was not until some time later that Rockefeller faced the cold legal facts.

Names for the Foundation were suggested—the Simón Bolívar Foundation, in honor of one of the great Liberators of South America, was one of the first. Others included International Development Foundation, Universal Development Foundation, Economic Development Foundation, the Peoples Foundation, Basic Economy Foundation.

At one point fourteen names were submitted for clearance to the Secretary of State of New York—and all of them contained either "economic development" or "basic economy," which was indicative of the direction the group's thinking was taking.

Among the statements of purpose that were whipped out during those days was this one:

> The Foundation shall be dedicated to the economic and social advancement of the peoples throughout the world. It is dedicated to the dignity and the rights of man. It recognizes that poverty, hunger, sickness and ignorance in any part of the world are a constant threat to the welfare and security of all the world.

AIA is Born

At last the American International Association for Economic and Social Development was incorporated under the Membership Corporation Law of the State of New York on July 1, 1946. Rockefeller, Jamieson, Friele, Harrison and Lockwood were the original members and Kadow was named Director of Operations. Its purposes were spelled out as follows:

> Based upon a faith in the inherent dignity and worth of the individual and in the capacity and desire for self-improvement of human beings of whatever nationality, race, creed or color, and upon a conviction that the welfare of each nation and person in the modern world is closely related to the welfare and opportunities for advancement of all the people of the world, this Association is organized for the purpose of promoting self-development and better standards of living, together with understanding and cooperation, among peoples throughout the world.

Both the name and the statement of purpose were wordier than earlier versions, which is a common fault of documents produced by committees. But the document expressed the whole philosophy.

Rockefeller personally contributed $72,775 for the year 1946; his brother Winthrop joined him the second year as did four oil companies operating in Venezuela to the tune of $275,466. Before the program operation was terminated, Rockefeller and his family had made total contributions of $7,605,000; the oil companies accounted for $5,695,000 and other contributors, both corporations and individuals, had given $1,224,000 to make a grand total of $14,524,000 which AIA received and expended over a period of twenty-two years.

The contributions to joint programs by AIA's partners, federal and state governments, international organizations, and private groups and individuals cannot even be estimated, since they include, in addition to actual cash, goods and services, office space, traveling facilities, and personnel that worked on programs. In dollar value they amount to several times AIA's contributions.

AIA was in business but a slight hitch arose. Wise legal minds decided that AIA could not be the two-headed, schizophrenic operation that would have resulted. They decreed that the profit-making operation must be divorced from the non-profit. As Rockefeller later ruefully recalled:

> Our original idea of having everything under one philanthropic umbrella, with the money made by the business concerns supporting the other, didn't work out. The laws of the United States didn't permit it. These were all things that a lot of people knew about, but I had to work it out, step by step—the hard way.

So on January 9, 1947, the business operations were lumped together into an organization called International Basic Economy Corporation (IBEC) which also is a separate story. However, it is interesting to note that the first thing IBEC did made history. It combined a social mission with profit goals and insisted upon having a preamble written into its certificate of incorporation, a thing unheard of in Albany at that time. It was what Lockwood called Sunday language.

> We, desiring, in association with others to promote the economic development of various parts of the world, to increase the production and availability of goods, things and services

useful to the lives and livelihood of their peoples, and thus to better their standards of living, and believing that these aims can be furthered through a corporation dedicated to their fulfillment and employing scientific and modern methods and techniques, do hereby form a stock corporation.

Wordy—but the ideas are all there. And today, IBEC, which had revenue of over $200,000,000 in 1967 and with 130 subsidiaries in 33 countries, is still true to its preamble.

Part 2

EARLY DAYS

From the beginning AIA's program was catalytic—in an effort to teach and stimulate others to do things better by and for themselves. AIA believed that the responsibility for solving each country's problems was in the hands of the people of that country, and AIA's function comprised two parts: training people and developing institutions to do the job.

The very heart of all AIA programs has been the training effort. Technical assistance implies training and showing people how to use new and better methods of doing things. It also means stimulating people to become interested in applying new ideas and, in turn, to interest others in what they have learned.

"This means that AIA's personnel not only have to be competent professionally," says John Camp, "but they have to be able to teach others and to devise effective training methods and processes, all of this in the underdeveloped environment of Latin America."

People and Institutions

AIA's training activities have been carried on largely outside formal educational institutions except where teacher training has been involved or where new education methods have been introduced into a going educational institution.

Training activities were carried on at all levels, first at the job level itself, teaching farmers better practices, farm women better health and homemaking methods, and youngsters learning-while-doing projects. The next was training local technicians how to teach and work effectively with rural people, not in a classroom environment but on an informal basis on the farm and in the farm home and the rural community. A further step was the training of teacher trainers. Finally, there was the informal type of training carried on by AIA directors and technicians at all levels of public administration, from cabinet ministers on down, demonstrating how agricultural, health and education programs are organized and carried out in an orderly and effective manner.

Specifically, AIA's grass-roots level training was designed to introduce better farming practices and new methods to thousands of small farmers. Along with this went the training of equal numbers of farm and village women in better homemaking and health practices and the training of rural youth through 4-H club type programs.

The development and improvement of Latin American institutions to serve the needs of their people was another basic element in all AIA programs. Training rural people and technicians, while a worth-while activity in itself, is immeasurably more productive if an improved extension service, credit institution or other public service is developed to continue the work. With many Latin American countries only recently beginning to change their archaic government systems to provide modern institutions to serve the modern popular needs, there is a tremendous need to provide well-organized, efficient public services.

As a corollary to its training efforts, AIA endeavored to help Latin American countries create the types of institutions and services needed to meet the demands of their people, particularly in the agricultural, health and education fields. This was not a simple process of using U.S. organizations as models, although many Latin American countries have copied or adapted their service organizations from the U.S. Classic examples in the agricultural field are extension services and farm credit institutions.

14

An important aspect of AIA's contribution to institution building has been its ability to experiment, improvise and test out on a small scale the practicality or need for a service before it was established full-blown on a national basis. This meant that extension services and credit programs were proven first on the farms and in rural communities before they were expanded into national programs. Nutrition education techniques were tested in the rural communities and poor urban sections before becoming part of a national campaign. New methods or approaches in vocational teacher training were proven first in an experimental school selected for this purpose before being introduced into the national system.

This way of doing things was contrary to the usual governmental approach of creating the institution first on a national basis and then developing the program. Latin American governments and the laws that create their institutions of public service are generally quite rigid and do not allow for experimentation. With its flexibility and freedom to innovate, AIA has been able to help improve established institutions and assist in the creation of new ones on a sound organizational basis.

While institution building may sound like a prosaic and bureaucratic process, it is nonetheless an important part of economic and social development in the Latin American countries. Training people is not enough if they do not have modern, efficient organizations in which to work. AIA's efforts have been directed toward developing and improving institutions in which trained people can work more effectively.

Nelson Rockefeller himself had a simple way of defining what AIA was to stand for.

"The ideal of AIA is human welfare," he wrote, in the initial issue of *The AIA Record,* a periodical devoted to telling of AIA progress.

"Tomorrow's world, bright with promise of better living, needs new highways for the march of science and technology over the obstacles of language, race and customs. AIA is one way of bridging these gaps between people so that the benefits of science and the new technology can spread more widely over the earth."

By a process of natural selection the determination was made to concentrate AIA's programs in two countries: Venezuela and Brazil, the former because of Rockefeller's interest, commitment and knowledge, the latter because of Kadow's and Friele's experience and knowledge of the needs and potentials of that area. In addition they represented two diverse economies, with widely varied problems and assets. Brazil was coffee-poor, Venezuela was oil-rich. Brazil was huge, with large tracts still unexplored, Venezuela was small in comparison, with its farm and ranch lands scattered from the formidable Andes range to the Orinoco jungle.

The feeling was that any projects carried out in these two countries could serve as useful prototypes for almost any other underdeveloped area in the world.

First Projects

Just a month after AIA's incorporation papers had been signed, a virulent and sudden hog cholera epidemic broke out in Brazil and rapidly spread through the states of Rio Grande do Sul, Paraná, São Paulo, and parts of Minas Gerais. Harried Brazilian government officials appealed to Dee Jackson, a long-time resident of Brazil who had

L to R—Wallace K. Harrison, Francis A. Jamieson, John C. McClintock and Nelson Rockefeller take off for Latin America.

16

just been appointed AIA Brazil representative. Available vaccine supplies were rapidly running out, the government had little foreign currency available with which to import additional supplies, and other measures of control were proving ineffective. The Ministry of Agriculture saw the country's hog industry threatened with extinction.

AIA agreed to make available one of the U.S.'s leading veterinarians and supplies of vaccine. Early in October the specialist arrived in Rio de Janeiro and within days was making tests in the field, accompanied by the top Brazilian animal specialists. He determined the best vaccine, established a set of rules for the safeguarding of both the production and application of the vaccine and outlined strict procedures to reduce the hazards of contagion.

In December, Rockefeller, Jamieson and Kadow went to Brazil and on their return, at a January board meeting, were able to report:

> The emergency hog cholera project has been satisfactorily completed and as a result of the technical assistance given by the Association, the Brazilian government has enacted new laws which will greatly facilitate the control of hog cholera and has established on a proper basis both laboratory facilities and services for distributing and administering serums.

The total expenditure was $8,486.40.

Shortly after the initiation of the hog project, AIA authorized a program in home demonstration, to help improve Brazil's nutrition, domestic and personal hygiene, sanitation and child care, including the training of personnel to work in that field. Again the travelers were able to report to the January meeting that the Brazilian government had already started the tedious work of creating a new, autonomous home demonstration service, was interviewing applicants, reported that it had a long waiting list of institutions wanting to hire the graduates, and had started to build a school.

The same board meeting had the agreeable task of considering an offer by a Brazilian subsidiary of Corn Products Refining Co. to give the Association $25,000 a year for improved seed production (particularly hybrid seed), warehousing, nutrition and scientific and technical services. It was voted to accept the offer, thus paving the way for much larger and more impressive contributions by the oil companies in Venezuela.

17

The Corn Products gift actually resulted in development of a hybrid corn seed company which has become one of IBEC's most successful operations. From an initial output of 143 tons of seed in 1948, the company's production has risen steadily to 14,300 tons in 1967. It is by far the biggest commercial producer of hybrid corn seed in Brazil and one of the half-dozen largest in the world. Hybrid seed, which was practically unknown to Brazilian farmers when the company started, today is used in more than 30% of the area planted to corn—and about half the hybrid seed is IBEC's.

Incidentally, a second grant by Corn Products was accepted by AIA with the proviso that it be used in connection with nutrition alone and not for seed development, in order to avoid any suggestion that it was being used to benefit the donor company.

Rockefeller and various of his associates traveled back and forth to Brazil and Venezuela during these early months. He talked to government officials, high and low, he talked to social scientists, to educators, to farmers. He wanted to know what was needed, how AIA could help achieve it, and how much the locals would contribute to doing the job.

Rockefeller's own enthusiasm was matched by that of people who had genuine concern for their country's welfare. In fact, there was danger that hopes would outrun accomplishments thus leading to a disastrous letdown.

"My neck was stuck out about five miles," Rockefeller says of these first explorations.

Meanwhile an old friend, Dr. James Yen, who headed up the so-called Mass Education Movement, Inc. had been in touch with AIA hoping to get a literacy project off the ground. This proposal entitled "Aid to People's Film Project of Chinese Education Movement," called for a $100,000 contribution to produce and distribute audio-visual teaching materials in various fields including health, sanitation and nutrition. AIA had agreed to contribute the $100,000, provided eight motion picture companies contribute the same amount in blocked Chinese currency, and that another organization, United Service to China, designed to support Christian colleges, medical missions and mass education in China, contribute $90,000. This project remained on AIA books from October 30, 1946, until December 3,

1948, when it was apparent that the other two contributions would not be forthcoming.

This was the first and last time, with one later exception, that AIA went outside the Western Hemisphere. The other occasion was in 1955 when AIA embarked on a rural credit and farm rehabilitation program in India, in a joint venture with the Cooperative League of the USA. It was a modest little program, the core of which was a pilot demonstration area in some fifteen villages clustered at Mehrauli, near New Delhi. Small short-term loans to the poorest farmers and demonstration sessions were the principal techniques. The program worked on only two or three principal crops, emphasizing the need of improved seed and use of fertilizer and insecticides which were bought by the Indian Cooperative Union and distributed in the form of loans in kind.

As the local project personnel gained experience and became better trained, the program was broadened to include medium-term loans for such needs as oxen and farm equipment, and joint loans for wells and irrigation systems.

Administration of this program was turned over early to the Cooperative League and in 1960 AIA, primarily for reasons of logistics, severed its connections. It is still being carried out by the Indian Cooperative Union, supported by the U.S. League.

Furthermore, the Mehrauli project served as proving ground and prototype for a later widespread $10,000,000 program, financed by the Ford Foundation.

Training Young Farmers

The Inter-American Institute of Agricultural Sciences was an organization set up by the governments of the twenty-one American republics, with headquarters then in Turrialba, Costa Rica. Its primary purpose is to encourage and advance the development of agricultural sciences in the Americas through research, teaching and extension activities in the theory and practice of agriculture and related arts and sciences.

The idea of the Institute had been vigorously advanced by Henry A. Wallace, then Secretary of Agriculture and strongly supported by Rockefeller when he was Coordinator of Inter-American Affairs. His concern was that Latin America was unable to supply her own needs, much less make contributions to the wartime needs of the Allies.

With the enthusiastic support of leaders of the hemisphere the Institute came into being in 1942, a small and struggling organization trying to do a man-sized job. Its first director, Dr. Ralph Allee, was very anxious to have a demonstration farm, for both training and research purposes. But the slim budget that the twenty-one republics provided to the organization would not spring to such an expense. Coordinator Rockefeller, well aware of the importance of the work Allee was trying to do, made an indefinite promise just before he left Washington to return to private life that he would see what he could do to get some private help.

When AIA was set up this was one of his first thoughts, but his associates, somewhat more hardheaded, said that AIA had to have something to show for its generosity.

Venezuelan students receive instruction in the greenhouse at
Turrialba, Costa Rica.

In view of the fact that the decision had already been made to start work in Venezuela, it was decided to ask the Institute to train potential rural leaders from that country. And Dr. Allee was delighted with the prospect. As he said, "it is our conviction that no field within our very broad mandate is more important than that which involves the training of farmers and farm families to use the advances made by science."

To this end AIA and the Institute signed an agreement in June, 1947, under which AIA would provide $158,000 over a period of two years and the Institute agreed to set up a demonstration farm on the rich rolling acres at Turrialba to train not less than ten and not more than twenty young Venezuelans each year in the hard realities of making a living as farmers. The farm, a general demonstration one, was to be run on a sound business basis and was to include beef and dairy cattle, hogs, a creamery and dairy, a poultry enterprise, the production of fresh vegetables, fruits and feed crops as well as training in the use and maintenance of agricultural equipment.

The first group of trainees, ten of them, arrived in Turrialba in September, 1948, just nine months after the project was scheduled to start. The delay had been largely due to construction problems at the farm but also to the difficulties of determining exactly the type of student that was wanted and the exact curriculum that would be most advantageous. It was finally decided that the program should emphasize well-rounded training in all rural activities rather than training in specialties, and to limit to two the advanced students who would be accepted each year for specialization.

All of the young men selected had agricultural backgrounds, recognized the problems of rural living in their country and, above all, exhibited sincere intentions of returning to their own local areas where they could hopefully become leaders in helping to solve some of these problems. Although some administrative problems were developing by 1950, the students themselves seemed to be enjoying their experience and getting a great deal out of it. On their own volition an Alumni Association was set up, and a small newspaper, *The Bugle,* was published.

In 1950 there were twenty students, but Dr. Allee asked that the number be reduced to ten. He pleaded a forced reduction in his

Students learn how to display and sell their produce.

budget, but hoped that the number of students could eventually be increased, perhaps even reach twenty-five or thirty. AIA agreed and reduced the number of students to twelve.

By 1954, not only had the Institute's financial situation worsened so that it was more and more hard pressed to fulfill its commitments, but, in addition, a hard look at the program revealed certain basic weaknesses:

1. Training in agricultural skills, it was found, should really be performed nearer the place where the students are going to apply their training. Customs, climate and soil are all factors in the intelligent application of scientific knowledge.

2. The Institute was fundamentally a postgraduate and research-oriented institution and was not too well adapted to conduct undergraduate practical training.

3. On the whole the students returned to Venezuela to perform many useful tasks—the most effective of which seemed to be extension work. It was agreed that Institute training in this area would be more effective if raised to the graduate level.

22

So the agreement with the Institute was modified to provide for postgraduate training for not more than six students a year. In addition some short-course training in agricultural and related skills was offered.

But an even greater blow fell. Shortly after the agreement was signed and the Venezuelan Ministry of Agriculture had agreed to pay travel and living costs of the students, the governments of Venezuela and Costa Rica, because of political tensions, severed relations. Under the circumstances Venezuelan students were not permitted to study in Costa Rica.

So the agreement remained inoperative until 1958 when normal diplomatic relations were resumed. But even so, the Venezuelan government was reluctant to avail itself of the scholarships available— probably for reasons of political expediency.

So in 1961 what remained of the scholarship program was transferred to the newly established Mass Communications and the Rural Youth programs, about which more later.

Although the program did not pan out as envisioned, it provided training to eighty-two young agriculturists. Of the nineteen members of the first class, all except three returned to agricultural pursuits in their own country and in part have helped to account for the great increase in food production in Venezuela.

For example, Evelio Tovar, then a bright-eyed young man with boundless enthusiasm, was an early graduate of Turrialba. Today he is a bright-eyed mature man still with boundless enthusiasm after having put his training to use in twenty years of service to the agricultural development of his country. He is Executive Secretary of the Venezuelan 5-V Association (the Venezuelan equivalent of the 4-H Club Foundation of the U.S.).

Froilán Romero has a progressive cattle ranch south of Lake Maracaibo and is a leader among livestock producers; Pedro Bereciartu is a special advisor to the Minister of Agriculture and has been mentioned as a candidate for the presidency of the new Agricultural Development Bank; Alberto Bruzual is an expert in national parks for the Department of Renewable Resources and was one of the organizers of the first Latin American Conference on National Parks, held in Caracas in 1967; others are extension agents, teachers, farmers and specialists in various agricultural pursuits.

Even the three non-agriculturalists have made their mark—one is a writer of some fame and Cultural Director for the Government of the State of Bolivar; one is Director of the National Transit School of the Ministry of Communications; and the third runs a highly successful school for theatrical productions in Caracas.

Organization and Staff

By January, 1947, AIA had qualified in Brazil, had appointed a representative in Rio and had persuaded Dr. John B. Griffing, a long-time agricultural worker and resident of Brazil, to join the staff as the Association's very first technical man. He was later to head the whole program in Brazil.

Early in the year Rockefeller could report that his negotiations with the oil companies had resulted in agreements to provide $13,000,000 total contributions from them for programs in Venezuela.

By March, 1947, AIA had qualified in Venezuela, and John Camp, a forester by profession, with previous experience as head of the Institute of Inter-American Affairs', agricultural programs in Paraquay and Venezuela, was appointed the Association's representative.

From then on things moved fast in both countries. Programs were proposed, programs were disposed. Offices were engaged, furniture bought. Staff was hired locally when possible, and when not, U.S. specialists were lured to the new venture.

Some of these early pioneers who went to far-out places in both Brazil and Venezuela had some quick and dramatic indoctrination into new ways of life.

One staff member recalling a trip through the Andes "by car, taxi, bus, railroad, lake steamer, tri-motored Ford, and on foot," said:

One of my drivers would insistently lean on his horn as we entered a town for luncheon or the night. Why? To alert his cousins. He had a lot of female 'cousins.'

On a large farm near the southern end of Lake Maracaibo I was impressed by a tractor-drawn disc harrow and a giant boa cut up into six-inch lengths. Seems that the driver was harrowing

24

Para grass pasture when the boa's head appeared behind. The driver crawled on to the hood of the tractor praying that the harrow's discs would do the job they did.

I remember I had to leap over a dead cow to get into the front door of the "Hotel Universe and Both Poles" at Cumaná. One's bed was a hammock slung on hooks in the wall. Next morning everybody had to lift up their feet to let the water flow across the patio as each new guest washed and brushed his teeth in a sink that had no drain pipe.

In touchy political areas my son Charlie and I have discharged our shotguns under cover of exploding saints' day rockets. Shot ducks from trees in the llanos and in the swamps of northwestern Venezuela where I have seen Charlie race crocodiles to retrieve the canvasbacks.

We have killed crocodiles on the Apure and seen them savaged by piranhas and gone tiger hunting and brought home wild pig in lieu of. Also monkeys which didn't howl but cried like babies.

We have slept in hammocks in the open jungle and in smoke-filled black thatched huts, eating rabbit-iguana stew for breakfast while the family we stayed with had an orgy over a giant stork I had shot.

But despite exposure to jungle life, the staff survived. New members were even enticed into the fold. The end of the year saw the resignation of Kadow and the appointment of Robert W. Hudgens, a long-time worker in the New Deal-inspired Farm Security Administration of the U.S. Department of Agriculture, as director.

At this time the permanent structure of AIA was set. With one exception, its basic organization was not to change until it ceased operations at the end of 1968.

That one exception was the absorption of a non-profit entity named Ibec Research Institute into AIA in late 1957.

The Institute had been created by Rockefeller and his brother David back in 1950 to do technical agricultural research in very basic fields. The Institute, commonly known from its initials IRI, was set up to do scientific experimental work in order to bring about more efficient, and thus more bountiful farm production.

At the time IRI became the scientific research division of AIA in 1957, it was working on increasing high quality protein foods—meat, milk and eggs—through simultaneous studies on soil fertility, forage plants and animal nutrition.

Results of IRI's research were published in a series of technical bulletins and notes in English, Portuguese, and Spanish which were distributed to interested agricultural colleges, research and extension workers, and leading agriculturists in almost all countries of the world.

The merger of AIA and IRI was originally dictated by logic— both organizations were working in the same geographical location and in the same general field of rural rehabilitation. It was felt that the scientific findings of IRI which was working primarily in Brazil would need the extension effort of AIA to filter them down to the farmer in his field.

However, the difficulties of combining two such operationally diverse groups proved too much for efficiency and some five years later the merger was dissolved.

IRI went its own way in 1963, and today is continuing its work in Brazil, largely under contract with USAID. It has concentrated on building the research institutions of the Ministry of Agriculture and also state organizations. Currently IRI has about 30 U.S. scientists working with more than 200 Brazilian scientists on over 150 projects in all parts of the country. Furthermore, about 50 young Brazilian scientists are studying for M.S. or Ph.D. degrees in the United States.

In its work IRI has developed a legume "IRI 1022" which has been bred from various native plants at its experimental farm at Matão. This legume appears to have many desirable characteristics— animal acceptability, the ability to remain green during the cool dry winter in Central Brazil and, most important, the ability to fix atmospheric nitrogen. Other IRI experiments have proven that applications of nitrogen can more than double the production of beef from approximately 300 pounds per acre to nearly 700 pounds per acre. Obviously it is more economical to obtain nitrogen from the atmosphere than to apply chemical fertilizers. "IRI 1022" is the first step toward finding the ideal forage legume for the tropics.

IRI has concentrated considerable effort on the "campo cerrado" areas of Brazil, which are potentially arable land but are currently in scrub brush and used only for grazing. IRI has demonstrated that with lime and fertilizers, including micro-elements, the "campos cerrados" are capable of producing many crops. Over 100 bushels of corn per acre have been produced and the experimental station at Brasilia has grown a number of vegetable crops and pasture grasses on these soils.

We shall see later in this book how this work of IRI in the "campos cerrados" has complemented AIA's work in this same area.

Operational Techniques

By early in 1958, an important part of the operational philosophy of AIA was developed. Everybody agreed that it was of paramount importance to get the local government or agency or group or individual deeply involved in each program so that when AIA's pump priming ministrations were terminated there would be left not only the will but also the mechanics with which to carry the program forward.

The so-called "servicio" program developed by the Coordinator's Office during the war was the pattern AIA chose to follow. The servicio was an agency created under local laws, to which both the appropriate local government agency and the Coordinator's Office contributed funds, personnel and material. It had the advantage of autonomy and yet carried the umbrella of protection of the national government. The U.S. government later discarded the device, to the detriment of our foreign aid program in the opinion of many observers.

AIA took the servicio principle one step further and tried to create an actual legal entity with a life and character of its own to which the two partners contributed sometimes equally, sometimes disproportionately. While the servicio was a government-to-government arrangement, the AIA development represented a union of private non-profit and local government efforts.

The form of these legal entities varied from country to country and even within a country. Some were temporary, some were permanent. However, the primary objective was to insure as far as possible the continuance of the program by seeing to it that the local entities had a real, even though bureaucratic, investment in it.

AIA protected itself from local political control or influence by insisting on carefully defined goals and objectives written into the charters of these organizations. Also included in these charters were a veto power on the selection of the director and the right of approval of the annual budget and program of work. These provisions were accepted locally as long as AIA was a substantial participant in the program. However, even in the case of the Venezuelan entity where, at the end, AIA's participation was only on a token basis, the Venezuelan government was inclined to accept AIA advice and guidance because of its reputation for complete objectivity and its concern for national agricultural programs.

Another operating device that AIA developed was the Special Commission used first in Venezuela and later in Chile to carry out education programs. Here an effort was made to introduce needed reforms into national educational systems. These reforms had to be tested first on an experimental basis, so the Special Commission was created by agreement between AIA and the national Ministry of Education to do the experimental work. As the new methods and techniques were proven out, they were introduced into the country's educational system at the time the budget was being prepared and new education legislation was being proposed.

Thus in the highly sensitive area of education AIA was able to operate under the umbrella of an official agency of the government and still make its influence felt through membership on the Special Commission.

Still a third form of international cooperation wedded AIA to the Inter-American Institute of Agricultural Sciences of the Organization of American States (OAS) in 1958, in order to carry out three basic hemisphere-wide programs as we shall see later.

This was perhaps the trickiest partnership to work out, and is certainly unique in the history of international cooperation. The Institute is an inter-governmental organization with all that is entailed in having to respond to a board of directors chosen from among the twenty-three members of the OAS. Even though AIA and the Institute had common goals and objectives, how could an effective operating structure be set up by two such disparate organizations?

The solution lay in dividing the load: AIA designed and carried out programs that would assist the Institute in meeting its own goals and would assist the individual countries themselves in developing their own operational programs. AIA as a fairly freewheeling private group was in a much better position to do a quick and effective job, even experimental at times, than the larger, slower-moving Institute.

In return the Institute gave the programs its official sponsorship, the use of personnel and office space, and entree under the very highest auspices to the individual countries.

Another principle that was early set forth by AIA directors, and generally adhered to in all its programs, was the descending scale of financial contributions by AIA and the ascending scale of contributions by the local partner. This was perhaps one of the most effective devices that AIA pioneered. Again the bureaucracy of the system came to the aid of the program—it is much easier to get an established budget renewed than it is to get a brand new one initiated.

In each case a written agreement was signed between AIA and the cooperating agency. A glance at the appendix of this book will reveal that these agreements were models of brevity. AIA from the beginning insisted that these documents set forth the broad principles and the financial responsibilities. But all details of administrative and program operation were left to the discretion of the board of directors of the joint operation. AIA's philosophy was that if there were not enough trust between the partners, the arrangement wouldn't work anyway—no matter how many hundreds of pages the agreement ran.

Part 3

BRAZIL

One cool day in June, 1967, a select group of U.S. agricultural technicians and some of their Brazilian friends were lunching at the Gloria Hotel in Rio. The guest speaker was Victor Pellegrini, farm management specialist who at that time headed the Rural Economics Department of the Brazilian Ministry of Agriculture.

He spent some time lauding the work of AIA in Brazil. His audience nodded wisely if soporifically; they knew all about AIA and agreed with him.

"But do you know what is the best thing AIA ever did? It was to get out."

Pellegrini's audience suddenly woke up.

"When Nelson Rockefeller first came to Brazil and he and his colleagues set up AIA they all said that the goal was to get a program well-started, train people to do it, and then get out. And they have kept their promise."

To some people this would have been faint praise indeed. But to Walter Crawford, AIA's representative in Brazil, these were sweet words, for they indicated that a job had been done and that at least one Brazilian appreciated it.

30

The Brazil program really got going in November, 1946, when Rockefeller took some of his ideas down to Rio de Janeiro. It was like old home week for the gregarious Rockefeller who during his government service both as Coordinator and as Assistant Secretary of State had made warm and close friends, both personal and political, among all classes of Brazilian leaders.

In fact during Rockefeller's whirlwind 1946 tour of Rio, Oswaldo Aranha, a former Foreign Minister of Brazil, was heard to say, "My, it's nice to have an ambassador from the United States again."

Rockefeller tried out his ideas on anybody who would listen—government officials including President Dutra, businessmen, fazendeiros (large landowners) and even churchmen. He gave a cocktail party for 300-400 people. In Rockefeller's words, "Everybody was there—the old group, the new group, the right, the left," adding with commendable understatement, "The ideas which I was expressing were very well received in Brazil."

Jamieson, whose job, in addition to general policy guidance on all proposed new projects, also was to inform the public of what Rockefeller was up to, accompanied Rockefeller on this trip. His comment about this period was: "Rockefeller is probably the number one North American in the eyes of the average Brazilian, whether he is the man in the street or an influential businessman or a government leader."

Jamieson frequently referred in subsequent years to the fact that if he had made any mistakes in either Brazil or Venezuela—and he felt sure he had—they were mistakes of overselling.

"There was always the danger with Nelson's ebullience, the glamour of the name and the man himself that people would expect too much."

Sometimes the adulation in the public print was embarrassing to Rockefeller and his associates as well. As in the *Correio da Noite*, "a young, educated millionaire like Nelson A. Rockefeller could lead an adventurous and idle life. But he prefers to found companies, distribute wealth, and feed whole generations. And all this he does simply, without a trace of haughtiness. In his evangelical activities he seems to be almost a Luke in the service of God."

During his stay in Rio, Rockefeller was deeply troubled by the

31

"favelas," grim shantytowns that cluster precariously on the sides of the mountains that ring the incredibly beautiful bay of Rio de Janeiro. Though the people living in the favelas have a magnificent view, and a salubrious climate, they live in squalor that is duplicated in few places in the world. Most are without running water, without electricity and without hope.

Rockefeller was told that a considerable percentage of the occupants of the favelas were emigrants from the nearby state of Minas Gerais and from the Northeast. Minas Gerais, the country's wealthiest state in mineral resources (in fact its name means General Mines) had long been reckless with its forest and land resources. Originally 80% of the people of the state made their living through agriculture. But as the population growth outstripped agricultural development, farmers moved to Rio where their destitution dictated that they live in the favelas.

Rockefeller's eyes gleamed. Minas Gerais was something to keep in mind. Could he help to bring back some agricultural prosperity?

That gleam in Rockefeller's eye developed in time into a nationwide network of organizations devoted to the social and scientific improvement of the agricultural community.

By 1961 when AIA concluded its participation in what the Brazilians call the "Sistema CAR" the whole program had been organized and people trained to carry it out. AIA was no longer needed in these areas and, as Pellegrini remarked, AIA kept its promise.

Chapter 1

SANTA RITA AND SAO JOSE

The work of AIA in Brazil, although officially conducted from a São Paulo office, had its genesis on the farms, in the dirt and cobbled streets and in village hang-outs in two small communities—Santa Rita do Passa Quatro and São José do Rio Pardo.

Here AIA started its first agricultural extension service in Brazil, and, although it left much to be desired, it was the forerunner of a national program that was destined to spread across the country from the jungles of the Amazon to the coffee lands of southern Brazil, with over 1,000 trained extension workers serving half a million farm families.

Santa Rita and São José were typical south Brazilian towns—some 2,000 population each, backward in many ways but with a nucleus of citizens who had high hopes and aspirations for their children. Outside the towns there was very little inside plumbing but there was lots of sun. Some of the houses were pretty primitive but it was cool and comfortable under the trees in the back yard.

Dr. Griffing, who was known to everybody as "Dad" and considered an elder statesman by a number of people of the state of São Paulo, and who was also the father of AIA in Brazil, wrote a report in 1953 summarizing the successes and the failures of AIA during its first five years.

Apologizing for the lack of statistics, Dad commented:

When we have succeeded in helping rural people to help themselves, there is nothing more to report. Thus, the successful culmination of any phase of work would seem to be a failure, when reading statistical summaries which show nothing more being done.

We need, therefore, a view at this stage, not of the trees, but of the forest, and a view of the forest from the air.

33

His review indeed did prove that AIA had taught people to help themselves.

In the field of animal production alone the needs were dramatic. It took four years or more to raise a steer in Brazil to the eating point, while in the U.S. it took only two years, sometimes less. And dairy cows give as little as half the production that U.S. cows do. The first thing AIA did was to teach farmers to spray their cattle to rid the beasts of the debilitating, sometimes fatal, ticks with which they were thoroughly infested.

AIA determined the chemical that was most effective and least expensive, ascertained the proper dosage and developed a cheap and effective portable type of sprayer. Santa Rita and São José served as laboratories and demonstration centers in development of the projects. The folk of these two communities found quickly that spraying resulted in ridding the animals of the ticks and grubs that were sapping their strength. An immediate increase in milk production resulted from the removal of these enfeebling parasites.

In Santa Rita the spraying program was such a success that the farmers decided to set up a general rural community service on their own if AIA would help. They wanted guidance on feed, pasture, and other livestock problems. They appointed a committee and together with Dr. Griffing worked out an operating technique. By unanimous vote the farmers agreed to contribute three days' milk receipts a month to finance their share of the program. AIA agreed to provide an agronomist, two animal husbandry technicians, a nurse, and various items of equipment.

The word spread and in no time this community program was regularly spraying thirty-five herds, conducting an active agricultural advisory program, supervising the planting of vegetable gardens and fruit trees by ten boys' and girls' clubs. The State Public Health Service came in, taking over the cost of the nurse and providing part-time services of physicians and dentists who went out to established gathering places on the farms to treat the farmers and their families.

AIA ceased to participate in the program in 1956. Not all but some of the practices still continue.

Today spraying for ticks and grubs is standard operating procedure in most of Brazil. In the state of Rio Grande do Sul where beef

34

cattle of European origin are common the technique is almost a must.

Another simple technique that was tried out in Santa Rita and São José was the construction of the trench silo. Among the most serious problems for cattlemen in that part of Brazil is the six-month dry period when pastures go almost barren. Brazil's humidity precludes the making of hay, concentrates are scarce and expensive and, until recently, silage was rare because of prohibitive costs of construction of vertical silos. There was little official support for AIA's proposal to introduce trench silos, but finally, with certain persuasion such as the loan of equipment and technical help, seven hesitant farmers of Santa Rita took the risk in 1950. The results were spectacular: the trench silo cost 1/50th as much as the traditional monolith, cost less to fill, and if built right had a spoilage of less than 5%.

Nestle, the milk company, paid part of the cost to have a cartoon book on the "why and how" of trench silos prepared and published, and also hired technicians to go all over the state of São Paulo to teach farmers how to make them. Later the extension organizations ACAR and ABCAR adopted the practice with the result that the trench silo today is common all over the country.

Digging a trench silo on a São Paulo fazenda.

One of the first and most important and lasting reforms that AIA was responsible for in Brazil was the technique for aiding in the recuperation of the soil—in other words, combating the "cut-burn-destroy-move on" technique. AIA demonstrated the fact that the great agricultural frontier of Brazil is not the disappearing forest land in the distance, but rather the immense areas of land already cleared and developed near population centers and transportation. Some land in Brazil, although apparently worn out, may be restored with organic matter, chemical fertilizer and conservation practices in as short a time as three years so that it gives yields even exceeding those of the original virgin soil.

Dad Griffing liked to call this operation his "café com leite" (coffee with milk, a favorite Brazilian drink) program. In searching for something that the worn-out old coffee lands could support, the farmers, under his tutelage, had tried out dairy cattle. By confining the cattle, they collected not only the milk but also fertilizer which was used to help bring back some of the coffee land.

The overwhelmingly successful 4-S club movement in Brazil, modeled on the U.S. 4-H clubs, can trace some ancestory to the same little sun-drenched villages of Santa Rita and São José. Dad Griffing encouraged youngsters to form so-called agricultural clubs directed by trained agronomists and home economists. A set of rules was laid down for club agricultural projects: (1) they are *home* projects; (2) the production plot must be large enough to be of *economic importance;* (3) superior yields are made certain by coaching members in *best methods* and in supplying *superior seed;* and (4) the work, though in cooperation with schools, is oriented by an agronomist. Hybrid corn clubs and garden clubs, the first established, quickly paid off for the youngsters in corn and garden yields that far exceeded those of their fathers.

One of Dad Griffing's first helpers in all these projects was a tall, thin, intense young Brazilian agronomist, Marcos Pereira. At the beginning he was Dad Griffing's shadow; soon he relieved the older man of many of the more wearing chores; and when AIA withdrew from this program Pereira moved on in his chosen field. He became head agronomist and acting director for the national organization ABCAR, was head of training for IRI Research Institute and in

1968 was named head of the country's first regional development organization in Campos.

In the health service in Santa Rita that worked in cooperation with AIA's farm and home service, the São Paulo state Health Department provided a physician, a mobile truck and a supply of drugs, and AIA made available the services of a trained nurse who was later paid by the state. This team made periodic visits to some twenty posts in and around Santa Rita.

Working in a radius of approximately twenty miles from the clinic laboratory and headquarters in Santa Rita, the team motored each day to one or more of the posts, each of which was thus serviced every two weeks. The truck rumbled up to its station, which might be in a farmer's home, in a school or in a public plaza, and the doctor set up a table, unloading drugs and other supplies.

These clinics were attended usually by an average of thirty to one hundred people. Some of them came many kilometers by burro, horse or on foot to take advantage of the first modern medical treatment they had ever known.

Marcos Pereira and Dr. John B. Griffing admire the corn crop of two young farmers.

37

After giving vaccinations, checking blood pressure and looking for evidence of internal parasites, the doctor then doubled in brass for the agricultural extension agent. He brought out small seedlings and gave them to the youngsters gathered expectantly around him.

"This is a broccoli plant," he would explain. "When you get home plant it right away in your garden. Sr. Pereira says you must cover it for a while to keep it away from the hot sun while it gets accustomed to its new home."

When he had given his last vaccination and distributed his last plant the doctor dismantled his "office" and drove off with the nurse to the next stop.

The program ran into some difficulties when the Health Department physicians assigned to the program began to prefer giving routine medical treatment of immediate cases rather than doing the more onerous job of educating people to the need for sanitary practices such as building a privy and other measures which might prevent some of the more prevalent diseases, caused mostly by internal parasites. They were abetted sometimes by their superiors who felt that anything so simple could not be good and instinctively preferred something far more elaborate and expensive.

However, in due course and with considerable education, the philosophy of sanitation and preventive medicine won out in the Santa Rita and São José programs.

Dr. Griffing, who started out life as a Protestant agricultural missionary in China, was of the old school—a pure extensionist who believed in doing practically everything himself before having others do it. Many a long hour he spent with a spray machine strapped on his back, demonstrating to a group of farmers how to rid their cattle of parasites. Sometimes in the absence of a home economist helper he would undertake to demonstrate to the ladies how best to bathe babies, how to prepare more nutritious meals, how to construct some small comfort for their meagerly furnished homes.

Although a younger generation was apt to complain that Dad Griffing failed to delegate responsibility, that perhaps his methods were outmoded, no one doubted that his selfless devotion to the farmers of Santa Rita and São José helped to set the pattern for a future successful and permanent AIA operation.

In view of his background, Dr. Griffing was acutely aware of the importance of the missionary's role in developing countries, and despite his rather rigorously Protestant upbringing, made a special point to collaborating with the Catholics:

Professionally I have endeavored to serve on equal terms and with equal interest and sincerity all religious groups. I consider it important that we do so because they can make more effective use of our ideas for rural improvement than any other groups.

One of Dr. Griffing's missionary colleagues characterized him as, "a wonderful man, full of meat—yet so humble about it all."

Even after ill health forced his retirement to his home in South Carolina, Dr. Griffing plied AIA with valuable advice. Witness his evaluation of a would-be collaborator in Brazil:

Dr. Blank is very politically minded. His interest is *not* the "greatest good for the greatest number with little cost" but more jobs and higher salaries for his doctors and functionaries. His whole organization has been greatly padded with sinecure jobs.

Never far from the soil, Dr. Griffing, in one of his last communications with AIA reported:

Flash. I am just starting to make some compost with the aid of some new miracle hoky-poky bacterial material. I don't know whether it is the kind we have been hunting for or not but if the stuff can break down these tough oak leaves it certainly will be a miracle.

Chapter 2

ACAR

Hudgens, from his long years with Roosevelt's New Deal, had an almost religious faith in supervised agricultural credit. Back in the bleak days of the depression in the U.S., such a system had been proposed. The Department of Agriculture fell back upon the classical argument that an extension agent should not be a loan collector. The Hudgenses of that era argued that without a little money and some intelligent supervision the Okies of the modern world can never help themselves.

Because of the recalcitrant attitude of the Department of Agriculture, a New Deal Agency, the Farm Security Administration (now the Farmers Home Administration) was set up to do the job. Incidentally, this argument between the pure extensionists and the credit people is still going on today.

Hudgens argued that if supervised rural credit had worked in the U.S., why not give it a whirl in Brazil? Early in 1948 he studied the situation and felt that the state of Minas Gerais offered the factors that might make a supervised credit experiment feasible.

In September Rockefeller, with Jamieson and Rockefeller's youngest brother David, who was later to become president of Chase Manhattan bank, made another trip to Brazil. A chartered DC-3 took them on a truly barnstorming trip all over the country. Rockefeller wanted to see how all his projects were progressing; he wanted to talk to people; he wanted to see what else needed to be done; and he wanted to show David how exciting everything was.

While Jamieson and the others fought to find a half an hour for a cool drink or a quick nap, the two Rockefellers were shaking hands and making friends as though they were running for office. It was on this trip and in an era when the population pressures were only beginning to be felt, that Nelson Rockefeller frequently made use of

40

this analogy to hammer home his hope of agricultural development:

> Our own situation in the United States is a good example of a balanced development in agriculture supplementing the industrial evolution of our country. Before the evolution in the 18th century it took two farmers in the United States to produce the food necessary for one person living in the city. Today one farmer can produce the food for eight people living in the city. That same evolution must take place in Brazil.

Incidentally, it was on this trip that David's first deep interest in the problems of Latin America was aroused—an interest that was to manifest itself many years later in a progressive Latin American development program by the Chase.

Minas Gerais

The party landed in Belo Horizonte, capital of Minas Gerais, one afternoon in September. At the airport to meet them was the governor of the state, Milton Campos. His welcome was warm and genuine.

Rockefeller wasted no time. In the car on the way to the hotel he propounded his idea—setting AIA to work in Minas.

The governor more than welcomed the proposal that his state be the testing ground for this trial run. An agreement, under which a program was to be carried out for three years, with AIA contributing $75,000 each year and the state contributing in the first year $25,000, in the second $75,000 and in the third $125,000, was sealed with a handshake.

Walter Crawford, a veteran of five years of work in Latin America, including two years in Paraguay as part of John Camp's team, arrived in October, 1948, to be the director of the program.

And on December 6, 1948, the formal agreement was signed in the Palace of Liberty in Belo Horizonte by Hudgens for AIA and by Governor Campos for the state of Minas Gerais. Thus was born ACAR (Associação de Crédito e Assistência Rural, or Association of Credit and Rural Assistance).

The agreement spelled out the fundamental objective of the organization: "increasing of crop and livestock production and the improvement of economic and social conditions of rural life. This objective will be accomplished through the application of a dual as-

41

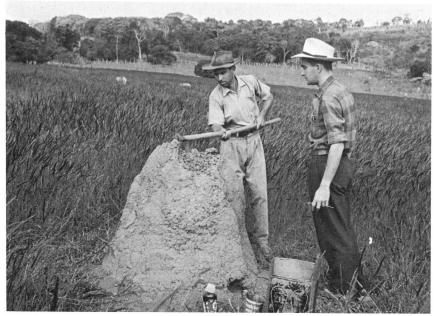
Destroying some of the monumental ant hills that infested Minas Gerais.

sistance, technical as well as financial. This dual assistance will facilitate the adoption of an adequate credit system for small crop and livestock producers and a plan of supervision that guarantees the efficient use of credit."

Crawford, a subscriber of Hudgens' philosophy of supervised agricultural credit, early got the state's agreement to put up the money to be used for this credit. But the bank refused to turn over the funds. One of the reasons the bank dragged its heels was that the interest rate to be charged the farmers (6% per annum) had very little appeal compared to the minimum of 12% and maximum of 25% that the bank could command for regular commercial loans. Biding his time, Crawford collected a staff—three North Americans and three Brazilians—and indoctrinated them in the philosophy of supervised credit. But in addition he kept them busy with many other jobs. One of the most effective was making an attack on the leaf-cutting ants that were plaguing the farmers of the state.

"The delay in getting credit funds was probably a blessing in disguise," recalls Crawford, "because our campaign to control the ants, and its success, impressed the farmers and, more important, gave them confidence in this strange, new foreign operation. By the time the credit funds came along and we had to ask a lot of questions they were more than willing to go along with us."

After a few months Affonso Paulino, of the Minas Gerais Savings Bank, volunteered to provide enough money for some thirty to forty loans for the first year. Paulino had become interested in the new ideas that Crawford had brought and decided to back him up. Every single loan made that first year was paid back at the appointed time, and the Savings Bank has been a major source of ACAR financing ever since. In recent years the Inter-American Development Bank has made two loans totaling more than $10,000,000 to the Savings Bank for ACAR loans.

The loans were all small and went to small- and medium-sized farmers and were for both operational needs and capital expenditures. The supervision of both the size and the application of the loans spelled the difference between success and failure. Of course extension work in all its phases was a large part of the work of ACAR and became an even bigger part in 1952 with the arrival of Santiago D. (Jimmy) Apodaca, who had come from 4-H work in his native state of New Mexico, and Aleta McDowell, who had been working in the state extension service in Wyoming and who was destined to become Mrs. Walter Crawford in 1958. Apodaca introduced the youth club movement as it is known today and Aleta worked out what has since become a model home economics program.

It was at this time that Hudgens introduced his famed "the man, the girl and the jeep" formula to extension work in Brazil. The man was the agricultural extensionist, the girl was the home economist and the jeep was the only vehicle that could make it through the rough country roads.

This formula was an innovation in Brazil and required constant and careful supervision. In the first place, it gave a woman a professional work status on a level with a man—something unheard of in rural areas. And secondly—was it moral?

The Hudgens' formula caused some difficulties in recruiting young women for jobs as local home supervisors. Most vociferous and effective of the objectors was the director of a secondary school of home economics near Rio. The school had a practical curriculum through which girls were taught to do housework, prepare food, take care of the sick, grow vegetables and fruits, make and care for clothing and care for domestic animals (cows, pigs, chickens, rabbits, etc.) But the director forcefully and successfully objected to girls from her school accepting jobs in ACAR because she believed such a system could only be immoral.

However, Aleta made a point of inviting her to an annual conference of all ACAR personnel. After watching the girls in action for a week the director volunteered that she would be happy to train girls for work with ACAR.

"By that time, however," reminisces Mrs. Crawford today, "we didn't need her help. We were training our own girls—and training them better."

However, high professional standards and specific job responsibilities of the man, the girl and the jeep combination resulted in eventual acceptance by farmers and rural leaders and fame for the system. For to this system can be attributed in large part the success that supervised credit and extension work have enjoyed, making Brazil's extension program one of the most outstanding in South America.

Community Centers

ACAR had its first crisis in its second year of existence, when Juscelino Kubitschek was elected to succeed Campos as governor. The two state members of the board of ACAR resigned as a matter of courtesy to the new administration, so there was no pipeline to the state government either for moral or financial support. For six months nothing happened. Then one day Henry W. Bagley, AIA's representative in São Paulo, told Crawford he had learned that Kubitschek was going to be traveling in the area of Mucambeiro. It so happened that ACAR was arranging for the inauguration of its first community center in Mucambeiro in the central part of the state. This was a forlorn little community in the middle of nowhere. The center itself was installed in what had formerly been the slave quarters of a wealthy fazenda, and not even the most loving ministrations of the home economists could make the place attractive.

Crawford pulled a judicious string or two and the governor agreed to attend the inauguration. It was a broiling day, but fortun-

Juscelino Kubitschek, governor of the state of Minas Gerais (later president of
Brazil) cutting the ribbon at the Mucambeiro community center
inauguration ceremony.

ately a local dealer had donated several cases of Coca-Cola, well iced. When the governor arrived, hot and tired and wondering why he had agreed to come, Crawford deftly led him through the throng of farmers and their families to a little bench in front of the building. It was the only small spot of shade in the entire courtyard. Crawford then produced a chilled bottle which Kubitschek grasped thankfully. Within minutes the governor was relaxed and had regained his normal good humor. When the chief home economist stumbled a bit in her speech in Portuguese, the governor came to her aid. He cut the ribbon that stretched across the doorway, made a speech, and henceforth became a devotee of ACAR and all it stood for.

There is a sequel to this event which is related in the next chapter and which proves that after many days you find the bread you cast upon the waters—in this case, Coca-Cola poured down a parched throat.

The job during the early years was physically exhausting. Roads were rough and often impassable even in four-wheel drive jeeps. Frequently the team had to make the last part of a trip on foot, carrying in their arms the equipment and supplies for demonstrations.

The wear and tear on ACAR personnel in making personal visits to individual homes led to the establishment of this first community center. The technicians had found that the farmers were not neighborly and did nothing together or for one another. Most families had no outside connections except for the church and they never visited one another's homes. ACAR soon recognized that the person-to-person contact was an expensive and inefficient way of doing the job. Also there were certain families that lived in the village and not upon their farms. These needed to be reached.

The community center idea was developed in the hopes of reaching more people by teaching in groups instead of individually, by providing better equipment for demonstration and in general making the programs known to townspeople and interested organizations, particularly the church whose understanding and support were essential.

"Mucambeiro was like a first or only child—spoiled," says Mrs. Crawford in recalling some of the mistakes in those early days.

One of the most distressing problems was the low level of sophistication of the people which the ACAR technicians at first did not understand. Many of the farmers were descendants of slaves, the agricultural level was very poor and unemployment ran high.

One of the ideas behind the community center was that the women themselves should run the operation. But in view of the non-existence of local leadership, the only way to keep the center operating was by assigning a home supervisor to it full time.

Three additional centers were set up in the state before it was finally decided to abandon the idea and return to working with people in their own home environment, seeking to get several people together in one home or in the local school house.

"Mucambeiro, like the others, failed because we didn't know enough when we started them," continues Mrs. Crawford. "In fact the important thing we learned was that community centers are good only when you have a sophisticated group of people to work with."

"But never forget Juscelino," interposes her husband, falling into the cozy Brazilian habit of calling presidents by their first names. "Mucambeiro was where we converted him, and without his political and moral support ACAR would never be where it is today."

"I agree," replies his wife. "And also we learned how to judge the size of the steps we took. Each time it would be a bit higher than the last but not so high that it was unsurmountable."

Home and Health

In those early days the hardest job was to convince people that things were good for them. There was the doting father who had refused to bother with installing a filter to make his water safe—"my parents used this water; it's good enough for me." But when his small son died of dysentery he was honest: "If I had only listened to you we'd still have our little boy."

There was the usual reluctance first to build and then to use a privy. One industrious farmer who had a good tobacco crop stored his tobacco in the fine new outhouse that a home economist had urged him to build. A grandmother, head of a large household, saved her money to buy a padlock for the door of her privy. "I'm not going to have all those kids dirtying it up."

Sue Taylor (later Mrs. Howard Murry), AIA consultant on home economics stationed in Caracas, came to Brazil in 1952 and started the country's first modern home economics course at the state agricultural university at Viçosa. Until her first class was graduated, the home economists that were available to ACAR were almost completely untrained—few of them even with the equivalent of high school educations. The general overall training course included training for both men and women and was designed to prepare students for jobs with ACAR. Specific training in agriculture was given for men and home economics for women. Some classes on health, nutrition, and sanitation were given jointly to men and women. There were approximately fifty students in that first class, with fifteen teachers recruited from the Ministries of Agriculture and Health, the State University and the ACAR staff.

At the same time the first college-level home economics training was initiated at the university, with a one-semester course. The next year a four-year course got under way and opened the door for the

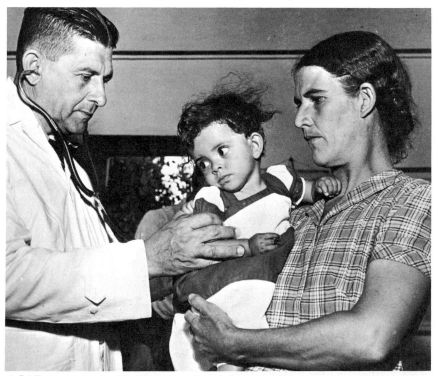

ACAR cooperated with the Minas Gerais health department in sending doctors, dentists and nurses to remote areas of the state to treat farmers and their families.

spread of the movement all over the country. Although neither AIA nor ACAR had responsibility for direction of the school both co-operated in every way possible, including furnishing teachers and equipment.

Subsequently six college-level schools of home economics have been opened in the country.

Through the years ACAR has provided scholarships to encourage women extension workers to study at the university and thus better prepare themselves for their jobs. The organization has also provided training for visiting students both from other states and from other countries either in formal courses or by in-service work.

Aleta left AIA in 1957 to undertake other assignments in the field of home economics but returned in 1960 on a part-time basis to work on technical educational material.

Her book, *Food Selection and Preparation,* was published in 1966 and has sold over 3,000 copies. This is the first authoritative and comprehensive Portuguese treatment of the kitchen arts and sciences. It presents simple factual information about the nature of foodstuffs, and how to preserve nutrients and quality while preparing and serving foods. Basic techniques in food handling and illustrative recipes are listed in great detail.

Growth

In spite of problems, money and otherwise, ACAR grew. From the four local offices set up that first year, it grew to 120 after ten years, and today boasts 20 regional and 180 local offices. ACAR technicians have penetrated into every corner of the state, the men carrying the word of improved farm practices and the girls the news of home and health improvements. The program has served as a model for the rest of the country and has served as a training ground for hundreds of other technicians.

Six years after its establishment, ACAR attracted the notice of the National Planning Association, which commissioned Dr. Arthur T. Mosher, then a Research Professor and Research Associate in Economic Development at the University of Chicago, to do a case study of ACAR. This was published in December, 1955.

49

Dr. Mosher cited the significant features of ACAR.

The ACAR program is one of only two technical cooperation programs which have made substantial use of the technique of supervised credit.

The most complete records of any extension program we have encountered are available from ACAR.

Much more attention has been directed to farm family welfare in the ACAR program than in other technical cooperation programs in agriculture.

The concept of rural home demonstration agents was introduced to Brazil by ACAR, and the program of ACAR has proved the value of such a service under Brazilian conditions.

The ACAR program has demonstrated that supervised credit and general extension education for nonborrower families can be combined in one program to the mutual advantage of both activities.

The popularity of ACAR's approach is a significant indication that ACAR has brought a ferment into a lagging national agricultural development program.

Dr. Mosher was particularly impressed by the increase in net worth of borrower families in the supervised credit program. The average net worth of 102 borrower families before receiving an ACAR loan was $4,423. At the end of the year in which the family received a loan it was $5,374, an increase of 21.5%.

Three years after Dr. Mosher's appraisal was published, a young economist, Clifton R. Wharton, Jr., who had been on the AIA staff as program analyst for five years, serving in both Venezuela and Brazil, chose ACAR as the subject for his Ph.D. dissertation at the University of Chicago. The title was impressive: "A Case Study of the Economic Impact of Technical Assistance: Capital and Technology in the Agricultural Development of Minas Gerais, Brazil."

But the contents were even more impressive.

Wharton's study covered two areas of the state: Curvelo and Ubá. His description of the 126 families from the two areas was this:

The typical or average Curvelo farm family joining the program can be pictured as follows: The father in his late thirties with about two years of primary schooling, a wife about the same

50

age, one son or daughter about thirteen, three or four other children, and usually a baby under one year. They lived in a house with a dirt floor; slept on four beds (one double). They had no electricity, sanitary privy, or running water. Such a family of six consumed about four and one-half pigs a year, about a chicken a week, and a little over a dozen eggs a week. They also consumed almost half their yearly manioc production, and about one-third the farm production of corn, beans and rice. The farmer owned his own land, sold about half of all the farm output he produced, but paid out some of the unsold output as shares for needed labor during harvest and planting.

The typical or average Ubá farm family joining the program would also consist of six persons with about the same age distribution. They would live in a somewhat better home than their counterpart in Curvelo. The farmer would own part of his land and probably rent some additional acreage. He would be heavily dependent upon tobacco and corn, which would account for two-thirds of all production. He would sell almost three-fourths of his total production—tobacco as his main cash crop. The rest would mainly be consumed by the family, largely pork, chickens, milk, eggs, beans, rice and manioc.

Upon joining the program the typical farmer secured a first year loan which averaged 20,000 cruzeiros ($800) in Ubá and 10,700 cruzeiros ($400), in Curvelo. The Ubá farmer divided his loans 54% for capital purchases and 46% for cash operating expenses—largely labor and fertilizer. The Curvelo farmer divided his 67% for capital purchase and 33% for cash operating expenses.

Now for the results of the credit and technical assistance that these farmers had received. While the agricultural production of Brazil as a whole increased during the five years of the study at the rate of 3.73% and the state of Minas Gerais at the rate of 2.63%, the average annual increase among the semi-subsistence farmers in the ACAR program was 21%!

Wharton further refined his figures to prove that for every cruzeiro in actual cash invested in the program, the actual output was Cr$6.50.

Incidentally, Dr. Wharton received his Ph.D.

Chapter 3

THE SINCEREST FLATTERY

ACAR had not been in business a year before other states wanted the same blessings. AIA had neither the financial nor personnel resources to undertake additional programs, but Crawford and his staff did everything they could to help with advice and guidance.

The first approach to AIA was from the state of Rio Grande do Sul early in the year 1950. AIA had to turn down the suggestion that it help organize the program and give financial support, but in 1955 civic-minded leaders headed by Kurt Weissheimer and state agencies succeeded in creating an organization similar to ACAR.

The Northeast

In the meantime the country's leaders were looking with worried eyes at the Northeast section of the country. This area, composed of eight of Brazil's twenty-two states, comprises a total area of 475,000 square miles with a population of 20,000,000 or 30% of that of Brazil. No other country of South America, except Argentina, even approaches this population figure. And the population density of the area is about 40 per square mile compared to 18 for the country as a whole.

The area lies entirely within the tropics and started its agricultural history on the coast with sugar-cane plantations, tended by slaves brought from Africa. As population increased it spread inland, establishing subsistence agriculture and cattle ranches. Incomes were supplemented by the harvesting and selling of native vegetable oils and fibers. No significant change in this pattern is found even today. Thus what was once a satisfactory though meager way of life, with greater population pressure and the exhaustion of always-limited soil resources, has become totally inadequate to meet the exigencies of man in a modern world.

Farming methods have not progressed much since colonial times.

For the majority the hoe and machete are the only tools. Clearing, planting, cultivating and harvesting are done by hand. Rarely is animal power used for anything except transportation, then only for breaking land in preparation for planting.

Social conditions are deplorable. While the 1950 census reported 48% of the population of Brazil could read and write, only 30% of the people in the Northeast were literate. Infant mortality is very high. Communicable diseases take a heavy toll, not only among children but also among adults, upon whom production depends. Even in favorable years, the population suffers from chronic malnutrition. Average daily caloric intake is 1,800 calories or less. During the periods of drought this situation becomes acute, with starvation not uncommon.

Among the conclusions that Crawford reached in his survey, *Agriculture in Brazil,* was this:

> There is a higher concentration of population than the resources can support at acceptable economic and social standards, indicating that resettlement of large numbers in more favorable areas of Brazil should be given high priority.

In 1954 came the first real push. Rómulo de Almeida, president of the Bank of the Northeast of Brazil, which had been created in 1953 to attack the emergency as well as the basic problems of the region, looked about at the drought-ridden Northeast and asked AIA to move in. Because of the problems, the size of the area and the number of states involved, AIA decided to join with the Bank of the Northeast and the Bank of Brazil in the formation of ANCAR (Associacão Nordestina de Crédito e Assistência Rural). AIA was not to have control of the organization nor responsibility for direction, but would be expected to participate actively as a member of the governing board and in conducting personnel training programs.

AIA made no financial contribution. It supplied only part-time personnel and the services of Bagley as a member of the board.

In reporting to the AIA board early in January, 1954, Crawford commented:

> This is a good opportunity to test out the effectiveness of spreading AIA work through an organization in which we are only a minor participant. There is a possibility of its failing and a good

These children of the Itaú district enjoy a school lunch with milk.

chance that it will be somewhat less successful than if we assumed the major responsibility as we have in Minas, but it will
cost AIA a good deal less this way and if it is reasonably successful, we will have made a step forward in shifting responsibility to local groups.

As things turned out, Crawford was more than prophetic.
ANCAR flourished, received substantial financial contributions from
the U.S., from the Bank of the Northeast, and from the federal government. A central office was established in Recife, capital of the state of
Pernambuco, under the direction of José Irineu Cabral, a native of
Pernambuco and at that time head of the Information Division of the
Ministry of Agriculture. Most of the initial activities revolved around
supervised credit to low-income families on an individual basis. The
entire operation was administered and supervised from Recife, without reference to the individual states. This led to many serious difficulties, so the pattern was changed and state-based organizations, with
the support of state governments, were set up beginning in 1955.
Today all eight states have their organizations—ANCAR-Ceará,
ANCAR-BA, etc.

ACAR-Minas helped a great deal in the training process in those early days, as it has ever since then. Its long experience in the field and its knowledge of some of the hazards and headaches of a new program qualified it uniquely to assist in the training program.

The following table summarzing the activities of ANCAR-Ceará serves to illustrate the growth of these state programs:

EXTENSION DATA

Year	Extension Offices		Extension Agents		4-S Clubs		Number of Counties Reached
	Regional	Local	Field	Central Office	Clubs	Members	
1954	1	5	12	—	—	—	—
1955	1	5	12	—	—	—	—
1956	1	5	12	—	—	—	—
1957	1	5	12	—	—	—	—
1958	2	9	23	2	—	—	15
1959	2	10	25	4	—	—	10
1960	2	10	22	9	2	40	18
1961	2	15	39	5	10	188	24
1962	2	18	43	14	14	263	25
1963	3	30	69	11	17	295	36
1964	6	36	85	13	20	386	69

"Car" Covers the Country

By early 1956 three more state organizations had been set up: the aforementioned Rio Grande do Sul (ASCAR), one in Santa Caterina (ACARESC) and one in Paraná (ACARPA) and several more were on the drawing boards.

One day in February, a few months after Kubitschek had been elected President of Brazil, Bagley and Crawford were in the AIA office in Rio when an agitated secretary came in to announce:

"The President wants you to come to the Catete Palace right away."

Bagley and Crawford raced over to the presidential palace in record time.

Kubitschek was awaiting them. Ostensibly he wanted to ask AIA for a contribution to his wife's social service organization. But quickly he asked about AIA progress. Before Crawford could take a deep breath for launching on his disquisition, the President burst out:

"I want to do the same thing for all of Brazil that we did for Minas Gerais. Will you help me do it?

"And we'll call it ANCAR—the National Association for Credit and Rural Assistance."

To gain time Bagley reminded him of the program for the Northeastern states, already called ANCAR.

"Very well," agreed the President. "Let's call it ABCAR—the Brazilian Association for Credit and Rural Assistance. The name makes no difference—as long as it is a CAR organization." Kubitschek had already, almost unconsciously, hit upon the "Sistema CAR."

He spoke glowingly of the "unlimited funds" in the Bank of Brazil, a government institution, and the importance of having an outside organization like AIA do the job, not the government, which he said would surely make a botch of it.

ACAR helped farmers provide watering ponds for their cattle.

56

At first Crawford and Bagley were a bit cool to the idea. They had had a plan for a national organization shortly after it was seen that ACAR was going to be a success. But when this seed fell on unfertile ground they had decided to support only the state organizations. As Bagley put it in his first report:

A federal ACAR would be an expensive, probably inefficient organization, subject to intense political pressures; it would probably have to try to serve regions where there is at present no demand or need for ACAR-type work; it would inevitably have to use a large number of weak employees, for lack of sufficient good ones.

AIA would be putting all its eggs in one basket, and that basket not only would be leaky but might be completely overturned with a change in the federal government.

However, as Bagley pointed out, this was neither his nor Crawford's final opinion. Two factors determined their final appraisal of the proposal: one was Kubitschek's alluring suggestions that there were plenty of funds available for loans to farmers; the other was a trip to Brazil by Nelson Rockefeller in April, 1956.

Rockefeller went to Belo Horizonte on April 12, and had a long talk with João Napoleão de Andrade, then president of ACAR and a long-time crony of President Kubitschek.

Andrade had arranged a meeting at his farm between Kubitschek and Rockefeller. But at the last minute the President had to cancel his trip.

Kubitschek, a highly controversial political figure, was under frequent attack in the opposition press that took gleeful advantage of the supposed meeting of these two vigorous and active international figures. The fact that the meeting did not take place and that David Rockefeller did not accompany his brother to Minas Gerais was of little concern to the editors.

"If the Rockefellers are in Brazil to discuss matters that are really of interest to the Brazilian state, the President of the Republic should receive them in the right place—why that undercover meeting in Minas and above all on a secluded farm?" was the editorial comment of *Diario de Noticias* of Rio.

And the *Informador Comercial wrote darkly,* "Mr. Juscelino

João Napoleão de Andrade receives a typical Brazilian "abraço" from Nelson Rockefeller while (right) Walter Crawford and Jimmy Apodaca beam their approval.

Kubitschek will meet the Rockefeller brothers at the João Napoleão de Andrade farm in Sete Lagoas. Mr. Andrade is the director of ACAR which belongs to the two Yankee millionaires . . . and as secrecy is one of the weapons of business no one will know why Juscelino chose such a far place—so distant from the Catete Palace —to talk to two Yankee sharks. It can't be good."

However, neither of these men was the type to be deterred by political opposition. They met the next day for lunch at the presidential palace, and Rockefeller agreed to participate in ABCAR. So on June 21, 1956, Crawford, for AIA, signed the final agreement that created ABCAR.

The signing was sealed by an exchange of cables between President Kubitschek and Rockefeller.

Rockefeller to Kubitschek: "After having worked with you for many years in Minas Gerais it is a privilege to join with you on a national scale in this work to further social and economic advance for rural Brazil under your inspired leadership."

Kubitschek to Rockefeller: "I reaffirm it gives me great satisfaction to count on your cooperation in the activities of ABCAR."

ABCAR's objectives were "to coordinate and stimulate":

a) Programs of Rural Extension in an effort to bring to rural families, through educational means, the knowledge necessary for improvement of agricultural and home management practices, thereby modifying their habits and attitudes as a means of attaining better social, cultural and economic standards of living.

b) Programs of Supervised Rural Credit in an effort to institute a system of credit based on the integral planning of the agricultural and home activities of rural families, as well as adequate supervision of agricultural development, in order to assure that the credit fulfills the function of assisting, technically and economically, small and medium-sized farmers to improve their standard of living.

ABCAR was charged with the task of obtaining the financial and technical resources from national and international organizations for distribution to the various regional and state member organizations that were carrying out programs of extension and rural credit, and also to foster the formation of additional agencies. However, ABCAR was not given authority to actually operate programs. This eliminated much of Bagley's and Crawford's initial misgivings.

Andrade was named president of the new organization, a spot he has held ever since.

On July 4, 1956 (an appropriate date for the Yankees on the staff) the *Brazil Herald* wrote:

An American idea for raising the living standards of farm people in Brazil, launched in Minas Gerais in 1949, has become an integral part of this country's rural development plans with the creation of the ABCAR. . . . It has the enthusiastic support of President Juscelino Kubitschek who has promised adequate funds not only for the small loans that are made to farmers but also for the operations of ABCAR and the field programs associated with it.

In the early days the rural dwellers commented on the "impropriety" of a man and a woman traveling over the back country unchaperoned but today such remarks are rare, as ACAR's specialists have convinced the farm people that they are there to work and have demonstrated that their work is useful.

The paper concludes its article on the practical note that "ACAR's records show better than 99% repayment of loans."

On the tenth anniversary of the ACAR program, Crawford was prompted to write: "The ACAR pattern for rural development has taken strong roots in Brazil," and cited among other achievements:

1) Extension programs now are operating in twelve of Brazil's twenty states.

2) Four hundred field technicians are bringing help to people in 200 counties of the country.

3) The federal, state and local governments are supplying more than $3,000,000 a year in support of the programs.

In the same year ACAR's record showed that loan repayments in Minas Gerais had averaged 99.97%.

Today ABCAR, which has enjoyed the full suport of every administration, controls a total of $10,000,000 in combined annual budgets and presides over a total of more than 1,000 employees. It is supported by many agencies, but no one organization has control. Thus, although it is *of* the government and *by* the government, it is operating *for* the government and *outside* the government. It is largely free of political pressures and is able to lead its own life with relative independence.

Through ABCAR comes 60% of the support for all of the state programs. Through its power of the purse ABCAR can withhold support from state organizations it thinks are not doing a good job and give it to states whose programs deserve greater support. Some of the state programs are better than others—usually due to the nature and ability of the director. The degree of success of a program has nothing to do with the economic health of the state. For example, Ceará, one of the country's poorest states, has one of the most active and best CAR programs. Two of the states, Santa Caterina and Espírito Santo, have almost 100% coverage—that is, an office within reach of every farm family in the state. ACAR in Minas Gerais, with 180 local offices, has 40% coverage.

Chapter 4

CONCLUSION

Crawford summarizes the two decades of AIA's work in Brazil thus:

> A long list of improved farm and home practices could be compiled, but these alone would not speak as loudly, or clearly, of the CAR program's real value as does the simple fact that in Brazil today, tomorrow and every day thousands of trained men and women work hard and intelligently to help farm families produce more and live better.

Everybody agrees that perhaps the most significant thing that the CAR idea has done is to indoctrinate key leaders in the country with the importance of technical assistance and credit in the development of agriculture.

Furthermore, the system has perfected administrative organizations for using both funds and people effectively. In general the CAR organizations, state and federal, are well accepted by the public and function smoothly.

Through these accomplishments a real service has been rendered to many thousands of rural people. Without this administrative backstopping, the public suport, including money, and the dedicated and enthusiastic service of the technicians who have contributed their knowledge and time, would long ago have been dissipated.

"It is sadly true that agricultural supply is actually retrogressing in Brazil," adds Crawford. "The agricultural problems are growing faster (primarily because of population pressures) than the CAR organizations. And the truth of the matter is that the organizations probably should not grow any faster than they are now doing."

But in spite of this there is real progress at the grass-roots where it counts. Water supplies have improved, indoor plumbing and outdoor privies have been installed, vegetable gardens have increased in number and quality, mothers and infants receive better pre- and post-natal care, consumption of protein foods (eggs, milk, meat, cheese) is up, fewer women are washing their clothes in parasite-infested streams.

And the rural people themselves are taking the initiative in trying to secure the things for a better life. The farmers are making good use of the small loans they get, their agricultural production is increasing. Neighbors actually get together to solve problems that affect them collectively as well as individually—for example, a new school build-in, getting more teachers, urging the local government to provide better roads, mail service and road signs. The rural family is not as isolated as formerly. It is more mobile, more in the mainstream of national life, especially the youth.

Part 4

VENEZUELA

The program in Venezuela actually began with a trip that Nelson Rockefeller made early in 1947 to discuss needs and potential remedies. From it grew a program which Rockefeller presented to President Rómulo Betancourt in June. This is how Rockefeller outlined it on paper from a long, yellow, lined pad:

I. OUR PROGRAM

    A. *Objectives*—Help

        1. Lower cost of living

        2. Raise standard of living

        3. Preserve freedom, human dignity and opportunity to improve life of individual by

        4. Increasing production of goods and services in demand on efficient economical basis. *If these things happen —then*

        5. Present Liberal government of Venezuela will serve as

an example of how to make most efficient use of private capital, management and technology to raise standard of living and create more opportunity for people.

6. Venezuela will go ahead faster than Mexico did—or Perón can.

B. *Method of Carrying out Program*

1. AIA—non-profit program

   a. Cooperative projects with government departments and agencies
   b. Agriculture, health, education
   c. Demonstration and training projects
   d. Designed to spread knowledge of modern methods in order to help individuals increase production

2. Technical Services

   a. Help government and private groups
   b. Secure and direct best technical talent in

   (1) planning
   (2) making studies
   (3) financing and
   (4) carrying out

   projects in public utility field on limited cost basis

3. VBEC (a subsidiary of IBEC)—to form companies on sound business basis

   a. These companies to be

   (1) founded and operated
       (a) on sound business principles
       (b) with broad sense of social responsibility
   (2) They will be organized
       (a) to meet specific economical needs
       (b) rather than on a basis of where most money could be made.

64

Late in 1947 the AIA board of directors appropriated $25,000 "for the purpose of conducting studies in Venezuela for the preparation of projects in the fields of training, information and education, all with a view of informing the Venezuelan people on the development and use of nutritive foods and improving agriculture and food production practices in Venezuela."

From this grew the Association's two foremost Venezuelan projects—CIDEA and CBR.

In the course of the months of discussion and negotiating, the political dilemma of the Venezuelan government was illustrated by the news that a Venezuelan advisor sent to Rockefeller:

> The publicity here about us and Creole has put the government in trouble with both Communists and Rightists. The government says it believes in free enterprise but that it must be a 'liberal and regulated free enterprise,' that capitalism in Venezuela had resulted in robbing her people through large profits and the government is determined to stop such exploitation.

On the other hand the conservative business and industrial community was deeply shocked by some of the Rockefeller proposals. In many quarters he, like some aristocrats before him, was considered a traitor to his class.

The AIA part of the program, with generous support from the oil companies, got under way in June, 1948, under the highest auspices. A diplomatic exchange of correspondence between President Rómulo Gallegos, who had succeeded in Betancourt, and Rockefeller lent a very lofty tone to the whole transaction.

Outlining the program proposed by AIA, as a result of conferences with ministries and departments of the Venezuelan government, Rockefeller concluded his letter thus, "Hoping for your personal happiness and for the progress and well-being of Venezuela, in this fruitful and transcendental hour in her history, I remain,"

In return President Gallegos assured Rockefeller that, "Even though the consequences can only be duly judged in the light of the results obtained, I do not hesitate to predict that they will be completely satisfying," adding that his "government will not spare its participation and support in guaranteeing, developing, and lending prestige to the work which your Association is carrying out in accordance with the aims which you have stated to me."

The details of the program were spelled out by Hudgens in a memo to his board concerning a "base program in Venezuela."

"Permanent gains in economic and social development can finally best be measured in numbers of individuals and families who have been helped to better lives, and the degree of development they have made," he wrote.

"There is also a need in AIA's total program for a 'distribution system for ideas' through which the beneficial results of experience or of any specialized project can be channeled to the point of ultimate good, the individual or family."

To this end a Community Service Program was proposed. Demonstration programs were to be placed strategically throughout the country, geared both to national organizations which would supply goods and services and to the local community. The scope of the program was infinite and the number of services endless:

> health services, including hospital and first-aid facilities;
> health education;
> sanitary engineering;
> sanitary facilities;
> guidance in homemaking, nutrition, and related fields;
> agricultural guidance and demonstration;
> credit facilities (in such fields as homemaking, home construction and improvement, crop and livestock production, farm operations and farm acquistion) including supervised credit;
> community planning and organization;
> guidance in community action;
> guidance in the organization and operation of cooperatives;
> planning and construction of individual and community water supplies;
> creation of recreational facilities;
> creation of needed educational facilities;
> and others which imagination and local needs will dictate.

In support of the community program, Hudgens proposed three activities:

1. Information programs.

2. Survey or investigative program. This would be short-term

research on pressing agricultural, health and educational problems.

3. Training program. This would include only practical training of farmer families and young people. The program at Turrialba fitted into this.

As things turned out the first supporting program became administratively independent while the second and third were merged with the community service program to form CBR.

When AIA went into Venezuela, its social and economic situation was unique. Seventy-eight percent of her 5,000,000 people lived in one-fifth of the area—in the northern mountainous and coastal regions of the country. Although Venezuela was and is largely an agricultural country, it is mainly dependent on its rich oil resources, from which at that time were derived more than half the total national income and over 70% of the government revenue. It had 250,000 farms, of which 35,000 were livestock ranches. Sixty percent of the

Girls and boys, members of a nutrition club in Caracas, learn to identify leafy and root vegetables.

country's rural families were tenants, sharecroppers and squatters, the latter known as *conuqueros*.

And the country was importing over a third of the foodstuffs consumed by its people, including items of such prime necessity as corn, rice, beans, potatoes, sugar, dairy products, oils and wheat flour.

Although about six out of every ten Venezuelans depended upon the soil for their livelihood, the typical Venezuelan farmer was unable to maintain an adequate level of living with the amount of land and methods of cultivation then available to him.

The then president of the National Agrarian Institute who was also chairman of the board of CBR, himself referred to the "sad reality confronting our countryside, traditionally lashed by a series of misfortunes, malnutrition, disease, ignorance, unsanitary housing, a low scale of production and abusive exploitation of its natural resources."

Sue Taylor, the home management technician of CBR whose tall, blonde figure was to become a strange contrast to the brunette, shorter Venezuelans as she made her way through the countryside, put the problem in an intensely human way:

> Most rural families live in huts made of mud and caña brava (wild cane, something like bamboo). The majority of these houses have only dirt floors, no windows and frequently only one room.
>
> There is almost no furniture, often only one or two chairs and a canvas bed which folds up in the daytime to make room in the tiny house. Many children sleep on the dirt floors. Sanitary conditions are bad. Pigs, chickens, dogs and children often run together in the house. Water is perhaps the number one problem of all rural families.
>
> Lack of family stability often makes it difficult to work in a home. In one group of nineteen families, only three were legally married. Two of the group called themselves bachelors and twelve had "companions." In some homes the children did not know who their real fathers were. In a few cases, they did not even know their mothers. The average family consists of five or six members, in many there are grandparents and older sisters who also have their "natural" children.

However, the picture was not entirely hopeless. There were large areas of potentially productive land in Venezuela that were either under-utilized or out of production altogether. By helping the individual farmer make more efficient use of his land and by attempting to bring unused land into production, Hudgens, Camp and their associates felt that not only could production be substantially increased but that the individual farmer's position and the economic health of the country could be significantly improved.

And even Sue Taylor found an eagerness to learn and very soon noted small day to day improvements—a family boiling its drinking water, another planting a home garden, still another eyeing wistfully the neighbor's sanitary privy.

"A change in attitude and a gradual development of managerial ability are not accomplishments to be noted by the casual eye," she reported. "Rather, it is the type of progress one feels and senses in the everyday work with the family."

Chapter 1

CIDEA

Early in the Venezuelan experience it was recognized that knowledge and technology had far outstripped the means of getting it disseminated. This was particularly true in the field of food production and consumption. A large proportion of the Venezuelan population was undernourished and many actually suffered from malnutrition. It was going to take time to increase the production of rice, beans, meat, dairy products, fruits, vegetables, and all the other elements so urgently needed. The immediate answer was to make better use of what resources were available.

Camp talked to Jamieson about it—and a new program evolved, an information program to be known as CIDEA (Consejo Interamericano de Educación Altimenticia, or Inter-American Council on Nutrition Education).

The preamble of the certificate of organization describes succinctly CIDEA's purpose:

> From studies which have been made up to the present time by various governmental and private organizations it has been learned that the food problem in Venezuela consists essentially in the low consumption of protective foods such as milk, butter, cheese, meat, fish, vegetables and fruits. Only the consumption of certain energy foods, such as papelón (coarse, raw sugar,) beans, etc., is relatively adequate except during periods of transitory shortage. Therefore, one can well understand that the Venezuelan is weakened by the deficiency of those foods which are needed to maintain his vitality. . . .

> The American International Association is offering its immediate collaboration in the organization of a campaign, within an information and education program, to create among lower income groups a consciousness of their ability to improve their own living standards. Through proved media of information, people

70

would be made aware of the advantage to themselves of improving the common diet by use of available but usually unrecognized sources of nourishment.

CIDEA officially came into existence on June 4, 1948, when José Ortega Durán, director of INPAP (Instituto Pro-Alimentación Popular, or Institute of Public Nutrition) and John Camp signed a contract for three years. Recognizing that nutrition and health were inextricably mixed together, the Minister of Health, Antonio Martin Araujo, was an important figure in the negotiations. As a matter of fact, through his interest in the program and subsequent witnessing its success in the field of nutrition, he was instrumental in having the scope enlarged to include health.

A. Edward Stuntz, original director, describes the CIDEA birth:

In Venezuela I had brought a small group of media people into the nutrition information program (I was the sole North American). We started out with one typewriter (a portable I had brought from New York). Our offices were in servants' quarters atop one of Caracas' old colonial buildings. We sat in deck chairs or paced the open roof vying for the right of way with the janitor's chickens. There we formulated CIDEA's policy—the right of the Venezuelan people to know anything about food and kindred subjects that would help them live more comfortably—and the sustained coverage of these topics.

A year and a half later, a small fleet of CIDEA mobile units was taking pamphlets, motion pictures, radio discs and lecturers to the remote corners of the country. School nutrition clubs, with hundreds of eager members, had been set up and teachers' courses in nutrition instruction had been written and were introduced in the regular curricula in most of the nation's schools. The radio stations of the country were demanding CIDEA scripts for which some 56,000 children and 15,000 laborers were known listeners on a regular basis, and the press was printing all the nutrition material the staff could provide.

Problems

It was not all smooth sailing. Like politicians in whatever country, those in Venezuela were not slow to recognize that the CIDEA apparatus provided a ready-made and built-in propaganda machine for

The CIDEA trailer proclaims that "to eat well does not mean to eat a lot or to eat expensively" and that "a good diet is the foundation of health."

the chosen party. Jamieson and Stuntz made elaborate and emotional speeches on the ethics of journalism, on the difference between propaganda and information, and the importance of keeping the faith with people who needed nutrition information and not political persuasion.

Another hurdle was the then common practice of a press agent in Venezuela paying a newspaper to run his release. Neither the newspapers nor his colleagues could understand when Stuntz blandly expected his releases to be printed on their merit and without payment.

Holding firm to principles paid off, however, and soon the papers were begging for material, and the politicians were surprised and pleased when their constituents recognized them, not by their political hue but by their association with the nutrition information program.

CIDEA's original intention had been to make use of every conceivable information channel—press, magazines, radio, movies, television, comic books, flannel and flip boards, scholarly journals, books both commercial and text, and word of mouth—to get the nutrition story across.

Initially it had no idea of going into physical operations. However, a lady home economist and an extension agent-type man made a survey. They reported that a proper information program could not be disseminated by the printed word or other educational methods alone, nor could other organizations be relied upon to carry out the program with the single-mindedness they felt the program deserved.

They were convinced that CIDEA needed a day-to-day, person-to-person effort, that is, physical establishments to prove its point and to convince the skeptics.

So, with some doubts in the minds of the proponents of pure information versus extension work, three such experimental centers were set up around the country. Although the program reverted three years later to its original *modus operandi,* a great deal had been learned and developed during these experimental days, not the least being the Nutrition Club Movement—which has since burgeoned into big business and today blankets the country.

Mobile Units

"If you possess a special combination of mechanical ingenuity, a love for people and the open road, an ability to think on your feet, a comedian's sense of timing and a feeling for vitamins, you can be a sound-truck operator for CIDEA."

This was the way one CIDEA driver summed up the job of the master-of-ceremonies-driver-mechanics who operated CIDEA mobile units. Each unit consisted of a station wagon with its back seats removed to make room for the equipment—a 16-mm. sound projector, microphone, turntable, generator, films, records and a supply of printed material. From the brilliant yellow roof sprouted a loudspeaker.

Coming into town at midday, the operator determined the best time for the program with the help of the mayor, the doctor or a civic leader. He usually scheduled the show for just after dusk, when the day's work was over and when the movies could be projected on the whitewashed wall of a building facing the plaza.

He then spent the afternoon driving slowly through the streets and in the outlying section, playing recorded music over the loud-

A mobile unit operator gets an assist from a young friend in Táchira.

speaker and barking: "Come to see CIDEA movies tonight in the plaza. Absolutely free."

By the time the crowd started arriving in the plaza, the driver had his equipment set up and was broadcasting popular tunes. The program might start with an animated cartoon on pure water, showing why drinking water should be boiled, what happens when it isn't, the virtues of bathing and the importance of sanitary toilets. This might be followed by a simple film on vaccination or a nutrition short explaining some principles of good diet. There was usually one pure entertainment film—a cartoon or a sports short. Interspersed between the movies there might be brief recorded talks or perhaps a leading member of the community spoke over the loudspeaker on some special local problem.

Once in a small village in the state of Carabobo, the operator discovered that a smallpox outbreak was threatening to become epidemic, and the town officials were anxious to get everybody to the clinic for vaccination. Fortunately he had a film on vaccination which he showed that night on the plaza. He also explained its lesson in terms of the local crisis. The doctor was delighted at the record-breaking crowd that lined up at the clinic the next morning, and credited the operator's quick action with having averted what might have been a most serious health problem.

The operator also enlisted the help of enthusiastic youngsters to distribute brightly-illustrated educational pamphlets to keep the CIDEA message fresh until his next visit.

One driver who had driven to a remote part of the state of Zulia, only a few miles away from the savage Motilone Indian country, set up his equipment in a little village where, he learned later, films had never been shown before. During the entertainment feature, where a cowboy hero meets the villian in life-or-death combat, the driver was startled to hear pistol fire whistling past his head.

"One of the spectators seated near the back row of benches in the plaza," he said, "had pulled a six-shooter out of his belt and was blazing away at the screen. After the smoke and commotion had cleared, I explained to everyone that these were not real flesh-and-blood people. Luckily I had a spare screen in the truck, which I set up, and the show went on."

The superintendent of schools in one district of Venezuela reported that the attendance at CIDEA films was so good that the commercial movie house manager was complaining about the competition. He also reported that the nutrition habits engendered in youngsters at school and in their nutrition clubs carried over into their homes.

"Sometimes their elders will give them arguments," he said, "saying that black beans and rice were good enough for us, but the kids stick to their guns and demand vegetables."

Comics

One of the many techniques that CIDEA, as well as Dad Griffing in Brazil in his work in Santa Rita and São José, experimented with was the comic strip technique. This was tried for two reasons: because of its inherent appeal and also because of the need to reach a largely illiterate or semi-literate audience.

Dr. Griffing had produced a comic book giving full directions on how to build a trench silo. The amazing thing was that it worked, and today there are thousands of trench silos in use that were constructed in conformity with the directions in this comic book.

For many years a comic book *Juancito Salud* (Johnny Good Health) was a best seller in Venezuela.

Papers and Radio

Venezuela was blessed with a substantial number of newspapers and radio stations when CIDEA went into operation. There were ten dailies in Caracas and nineteen published in the interior. In addition, there were many weeklies of many hues.

An impressive number of radio broadcasting stations, all with short-wave and some of relatively strong power, existed—thirty-one in all, ten of which were in the Caracas area.

Fortunately in those days in Venezuela a radio receiving set seemed to be an indispensable item of furniture of nearly every Venezuelan home, however humble. It was not unusual to see Caracas families, living under bridges and with no other roof, whose radio sets were the most prized possessions. Bars, cafes, schools, clubs, recreation and community centers also had radio receiving sets, thus vastly multiplying the potential audience.

Every possible type of program was used on radio. A popular children's program "Adventure of the Valiant Vitamin," offering prizes and membership in a nutrition and health club, drew an average of 1,200 letters and postcards a month. Other ventures included a program "Health, Food and Money for You," a round-table quiz show on nutrition and public health, daily nutrition news bulletins and spot announcements.

Famous people were dragooned to help with the cause. For example, Alfonso "Chico" Carrasquel, one of Venezuela's first contributions to major league baseball, and a local hero, testified on radio and in print to the benefits of a sound diet. He appeared personally at nutrition club meetings and nearly always broke them up by the enthusiastic reception he got.

By 1951 the demand for nutritional and health material to be disseminated through all media—radio, newspapers, magazines, schools—had reached such a point that a special service was set up in New York to collect and prepare material for use in the Venezuelan service. A periodic *CIDEA Newsletter* was issued during the years 1951-56 and covered every possible facet of the nutrition and health fields, as witness some of the titles:

"FAO Project Forecasts New Foods from Old Plants."
"Home Pasteurization of Milk Practicable."
"How Not to be Struck by Lightning."
"Find Cigarettes, Alcohol Factors in Larynx Cancer."
"More Proteins, Fewer Calories for Oldsters' Diet."

100% Venezuelan

On January 30, 1956, AIA withdrew from CIDEA, the whole operation being taken over by the National Nutrition Institute of the Ministry of Health with Dr. Alí Romero, who had been assistant director from the beginning, named the first Venezuelan director. CIDEA has remained a separate entity within the Ministry's National Nutrition Institute and has also retained its name. Today it is responsible for some 2,000 nutrition clubs throughout the country and sponsors 4,000 radio programs a year for a total air time of more than 500 air hours ·

A movie audience in a small Andean town.

devoted to health and nutrition. Most of these are five-minute educational spots.

By 1966, 1,175 extension workers and 2,765 home demonstrators were trained in the basics of good health and nutrition. A total of sixty pamphlets and other publications were published. These include *Paths to Health,* an exhaustive syllabus for teachers on how to establish and run health and nutrition projects and centers for the benefit of youngsters of all ages.

As testimony to the effectiveness of twenty years of disseminating the story of good nutrition there are a few figures, for which CIDEA does not pretend to take credit but to which it rightly feels it has contributed.

78

For example, the increases in the production (in 1,000 metric tons) of some food crops of special dietary significance are of interest:

Year	Sesame	Bananas	Plaintains	Other Fruits	Onions	Tomatoes	Other Vegetables
1950	8.2	252.0	132.7	N.D.*	N.D.	N.D.	N.D.
1955	9.1	358.4	183.0	N.D.	N.D.	N.D.	N.D.
1960	16.3	381.4	235.6	83.2	23.2	49.3	41.8
1965	54.1	430.4	547.1	106.9	34.9	72.1	46.7
Index of Increase from 1950 to 1965	660%	171%	412%	N.D.	N.D.	N.D.	N.D.

Source: Ministry of Agriculture, Annual Agricultural Statistics Reports, Caracas, Venezuela.
*N.D.—No data.

And the consumption changes of some other products give an indication of nutritional progress:

	Average Consumption per Capita								
Year	Milled Rice (Kgs.)	Refined Sugar (Kgs.)	Vegetable Oils and Fats (Kgs.)	Beef (Kgs.)	Pork (Kgs.)	Dairy Products Liquid Milk Equiv. (Ltrs.)	Eggs (Units)	Corn (Kgs.)	Potatoes (Kgs.)
1950	7.3	18.5	4.5	14.5	4.6	48.5	36.5	64.1	12.7
1955	4.4	23.0	7.4	13.4	3.7	84.9	55.6	51.7	12.3
1960	10.5	28.9	8.1	16.6	4.4	94.3	62.0	58.8	14.5
1965	14.9	N.D.	N.D.	18.6	4.1	107.0	67.0	59.7	15.5
Index of Increase from 1950 to 1965	204%	156%[1]	180%[1]	128%	(—11%)	221%	184%	(—7%)	122%

Source: Data to 1960 from: CBR "Long Term Forecasts of the Supply and Demand of Agricultural and Livestock Products in Venezuela" Caracas, December, 1965.
    Data for 1965 from: CBR "Present Status and Possibilities of Agricultural Development in Venezuela," Caracas, March, 1967.

[1] Change between 1950 and 1960 calculated because 1965 data not available.

Chapter 2

CBR

Just a month after CIDEA had seen the light of day its sister organization, the non-profit Venezuelan civil society, CBR (so-called from the initials of its name in Spanish, Consejo de Bienestar Rural, or Council of Rural Welfare) was set up by agreement between the Technical Institute for Immigration and Colonization (later to become the National Agrarian Institute) and AIA.

The agreement was to run for three years. It provided for a board of directors divided equally between Venezuelan government members and AIA representatives. Its president was to be designated by the Venezuelan government and its executive director by AIA.

A fundamental financial arrangement was included in the contract: the gradually diminishing size of the AIA contribution, and the gradually increasing commitment of the Venezuelan government.

The contract was destined to be renewed ten times before AIA withdrew completely in 1968. From an annual contribution as high as $375,000, AIA's final contribution amounted to $22,000 while the Venezuelan government's ranged from $333,000 to $750,000.

The charter defined the organization's aims:

> To improve Venezuelan living conditions through a program of rural rehabilitation and supervised credit through:
> a. Development of agricultural production
> b. Improvement of the physical environment
> c. Technical guidance and
> d. Training and education by means of community service.

As in all AIA programs, training and education were at the heart of the CBR operation. The Venezuelan government had the beginnings of an agricultural extension service, the nucleus of a rural youth program and local health services. But none of them incorporated the training precept—either of the prime recipients or of future trainers. In this CBR pioneered. The training function was inserted at all levels, from the illiterate *campesino* to high government officials.

CBR was destined to have an on-again-off-again quality, primarily because it adhered so strongly and effectively to the AIA philosophy of developing a program, involving local people and then turning the program over to them.

Originally CBR planned to set up experimental services in five states of the country: Carabobo, Táchira, Nueva Esparta, Lara and Bolívar. And the program activities were to include supervised credit, as the core of all family and farm development, tractor training, community centers, and improved farm practices, such as use of fertilizers. Above all, CBR was to remain flexible and be able to jump in any direction that was indicated.

Supervised Credit

The first project undertaken was a program of supervised credit carried out in cooperation with the Agricultural and Livestock Bank under a bilateral agreement. This program was based on the very simple premise that farmers without land, tools and techniques are not very productive; but even if they have land, tools and techniques, unless they know how to make maximum use of them, they are still not very productive.

With a small amount of money a man may acquire the tools he so critically needs, the small parcel of land that can make the difference between success and failure, or plant the home garden that can give him and his family a healthier nutritional level.

A CBR technician worked with a farmer applicant and developed a work plan which was then presented to the Bank. The Bank provided funds, at 5% interest, handled disbursements and collections, while the CBR agronomist followed through with his farmer, to make sure that the original plan was being followed.

This program was operated for six years, until 1954. It was terminated only because the restrictive laws and banking regulations made it almost impossible to operate. In other words it was just a bit ahead of its time. Since then the legal structure has been amended, a body of technicians trained in giving the necessary supervision has been created, and, most important perhaps, Venezuelan officials have learned to see the value in this form of credit. Ten years after this program was ended, as we shall see later, Venezuela was to embark on a $20,000,000 supervised credit program, patterned faithfully on the earlier experience.

But in the early days it was an uphill job. Hudgens' trio (man, woman and jeep) scoured the back country and sought out farmers. Their reception at first was far from friendly.

But the teams persisted and during its lifetime this program made 1,047 loans for a total of Bs. 4,056,000 ($1,349,000). Over 91% of these loans were repaid—a rate that compared most favorably with the repayment rate of ordinary loans made by the Bank.

Even bankers were amazed at the effectiveness of making credit available to people with very limited resources and at the rate of repayment of these high risk loans. The before and after records of these farm families told the story: many families, with the aid of a supervised loan, had changed their standard of living from one of desperation to one of at least adequacy, and subsequently had risen to positions of honor in their communities.

His ever-present machete under his arm, this farmer shows what supervised credit and counseling on fertilizers and insect elimination can do for his cotton crop.

82

Early in the program CBR started making detailed studies to determine the exact status of families before and after receiving loans. In October, 1951, an analysis was made of twenty-six formerly landless families who had been given a year's training by CBR in the Lake Valencia region, and then presented with a parcel of land from a large government-owned tract and a loan. Here are the figures before receiving the loan and one year after the loan, measured by the indices of size of farm, net worth and net family cash income:

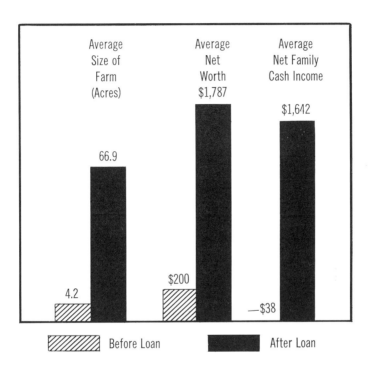

A year later an analysis was made of 60 families who had participated in the supervised credit program for two crop years and 189 who had received loans for only one year. The families who were chosen by lot for the survey were from four states: Carabobo, Táchira, Bolívar and Lara. Here are some of the results:

Two-Year Families: (60 Families)
    Ninety-two percent increase in average size of farm:
        1949—25.5 acres   1951—49.0 acres

Average gross farm income increased from $1,417 in 1949 to $4,410 in 1951.

Average net family income increased from $408 in 1949 to $1,804 in 1951.

Eighty percent of the families now have sanitary latrines.

Seventy-eight percent of the families have home gardens.

One-Year Families: (189 Families)

Sixteen percent increase in average size of farm:
1950—31.3 acres   1951—37.3 acres

Average gross farm income increased from $1,088 in 1950 to $2,431 in 1951.

Average net family income increased from $379 in 1950 to $1,604 in 1951.

Forty-five rooms were added to the 189 homes.

Ninety-five beds were built.

One of the secrets that AIA instilled in the CBR operation was to gauge the individual carefully, to guide him into a task that, while a challenge to him, was not one so far beyond his experience that he was frustrated by its very complexities. Usually the farmer was led on to more and more ambitious programs, eventually to handle the improvement of his place with a minimum of advice.

The loans were small in most cases, although occasionally a farmer was judged ready for a more substantial amount of money. The loans permitted the farmers to buy equipment and tools, a cow or some pigs, good seed and fertilizer to grow his own crops, nursery stock from which to develop an orchard, a hive of bees from which he could start a paying honey business, or to dig a well to provide his ailing family with pure water, or to build a sanitary privy.

Hudgens, remembering that thousands of U.S. farmers had been saved from complete ruin in the dark days of the depression by supervised credit, put his complete faith in this device. Some have subsequently thought perhaps AIA oversold the Venezuelan government on the cure-all properties of supervised credit, particularly after apathy had forced the program to close down. Others say that it was the single most important mechanism that AIA developed in Venezuela, for, in addition to leaving a firm foundation for future programs, it also revealed some very basic needs that existed in the pattern of Venezuelan agricultural development. Many of these needs came as a great surprise to the North-American trained AIA technicians working in CBR, accustomed as they were to a much more sophisticated level of agricultural development. Things that AIA's staff members took for granted—such as tools, roads, marketing facilities—they suddenly discovered had to be created from scratch.

In addition, all manner of unforeseen local problems cropped up—lack of water on Isla Margarita, soil erosion in the Andes where centuries of clearing and planting had washed away what little top soil there was, the absence of access roads to rural communities.

These discoveries led to concomitant programs which have stood both CBR and the whole country in very good stead indeed.

When political developments resulted in the overthrow of the liberal party, the Acción Democrática (or Democratic Action), the installation of an interim, troika-like military junta, and finally the advent of the oppressive Pérez Jiménez regime which almost forced the temporary discontinuance of supervised credit, the contributory programs assumed greater and greater importance. Successors to Acción Democrática felt these programs cost them very little, caused no great problems, and brought considerable kudos in public relations.

Community Centers

Both CBR and the Venezuelan government were anxious to get some principles of modern home economics introduced into individual farm families. However, home economists were rudely rebuffed when they tried to ingratiate themselves into the farm home. This perhaps stemmed from a natural reluctance to welcome strangers, a shame of the poor conditions of their homes, and also a fear of what was new. Even when the girls were given the welcome mat, they found their job almost impossible because of lack of tools and equipment of the simplest kind.

As in Brazil, it was felt that the answer to this was a community center where women could come, usually with their children, to see demonstrations, to learn how to do for themselves, and perhaps to become a significant and successful part of the community. For some reason never quite identified, the families most resistant to an invasion

85

Personal hygiene starts early at the Yagua community center.

of their homes participated with eagerness when it was put on a community basis.

And the home economists had an easier time of it and could serve a greater number of families. In a very short time the women were asking the technician at the center to come to their homes in order to diagnose problems and offer suggestions for solution.

Early in the community center program, CBR devised the charter that was to guide all the girls who worked in these centers:

Today the question is not to solve problems *for* people, nor to solve problems *with* people, but to help people solve their own problems.

Both men and women participated in the actual work of building the center—whether it was remodeling and equipping an old building or creating one from scratch. In some communities enthusiasm ran so high that night and Sunday work was in order. Whole families turned up. The children were herded together in custody of one of the mothers. The men went to work with hammer and saw, and the women sewed curtains, made simple furniture—makeshift tables, chairs and workbenches—built the fires to boil the water, and urged everybody to use the sanitary privy.

The centers were modestly furnished in an effort to show local families how they could make their own homes more pleasant and comfortable with very little money. Most of the furniture at the centers was built as demonstration lessons in carpentry and improvised equipment for the women and girls. Boxes, barrels, tin cans, inexpensive oil cloth and feed sacks went into much of the furnishings; and families that were too poor to invest in chairs, beds, cupboards were soon making such furnishings for their bare homes.

The girls and women were so thrilled at the opportunity to learn how to sew that they showed up at the center full of enthusiasm and armed with satins, brocades and other costly and perishable materials, secured at heaven only knows what sacrifice. Denise Dabrowski, a stocky little no-nonsense home economist stationed at the center in Caripito firmly laid down the law that attractive and becoming dresses could be made out of cotton and other materials that were washable, would wear well and were much more suitable to the oppressive heat of the area.

The centers served as school rooms for the home economist to teach improved home management methods, conduct special courses in nutrition, health and sanitation, and direct other activities. They were also used for apprentice training of employees of the Ministries of Agriculture and Health and Sanitation and some state governments.

In addition, the villagers themselves used the centers for town meetings where questions of local import were threshed out, for occasional get-togethers to welcome a victorious soccer team, to celebrate a local saint's day, or just to have fun.

During the six years that CBR operated this demonstration program, it established twenty-one centers in cooperation with state governments and other organizations in all the various areas of the country—in the Andes, on the island of Margarita, in the rich farming area around Valencia and Maracay.

In 1954, when CBR withdrew from this activity, all the centers were turned over to state and local groups for management. Most of the original ones are still going strong and have been joined by some 250 more. In fact, today a Department of Community Development and Planning is attached to the Office of the President, to nurture and encourage similar centers, both rural and urban.

Head Start—Venezuelan Style

Early in the program Sue Taylor discovered that between weaning and entering school a child's health and nutrition level declined sharply.

She called her home economists together (at the time there were about ten deployed in all parts of the country) propounded her theory and asked them to explore their own areas and come up with some suggestions.

The findings were that federal health clinics gave mothers pre- and post-natal assistance until the time the baby was weaned. The mother was then on her own until the youngster went to school, when he was enrolled in a school lunch program. It became evident that the mothers' lack of knowledge resulted in a serious health decline during this interim period.

This led to a pre-school breakfast program initiated in twelve of the community centers. A basic part of the program was to teach the children, and through them the mothers, improved nutrition, sanitary food preparation, personal cleanliness and general self-improvement.

Perhaps the curriculum sounds a little dull, but it was far from it for the youngsters. The first thing a visitor to a center saw was a neat row of tiny toothbrushes, a similar line of clean little towels and combs, and a stack of individual drinking cups. The joy a child took in his first encounter with a toothbrush knew no bounds, particularly when he found it worked equally well on his chin and eyebrows.

All in all, many thousands of meals were served and hundreds of mothers learned better health and food habits by working in the centers.

Although CBR withdrew from the program in 1954, it has been continued as an integral part of the Ministry of Health's program. Like our own Head Start program, this has a built-in termination point—in Venezuela when the whole country is brought to an ideal nutritional level.

Rural Roads

Where does a road lead? For the farmer it leads to market, for the housewife it goes to a shopping center and for a child to school.

To the early CBR extension workers it was something that didn't exist and hence led nowhere. Even Hudgens' jeep couldn't get through some of the trails that led from farm area to farm area, and both the man and the girl had to take to foot or horseback.

Because so many communities were connected only by mule trails, the farmers' transportation costs were disproportionately high, they were limited in the type of products they could market and, most important, in the amount of produce they could carry.

All-weather road building was expensive and the costs were way beyond the means of most state and local governments.

John Camp, recalling his early days as a forester in the U.S. Northwest, remembered the logging roads that bulldozers quickly cut through a forest area, and decided to give it a whirl. The state of Táchira, deep in the Andes, was chosen for the trial run because the problem there was particularly acute.

CBR agreed to survey a road, bulldoze it, and in the course of it to train machine operators to perform such operations as sidecasting, ditching, bulldozing, leveling and grading. The state of Táchira agreed to foot the modest bill.

The first road, that connected little farms and villages in the mountainous region near San Cristóbal to the main Trans-Andean Highway and that brought in hundreds of commercial trucks, spelled new life and new hope. Hundreds of farmers who at one time took their produce to market on muleback over narrow, winding trails, now had a more efficient and low-cost means of transportation. The road did away with endless hours, rain or shine, of journey to the nearest market. Produce and flowers arrived at the market crisp and fresh. Farm machinery for more efficient cultivation of the land, and household utensils for improved home living, were brought in over the road. The construction of the church, so desired by the devout families of the region and undertaken with great effort and sacrifice for years, was accelerated and soon completed. More children could attend school and a doctor was available on short notice.

"Those first roads were made by guess and by God," says Camp.

A CBR farm-to-market road winds through the foothills of
the Andes in western Venezuela.

"But we got them done, and done quickly. The idea soon spread to other states and eventually became a more up-to-date and finished program."

Camp himself confesses to surprise at the ingenuity of some of the technicians trying to work against time. He recalls that one of the workers resorted to toilet paper to establish the line to be cut through. Every morning before he went into the bush, he visited the local store and laid in three dozen rolls. One morning the storekeeper drew his customer aside, lowered his voice and confided, "You know, I have something that will cure that."

Today Venezuela has the best secondary road network in South America. This system has succeeded not only in getting produce to the market more quickly and efficiently but has also opened up whole new agricultural areas. Not the least of its achievements has been to make the difference for the individual farmer between living in a real community or in isolation on a mountain slope or in a jungle clearing.

Tractor Driver Training

In 1948, the Venezuelan government asked CBR to lend a hand in helping to settle farm families on a large acreage of land skirting Lake Valencia in the state of Carabobo. There were some 170 families with a total population of around 800 involved. Originally the government

The practice area near the farm machinery training center.

91

attempted to settle and rehabilitate these folk through cooperative groups, members of which were paid day laborers' wages and were to participate in any profits from the operation. Despite a large investment in loans to the cooperatives, the farmers were not making enough to improve their standards of living. In other words, the system was not working. It was at this point that CBR was invited to make an analysis.

Among the many things that were lacking to the farm families was a knowledge of farm machinery, its use and care. A tractor school was set up in a couple of quonset huts, at the little town of Guacara.

The government colonization agency supplied thirty-two new tractors and other farm equipment while CBR supplied the teaching manpower. Candidates for the training school came by bicycle, burro and on foot to their daily half-day class for two weeks. Nearly 40% of them were illiterate and none had ever driven a truck, car or jeep before.

The men were taught how to handle the machines, how to check tires, motor oil, transmission oil, gasoline, water, battery, airfilter and how to grease and adjust the machines. Fifty were trained in the first two weeks and were promptly put in the fields to plow and disk some sixty hectares of the land.

A change of government has resulted in the return of the land on which these farmers were located to the original wealthy, large landowners. Many of the more efficient farmers, who had been trained by CBR, were resettled at a later agricultural colony at Turén, in the state of Portuguesa.

Meanwhile, the Yaracuy valley, which was undergoing a rapid change in agricultural practices, from a primitive hand-tool system to mechanized operations, was facing a serious shortage of skilled people to handle and maintain tractors and other heavy farm equipment. The state turned immediately to CBR for help. And within a matter of weeks CBR had set up two completely mobile machinery training units as part of the many activities going on in its center at San Felipe. CBR supplied both the tractors and equipment (with the cooperation of local machinery companies who sold CBR the equipment at or below cost) as well as teaching.

The mobile training units later moved to the states of Guárico

Where small acreage did not warrant the use of tractors, CBR gave
training in use of animal-drawn implements.

and Aragua and, in all, trained nearly 2,000 drivers whose earning
powers have since doubled.

In addition to the training of drivers and mechanics, this program provided a farm machinery service to small farmers in the area
and contributed to the orientation of future land reform activities of
the Venezuelan government.

In some cases where, for one reason or another, a mechanical
program was not feasible, CBR gave special training in the use of
animal-drawn implements.

CBR completed its function in this program in 1956 and, although the Ministry of Agriculture maintains a token mobile service, Camp feels that the program never really caught on.

"Some officials," he comments, "thought you could only train
these tractor drivers at a fixed place. We felt that it was better to take
the units around to areas where the service was needed. After all, you
can reach the saturation point of tractor drivers in a very short time.

"Also these same officials thought it was a good idea to give a
graduate of a two-week course a diploma. And of course by then the
guy didn't want to *be* a tractor driver—he wanted to be an executive
and hang his diploma on the wall."

93

Perhaps one of the most far-reaching programs that CBR has carried out has been its special studies. This developed early, when AIA technicians were faced with the problem of designing programs, making recommendations and carrying out activities without adequate background information.

They might set up a splendid project of growing rutabaga and suddenly discover that the soil was quite unsuited to that esoteric vegetable. All sorts of interesting developments were suggested for the arid but pearl-rich little island of Margarita off the northeast coast. Then it was discovered that the lack of water was more serious than anybody had recognized.

This all led to special agricultural resource studies which have developed into an important body of basic research data on which all potential agricultural development is now based.

In time various government agencies began requesting CBR assistance in basic research, and soon CBR had a whole staff of specialists engaged in making special studies. These varied both in scope and depth of treatment, depending on the needs. However, they fell mainly into four broad categories:

1) Regional Resource Studies: e.g., *Agricultural Resources of the State of Yaracuy; Economic and Social Problems of the Andes* (in two volumes, this has been much in demand in Venezuela since its publication in 1955); *Agricultural and Forest Resources of the State of Barinas.*

2) Specific Agricultural Industry Studies: e.g., *The Livestock Industry in Venezuela; Cost of Corn Production; The Classification of Tobacco in Venezuela.*

3) General and Specific Agricultural or Community Problem Studies: e.g., *Possibilities of the Organization of Cooperatives in the Federal Colonies; Agricultural and Livestock Atlas of Venezuela; Analysis of Governmental Policies Concerning the Prices and Marketing of the Milk Industry of Venezuela.*

4) Administrative Organization Studies: e.g., *Administrative Studies of the Forestry Service and the Extension Service of the Ministry of Agriculture; Agricultural Research in Venezuela; A Department of Irrigation in the National Agrarian Institute.*

A complete list of these studies appears in the appendix.

In addition to the CBR staff itself, the organization called upon outsiders with international experience in special areas. Also there were always several Venezuelans affiliated with each study, so that the program had an in-service training function connected with it. Many of these fledgling researchers have since moved on to positions of importance in the academic and agricultural circles of the country.

While some of the reports have been prepared for the solution of immediate problems, most of them have been made with a long-range viewpoint and their effectiveness is hard to measure. However, indications are that their use is widespread and growing every year.

In 1966, several years after AIA had turned the direction of CBR entirely over to the Venezuelans and retained only an advisory connection, the organization made an analysis of all the studies and special research projects it had turned out since 1948. There were 67 studies and 339 experts (of whom 203 were Venezuelans) had worked on them from periods ranging from a few weeks to two years.

The author, Ricardo Gondelles A., director of the studies program since 1961, comments:

> One of the most important results of these studies is the growing evidence of a changing attitude on the part of rural people. They are now showing themselves more amenable to using modern methods in approaching the various social and economic problems which confront them. This changed attitude can be traced, to a certain extent, to the special studies, inasmuch as they have presented reasonable ideas in a simple, clear form and suggested substantial changes firmly based in scientific research.

According to Gondelles' survey most of these studies, instead of gathering dust in somebody's desk drawer, are well-thumbed and overworked reference books which not only the theoretical planner but also the man in the field consults.

For example, *The Livestock Industry in Venezuela* is "generally considered as one of the classic and most authoritative works of its kind and constitutes an essential reference work for all working in the field."

The monumental study on the Andes region—a study of all the factors, economic, social, geographic, physical and cultural, that make the Andean region what it is—was the first such study ever made in Venezuela. This interdisciplinary study is today a basic document on which the newly formed Development Corporation for the Andes has based all its plans and programs for the future of the area.

In 1959 a team of specialists, headed by Louis E. Heaton, a hard-working, amiable agricultural economist, original director of the special studies program, pushed their way through the jungles, across the flat, dry grasslands and into high timberland in the area of Venezuela known as Guayana, south of the Orinoco, adjacent to former British Guiana, now independent Guyana. The study that resulted two years later, *Agricultural and Forestry Survey of Guayana Area of Venezuela* (in seven volumes), has served as the basis for agricultural development plans of the Venezuelan Development Corporation for Guayana. It is a complete inventory of the land, forest and water resources of some thirty million acres of this wild, undeveloped region.

From this a full plan of exploitation of the forest resources and agricultural development under irrigation is being developed—to add to the nation's productivity.

Extension Training

By 1954 the political situation in Venezuela deteriorated to the point where both CBR and AIA realized that the supervised credit program had no chance of moving forward, at least for the time being. It was unanimously agreed, therefore, that CBR switch its course to another area where the need was just as great.

CBR had always been in one form of extension work or another—but primarily demonstration projects combined with supervised credit and community centers. It was hoped that from these demonstrations their influence would spread and government agencies and other organizations would adopt and expand the programs into national services.

This did not happen—primarily for one reason—namely, that there were insufficient well-trained professional and semi-professional technicians in the country.

So CBR took another deep breath and moved into a program of training extension technicians. The program was centered in the state of Aragua, where several agricultural schools were located. Two demonstration extension offices were established in the state to serve as laboratories for the training in both practical and applied aspects of extension, both in-service and pre-service courses.

The two centers, at Palo Negro and San Francisco de Asís, provided the surrounding farmers with a full program of services. Students visited farm families, organized 5-V clubs, demonstrated child care, taught sewing and poultry raising and trained voluntary community leaders. The in-service students were mostly employees of the Ministry of Agriculture, the National Agrarian Institute and the Agricultural Bank. These courses lasted anywhere from two weeks to three months.

The pre-service training in extension methods was provided for students taking the regular agricultural college courses, as well as the senior students in the vocational agricultural school and the Home Demonstration Agents School. Most of these students were preparing to enter the federal extension service. In addition to their formal

A Venezuelan farmer learns how to make his own adobe bricks and mortar with which he is rebuilding his unsanitary mud-thatch house.

and academic work at school, the students received practical training at the two centers. All told, about 500 technicians in agriculture, including extension, and in health and sanitation, were trained in the fifteen to twenty courses, both theoretical and practical, that were conducted. For college students the course lasted a full school year, while for the students at the vocational school and the Home Demonstration School the course was of three months' duration. Incidentally, CBR, through Dr. Alberto Fernández Yépez, taught the first extension course in the University School of Agronomy at Maracay.

Today extension training is an established part of the curriculum of all the agricultural colleges and high schools of the country.

Urban Community Center

The success of the rural community centers caught the eye of more than country people. People from towns and cities, where living conditions left much to be desired, wondered why the same principle would not apply in their communities.

So CBR was asked in early 1957 by the governor of the state of Zulia if it would undertake a specialized community project in one of the towns that was rapidly mushrooming, without plan or reason, on the periphery of the oil fields in western Venezuela. It was frankly an experiment—to see if the community resources of a poor industrial area could be marshalled to provide the needed education and cultural and recreational facilities.

The little town of Ciudad Ojeda, on the eastern shore of Lake Maracaibo, one of hundreds of small satellite communities that had grown up in the oil areas, was chosen for this project.

It was a sad little town that had grown from less than 2,000 persons in 1950 to over 15,000 in 1956. Aside from one movie house there were no facilities for public gatherings, and the standard of living was so low that none of the residents took pleasure in their homes which were nothing more than overcrowded shelters.

CBR sent one of its technicians, Elda Marquina, a bright-eyed bouncy enthusiast who had worked for several years in rural areas setting up and running community centers. Elda got hold of a few community leaders (there were pitifully few of them) and explained what she had in mind. Her enthusiasm communicated itself and the leaders organized a general public meeting to explain to everybody who would listen.

In time a central committee was named, the local school provided a small room for meetings, and committees were appointed to: 1) find a permanent home for the center; 2) promote news of the center; 3) develop activities for fund raising; and 4) write the charter.

Within a very short time all the committees reported success: an unfurnished house; lots of publicity through the press, radio, pamphlets and individual visits; the sum of Bs. 2,433.45 collected from a fine fiesta in which the whole village participated; and a charter and bylaws set forth.

Various local enterprises contributed materials and furniture and the 5-V club members painted the whole place, inside and out as well as the furniture.

By July, 1957, the center was in full swing. Courses in cooking and sewing were going on, as were demonstrations in home management, health and hygiene. The Lions Club had agreed to sponsor a children's nursery, five local physicians had agreed to give free medical consultation on a regular basis, a soft-drink company sponsored a "Birthday of the Month" for youngsters from two to ten years old.

When CBR bowed out in 1958, turning the operation over to the Zulia State Department of Education, Elda summarized her experience thus:

> From the very beginning the community took the center to its heart. The entire population, each according to his ability, helped in its organization and contributed to the progress of the institution, which became the pride of all Ojedans. During the two years that CBR ran the center, I would say that 90% of all the town's citizens took some part in the life of the center.

Information Program

The board of directors of CBR looked at CIDEA and, recognizing that it was doing a very special and effective job, decided to allot a good-sized part of its budget to an agricultural information program.

CBR had developed many new techniques, had spotted some of the difficulties in the agricultural picture, and then was faced with the problem of how to get the information across to the people who would most benefit from it—namely the farmers. This was where a

A wordless pamphlet, on the subject of selecting good corn seed, absorbs this Venezuelan peasant farmer.

program of communicating the "how-to-do" and "what-to-do" facts to the farmers was of critical importance.

Perhaps the first-person reminiscences of H. Schuyler Bradt, director of the program, tell the story best. Bradt, who came to CBR from a successful career of making training films for the U.S. Navy and business corporations, here outlines problems and experiences that, while encountered in CBR, were also common to CIDEA.

I was not an agricultural specialist nor did I know the agricultural problems of the country so it was agreed that the Ministry of Agriculture would assume complete responsibility for subject matter while I would take responsibility for format, media, language and the style of the messages to be promoted.

Very early in the game there was a full-dress showdown when I refused to turn the job into a public relations and publicity office for politicians. The air was quickly cleared and there was never further trouble from that direction.

The method of operation was simple. Agricultural problem areas were established and priority assigned. Upon each subject a technical bulletin was prepared and distributed to agricultural engineers, agricultural zone chiefs, and extension agents. Each bulletin was broken down into briefer, usuable, common-language messages and assigned to the communications channels considered most suitable.

While this was going on an agricultural technician of CBR and myself visited each of the 56 newspapers and 23 radio stations in Venezuela. First, interest had to be aroused in the altruistic aim of the program to improve agricultural production on a national basis. There were oil and money in Venezuela but money without agricultural technology, even primitive technology, does not produce food. The biggest communication feat, however, was to break through the age-old custom of the public media and to induce them to treat agricultural information as news rather than as advertising to be paid for by the inch, and in advance.

Once established, the newspaper campaign offered few difficulties. I believe that in a two-year period we harvested 3,100 clippings from 700 articles released. The papers plus a few magazines had a weekly circulation of 900,000. I have no way of guessing how many people read the releases but in any event it was the biggest snow-job I ever was connected with. Releases to Caracas papers were distributed by hand (these papers accounted for the major circulation throughout the country). Releases to smaller city dailies and to weeklies were mailed. Releases were produced on multilith of high quality and were distributed six days a week with frequent "specials." Photos were transmitted by mat.

During much of the time the campaign was operating, political feeling in Venezuela was intense, finally resulting in revolution. For reasons beyond my ken the information campaign, in all its parts, remained free of criticism in any form.

The radio campaign presented more problems. How do you get people to listen to a new program in the first place? Well, you launch it with newspaper stories (we should have also used posters but due to a strenuous work-load it escaped us) then you put the program on the air. Even here there are restrictions. If you broadcast a program at 5 A.M. before the farmer goes into the field, the electric current has not yet been turned on in a sizeable number of rural communities. If you try to reach a group audience of farmers, say at local bars Saturday afternoons, the timing has to be precise: not too early or the farmers won't be there and not too late or their receptivity will have become dulled for obvious reasons.

Instead of news announcements we elected to create interest by presenting five-minute soap operas five days a week. Content was about 80% agricultural and 20% home economics. We used a popular Venezuelan tune as identifying theme song. The announcer was the straight man, his counterpart a peasant who was not dumb by any means but who just did not have the knowledge available to him to solve his problems. There was also a middle-aged actress who helped out on the home economics. Sometimes the action was played straight, sometimes with comic relief, and on public holidays it was frequently pure entertainment. Occasionally there was a taped field interview.

In 1956 tape was not in common use in Venezuela so discs were made, a week's program being sent out by airmail in advance. This was expensive because the discs having once been played were of no further use. During my part in the campaign 66,000 discs were produced and distributed.

Aside from the technical, or source, pamphlets we produced a high-school level series and a second-grade level series. These were distributed via local extension offices. All were illustrated with drawings or photographs. I don't have the figures but we probably produced and distributed a million copies covering over 200 subjects.

For some reason it was easier to evaluate the pamphlets than the other media. Artistically, the simple, realistic drawings were more effective than sophisticated ones. Simple, realistic drawings were more effective than photographs which frequently contained too much extraneous detail. There did not seem to be much variation in effectiveness in the use of color as against black and white. We experimented with a pamphlet consisting entirely of drawings on the subject of better corn seed selection and found that it was understood by 42% of the 1,000 farmers who "read" it. With such a high percent we suspected that the sampling was contaminated by some extension agent interviewers who thought a low score reflected adversely on them. In any event, there was no record of the educational level of those interviewed nor was there a subsequent follow-up to see if those who understood the pamphlet actually put the information to practice. Of course, in an over-all, slam-bang campaign of these proportions in such a limited time there was no room for niceties such as pre-testing or evaluation.

The distribution of printed material was in the hands of the Ministry of Agriculture if, in truth, it was in any hands at all. We found quantities of pamphlets on coffee production in the eastern lowlands where corn is grown and other quantities of corn pamphlets blithely being broadcast in the Andes. Zones noted for high illiteracy were flooded with technical bulletins.

The AIA program produced the first Venezuelan comic books. The purpose was to try to increase membership in rural youth clubs. They were well distributed and enthusiastically received, some were even stolen and sold on the street. I believe the three comic books produced and distributed came to 300,000 copies. Posters were produced in relatively large quantities, usually to promote pamphlets and leaflets. Some were seen to have been tacked up with the printed legend upside down, pictures apparently being more important than words.

Two 20-minute films were made which together with several Ministry films were seen by a rural audience of a million over a two-year period. Following CIDEA's earlier lead, the films were shown from mobile units.

Contestant displays her prize-winning poster urging the destruction of flies, particularly by burning trash and garbage.

The staff consisted of a director, two assistant directors, two artists, three radio actors, two recording technicians, a multilith operator, a reporter and two secretaries. On looking back it seems incredible that such a small group could have produced such a great quantity of work. This all-Venezuelan staff was loyal and enthusiastic beyond my greatest hopes.

It has been said that the quality and sheer bulk of the CBR agricultural information campaign put CBR on the map throughout Latin America.

What it did for agricultural production in Venezuela will probably never be known. It certainly trained a number of Venezuelans in agricultural information methods and techniques. Indirectly it provided a first step in putting AIA's programs on a hemisphere-wide basis. In any event, specific evaluation of the information campaign would have been difficult, if indeed possible, as the country was in revolution as the campaign closed.

The conclusions reached as a result of the Venezuelan campaign and other information programs put on by various entities in Latin America and throughout the world by United States agencies were:

1. All-out crash information programs are not always effective because of:
   a. Lack of knowledge of the audience.
   b. Prohibitive cost which can only be born by wealthy nations or U.S. foreign aid.
   c. The inclination to train foreign technicians in the United States where such training is not always applicable to local conditions.
   d. Over training, such as at the Ph.D. level, where the recipients either do not return to their own countries or do return and find no one at their educational level to understand what they are talking about.

Recommendations were to:

1. Train directors of information in the various ministries in basic information theory and techniques. Almost all of these people were either newspaper reporters or radio announcers and were only high-school graduates.

2. Find out more about how people in Latin America accept new ideas and adopt new practices.

3. Train qualified Latin American, information specialists in Latin America to the Master's Degree level to strengthen

the faculties of agricultural universities and to provide a corps of qualified information teachers to replace U.S. instructors.

4. Put AIA's information program on a Latin American-wide basis.

Thus was laid the basis for the new step forward by AIA in the information field, which will be described later.

Housing, Youth, Land Reform

No matter where CBR technicians turned they found that one of the greatest deterrents to improvement in the rural areas was housing. Not only was it unsanitary, it was inadequate and depressing. For the first time in the history of Venezuela an experimental program of rural housing was tried out.

The program started in the village of Magdalena in the state of Aragua, a cooperative effort of CBR with the Mendoza Foundation and the Malaria Control Division of the Ministry of Health. It began as a small, experimental effort using so-called "aided self-help" methods. The government subsidized part of the cost and the village family itself contributed labor and footed the bill for the rest. CBR and the Ministry of Health contributed technical assistance, education in construction methods, home furnishings, home management, etc., while the Mendoza Foundation helped with cement and building materials. The families were responsible for the actual cost of all materials used in construction and the employment of skilled workers for certain jobs that the families themselves could not do, such as fitting windows and doors, roofing, etc.

An initial start was made with six families and the success of the project inspired thirty other families to similar construction. The families grouped together to raise their houses cooperatively. As in any pioneer effort, the "bee" principle stood them in good stead here. Comfortable houses were built at an average cash cost to a family of Bs. 3,350, or about $1,000. These funds were provided on loan from the government to be repaid in ten years without interest.

From these experimental efforts the Venezuelan government has since developed a national program of rural housing, based on the aided self-help principle. On March 14, 1968, this program celebrated

105

Dr. Edgardo Mondolfi, CBR Director and Jorge Marcano review the
5-V club members of Pimpinela.

its tenth anniversary by completing its 70,000th house and inaugurating a new land reform settlement in Guárico State, with President Raúl Leoni officiating.

There were two other areas in which CBR's contribution, while not of prime importance in its early program, gradually became of greater and greater significance.

One was the development of the rural youth movement. Even before AIA came into the picture there had been a 5-V club movement in the country (the V's stand for Valor—bravery, Vigor—strength, Verdad—truth, Verguenza—honor, Venezuela). But it had been primarily a social operation and run in connection with the schools. An extension agent would organize a 5-V group in a community, chalk up another accomplishment on his worksheet, arrange one or two recreational or sports events and let it go at that.

With the advent of CBR and its philosophy of training and education, the youth clubs took on a whole new meaning. The youngsters were taught to grow vegetables, sew clothes for a family, raise pigs, and make furniture in their own homes and on their own farms. Through youthful enthusiasm many a parent was stimulated to search for a better life.

It was during this developmental period that Howard E. Law,

who was at that time director of CBR and was destined to become the father of the hemisphere-wide rural youth program, recognized the need for the parents, the community, the business leaders to become interested supporters and actively concerned with the youth club program. Law's quiet but dogged perseverance led, in 1960, to the formation of the 5-V Association. This nation-wide group of civic-minded citizens has since then given tremendous encouragement and also something more substantial—the leadership and financial support needed in a developing society.

We will see later how this movement has spread all over the hemisphere.

Perhaps the most important, albeit unofficial, job that CBR did was the influence it had on the agrarian reform movement in Venezuela. Through the quiet counseling, demonstrations, the special studies and learning through doing, a rational pattern of land tenure and redistribution was adopted by Venezuela.

She was the first country to pass an integral or comprehensive agrarian reform law which covered all aspects of restructuring the rural economy. The preamble of this law, which was passed in 1960, served as the basis for the declaration on agrarian reform in the Charter of Punta del Este which established the Alliance for Progress in 1961.

Land reform is much more than a simple transfer of acreage from one ownership to many. The key lies in the training and other services that are furnished the new landowner. To be of lasting value the program must put knowledge into his head and opportunity within his grasp. It does no permanent good to give land to a man who does not know how to make it produce food that his family can eat and crops that he can sell.

This means that carefully developed systems of training in agriculture, nutrition and health, and the results of crop and market research must be available to the new farmers and their families. Involved here are farm and home extension services, supervised credit, education for the children, youth clubs, farm-to-market roads, community health services.

Underlying all these are the facts about the resources of the area to be settled by a land reform project: the soils, water supplies, timber, minerals. Without such basic information the project may be a hit-or-miss proposition at a time, in the 1960's, and a place, in Latin America, where a miss could have spelled disaster.

In other words, everything that CBR was doing was to contribute to a sound and evolutionary program of land redistribution. The pattern offered at the other extreme (Cuba) of only taking land away from those who have it and handing it over to those who don't apparently has not worked out to the economic or social advantage of the citizens.

Evaluation

The place that CBR holds in the permanent structure of the Venezuelan government is attested by the acclaim with which its twentieth anniversary was celebrated. Eight leading figures in government and

5-V club members working in their vegetable plots.

108

agriculture, of widely varying political affiliations and economic interests, took the occasion in October, 1967, to publish their appreciation of the work that CBR had done and to wish it a long life.

One official who had been Minister of Agriculture at the time CBR was set up and who was one of the most enthusiastic original supporters of the idea confessed to "greatest satisfaction in having contributed to the founding of CBR, in seeing the point to which it has arrived after such modest beginnings."

Another former Minister of Agriculture said that a CBR study on livestock in Venezuela had served as the base on which the country's present widespread and very successful livestock development plan was being carried forward.

The "practical solutions to the great regional and national problems of the country" offered by CBR were hailed by the Minister of Development, who added that it was thanks to the policies of CBR in cooperation with the federal government that "a national conscience as to the social and economic importance of agricultural planning had been successfully created."

Another former Minister of Agriculture cited CBR's freedom from preconceived ideas and established ideologies as an important factor in its success, adding that CBR had three special qualifications:

1. Administrative flexibility which permits it to operate without the miles of red tape which usually fetter a bureaucracy.

2. Its freedom to negotiate as it sees fit, which permits it to contract for experts and studies as they are required.

3. Its ability to carry out its work without political compromises and its ability to remain outside all ideological controversies.

Chapter 3

VOCATIONAL TRAINING

Early in the program in Venezuela it was recognized that the greatest deterrent to progress was the lack of trained people at all levels and in all fields: agriculture, trades, professions, business and industry, and public administration. John Camp highlighted this in a report in 1953:

> AIA's work relates especially to the fields of agriculture, health and education where the lack of trained people is especially acute. One reason for this is that until about twenty years ago Venezuela had no health or agricultural services and no free public education system. Another reason is that the professions associated with these activities offer less remuneration than business and professional work in other fields.

> From practically nothing twenty years ago, the Venezuelan government is now spending about $140,000,000 a year on its health, agriculture and education services. However, it takes five to seven years to train professional personnel for public health and agricultural services and four years for school teachers. In spite of the present availability of funds there are not enough nurses, agronomists or school teachers and at the present rate that they are being trained, there will not be enough for another generation.

> The result is that there are untrained people holding down important jobs that require professional or at least vocational training and there are even schools, hospitals and agricultural agencies that cannot be opened because of the lack of trained personnel.

AIA, never an organization to see a problem without jumping in to do something about it, set forth an elaborate proposal to help the Ministry of Education to implement its planned reorganization of two of the basic educational systems of the country, namely, rural primary education and vocational trade and industrial education.

The proposal did not pretend to do the entire job, but rather to provide the Ministry with a demonstration in selected geographic areas of what the eventual transformation should be and with the technical resources requred for achieving it, including the trained Venezuelan personnel needed for extending the demonstration to other areas.

As Ernest E. Maes, who was slated to become director of all AIA educational programs, said, "the function of the program would be that of placing a train on the tracks, facing it in the right direction, and providing it with an adequately trained crew."

However, AIA's board of directors looked twice at the ambitious scope of the project and suggested that it be trimmed to a more wieldy size. Since the Ministry of Education also was reluctant to embark on such a revolutionary program, it was decided to confine the job to vocational trade and industrial education for a two-year period. The agreement was signed in June, 1954. It was later extended for an additional fifteen months.

Maes, an enthusiast of boundless energy, promptly went to work to set up the program. An educator of distinguished standing, Maes brought to the job nearly twenty years of experience in Latin America. Particularly his work with the Inter-American Education Foundation (later combined with the Institute of Inter-American Affairs) stood him and AIA in good stead. For this organization had developed, from scratch, similar programs in Bolivia, Chile, Ecuador, Peru, Paraguay, Haiti and all the Central American countries and had provided an eight-year accumulation of proven teaching materials which could be easily adapted for Venezuelan use.

Demonstration School

Maes, with the help of Lyle B. Pember, a California vocational education specialist, set up a trade and industrial teacher training center and a demonstration trade school in Valencia, with the Ministry of Education providing fourteen selected Venezuelan vocational teachers who were to be the first training staff. The Ministry also made available the tools, equipment and supplies needed for the several shops and classroom.

The newly established center in Valencia organized the teachers' workshops during vacation periods—gladly attended by shop teachers

111

from all over the country who welcomed a chance to really learn how to do their job. An ambitious program of preparation of teaching materials, including manuals, guides on industrial teaching methods, job analysis, lesson plans, visual aids, instruction sheets, etc., was carried out by the center.

The demonstration school developed such an attractive program that students from all over the area began clamoring for admittance. Youngsters were enchanted with the practical and useful things they were learning—things that they could put to immediate use in their own homes. The success of the vocational aspects of their training made them more open-minded about the more academic learning— such as reading and writing. The general subjects had some meaning to them since, for the first time, they had a reason to want to read— otherwise how would they absorb the instructions on how to make a table or fix a carburetor or repair a broken switch?

Teachers attend a summer course in shop practice in Valencia.

At the end of the first year the following accomplishments had been chalked up:

1. The Experimental Institute of Industrial Education, which included both teacher training and the demonstration school, was running in high gear, with all operating scuffles between AIA and the Ministry of Education completely ironed out.

2. A $700,000 program for building and equipping shops, classroom and dormitory facilities at the Institute was under way.

3. Thirty-six shop teachers and four science and mathematics teachers had participated in the first vacation course.

4. An effective liaison had been set up with Venezuelan industry which had opened its shops and factories to the teacher trainers who needed experience.

5. Six basic manuals had been translated or adapted.

In September, 1957, just three years and three months after it had started, AIA terminated its part in the project and turned over to the Ministry of Education a flourishing and on-going program.

By this time the demonstration school had grown from the initial thirty-nine students to 340 and plans were already made to increase it to 500 in order to meet the demand from all over the country. In addition to a group of trained teacher trainers that had been incorporated into the staff of the Ministry of Education, the program had provided training for some 350 shop teachers in four summer vacation courses. Forty teachers had received intensive one-year training courses and were working in trade schools throughout the country. An impressive library of eighteen teachers' manuals had been either reproduced or translated and were in use all over the country. These ranged in scope from "Psychology for Industrial Teachers" to "Preparation of the Industrial Worker to Teach" to "Education for the Home."

This program, generally regarded as almost a model of what a technical cooperation program should be, probably owed its success to sound planning and early integration of all facets of its work into the Ministry itself. From the beginning AIA provided only those elements of the program which were by nature impermanent or non-recurring. This included technical specialists to train the local staff, the basic technical library and the services of AIA technicians.

A job analysis course requires concentration for the teacher-students.

No attempt was made at any time to impose the U.S. system in Venezuela. What was done was an adaptation of the U.S. system to the Venezuelan picture.

"Interestingly enough," summarized Maes, "the result was very close in principle to the U.S. program, but with many variations in details. Those variations were the contributions of the Venezuelan members of the staff and, because of it, they consider the resulting program as theirs."

A look at the program today, 1968, ten years after AIA relinquished it, shows that it has grown explosively. The number of vocational schools has risen from ten to over thirty. In 1958 the Ministry created the Technical Department in the Vocational Education Division, in large part staffed by AIA trained teachers. All the vocational courses, including the elementary shop courses, have been developed by this department, and all the teaching materials have derived from the original program.

In 1960, because of a greatly increased budget for additional vocational schools, the Ministry had to use the teacher trainers as directors of the new schools. This again resulted in a shortage of teachers, so in 1965 the Ministry reactivated the teacher training program on the pattern developed by AIA in 1954.

Chapter 4

CONCLUSION

Since 1960 AIA's Venezuela operations have been inextricably mixed up with the hemispherically expanded program that is described in the following section. Only with CBR did AIA keep up a formal relationship, signing an agreement every two years. AIA's financial contribution was reduced each contract term until it reached the token point of $22,000. The important part of the contract was the continued consultative services of Louis Heaton.

CBR—Post-AIA

In 1960 Edgardo Mondolfi became the first Venezuelan director of CBR, succeeding Howard Law who moved to head up the expanded Rural Youth Program based in Costa Rica. Mondolfi, an animal husbandry technician and an intense and dedicated student of the agricultural scene in Venezuela, brought to his job fifteen years of experience, coming to CBR from the number two post in the Ministry of Agriculture. During his eight years of tenure in the job, he has succeeded in weathering political changes and has consistently directed CBR's efforts into new and pioneering programs, which have brought acclaim and credit to the organization not only in Venezuela but also throughout the hemisphere.

Among the accomplishments that CBR is responsible for since AIA relinquished control are an impressive fruit development program through which CBR instituted fruit tree nurseries, distributed thousands of pounds of seeds, thousands of grafted stock of fruit trees and slips, arranged for credit and conducted hundreds of demonstrations and training sessions for potential fruit growers and, in general, laid the groundwork for a thriving fruit culture in all parts of the country, particularly in the Andes.

The program has recently been transferred to the Ministry of

115

Agriculture, except for that part in the Andes which has been turned over to the Andes Regional Development Corporation.

Another important job CBR has done has been a training and demonstration program for agrarian reform technicians. This work is based on two land settlement colonies in the state of Portuguesa with a total of 500 families. CBR technicians have conducted hundreds of farmers', homemakers' and youth leaders' meetings, have distributed thousands of pieces of training literature, and have otherwise prepared hundreds of specialists for their tricky jobs of helping the beneficiaries of agrarian reform to make the most of their new opportunities.

Mondolfi's greatest headache these days is the raiding of his CBR-trained staff. Fernando Rondón, CBR assistant director, is the latest loss. Rondón, who has accepted an important position as liaison officer with the Intergovernmental Committee for European Migration, in Buenos Aires, was one of CBR's first employees and spent most of his mature professional life with the organization. He worked in one of the first field offices in 1948 at San Cristóbal, in the high, cold Andean state of Táchira. His calm assurance that no matter how impossible something was it could be done, was a constant source of encouragement to the sometimes frustrated, always overworked, men and women who were trying to create CBR out of whole cloth.

Review and Evaluation

From the beginning AIA constantly reviewed its program, evaluated the job it was doing and conducted agonizing self-appraisals.

"My personal feeling," wrote Rockefeller in 1950, "is that AIA has only two functions. One is as a pioneer in the type of work we're presently doing. For the long pull it seems to me that this field is clearly a government field.

"The other is doing this work in this field for U.S. private enterprise clearly as a public relations program abroad in countries where the U.S. private companies have interest. This latter may justify the continuation of AIA if it is good enough to merit their support. Under these circumstances it would be a foundation working in the field of rural welfare on a contract basis like the non-profit research laboratories."

116

In 1951, AIA asked John French, a lawyer, and Arthur Jones, a long-time advisor to the Rockefeller family, to make an appraisal of AIA programs in Venezuela.

Specifically, a memo from Rockefeller asked that they make:

1. An appraisal of the degrees to which the various programs have accomplished their stated social, economic and public relations objectives.

2. An analysis of the expense of each of the programs with particular reference to cost per individual, or family, of services rendered.

3. An appraisal of whether the services rendered in each program were justified in the light of the cost per person or family.

4. An opinion as to whether the cost of the services under each program could be substantially reduced in any future work and, if so, an analysis of how.

The report came very early in the game—most of the Venezuelan programs were less than two years old so that a true evaluation was hardly possible. However, the consensus of the two evaluators was that a "promising start has been made toward AIA's objective of bettering the economic and social well-being of Venezuela and its people."

"Furthermore," the report added, "the programs appear to be possible of adaptation and adoption on a broad scale by the Venezuelan government."

Some valid criticisms of high administrative costs compared to program expenses were taken to heart and some tightening up and streamlining of overhead apparatus was instituted.

In conclusion, let's look at a few figures that may indicate the impact that AIA has had on the country as a whole. Not even AIA's most enthusiastic supporter claims that it alone is responsible for the startling improvement. There were dedicated government officials who pushed hard for reforms; there were bankers and banks that used imagination and faith in making loans; and, above all, there were the young men and women who stormed all over the hinterland taking the message of better farming methods and better home conditions to farmers and their families.

117

Here then are the indices of agricultural production in Venezuela by segments of the total agricultural sector, 1948 to 1966 (1948 equals 100).

Year	Crop Production	Livestock and Livestock Products	Fish Products	Forestry Products	Total Agricultural Sector
1948	100.0	100.0	100.0	100.0	100.0
1950	101.3	119.1	72.7	115.7	103.9
1955	128.3	162.6	88.7	138.5	133.4
1960	147.1	209.7	121.5	155.9	186.0
1965	203.2	300.8	156.9	190.9	248.2
1966	217.7	321.2	169.5	201.0	261.5

Source: Annual Reports of the Banco Central de Venezuela.

Indicators of improved agricultural practices that have particularly pleased AIA technicians are charted below:

A. **Improved and More Intensive Livestock Operations**

Increases in Use of Feed Concentrates (1950 to 1965)

Year	Production of Feed Concentrates (1000 Metric tons)		
	For Cattle	For Hogs	For Poultry
1950	9,980	231	4,121
1955	32,239	738	33,475
1960	40,495	14,543	114,914
1965	70,571	59,569	306,721
Index of Increase from 1950 to 1965	707% (7 fold increase)	25787% (258 fold increase)	7443% (74 fold increase)

B. **Improved Crop Production Practices**

1. **Fertilizer Use in the Country:**
   Increase in Use of Chemical Fertilizer Nutrients 1960 to 1965
   1960—21,150 Met. Tons; 1965—36,605 Met. Tons: Index for increase in use over the 5 year period—173% (1.7 fold increase)

118

2. **Insecticide and Fungicide Use: Increase in Use 1960 to 1965**
   1960—5.3 Met. Tons; 1965—10.5 Met. Tons: Index of increase in use over the 5 year period—198% (2 fold increase)

3. **Herbicide Use: Increase from 1960 to 1965**
   1960—330 Met. Tons; 1965—3,869 Met. Tons: Index of increase in use over the 5 year period—1172% (12 fold increase)

4. **Tractors on Farms: Increase in Number 1950 to 1965**
   1950—3,930 farm tractors; 1960—13,800; and 1965—16,773: Index for increase in number—1950 to 1965—427% (4¼ fold increase)

Source: Ministry of Agriculture; Annual Agricultural Statistics Reports; Caracas, Venezuela for all data except items B-3 and B-4 which were taken from CBR; "Present Status and Possibilities of Agricultural Development in Venezuela" Caracas, March, 1967.

An interesting footnote to the story in Venezuela is that when AIA first went to the country there were no private foundations as we know them in this country. Today there are twenty-eight.

The first to be established, in 1951, was set up by a wealthy and public-minded citizen, Eugenio Mendoza. Mendoza talked over his plans with his long-time friend Rockefeller and picked up a few pointers on both organization and philosophy for the new foundation.

Two oil companies also subsequently set up their own foundations, Creole and Shell, the former to "develop education, culture and science," the latter to "contribute to the agricultural development of the country by means of scientific research and its distribution."

Part 5

EXPANSION

In 1957, ten years after the birth of AIA, staff members and a couple of board members looked around them with considerable, but justified, complacency to see what they had wrought in Brazil and Venezuela. They liked what they saw and, like proud initiators, began casting about to see how their work could be expanded.

They wanted a hospitable, international organization, whose goals coincided with AIA's, which could provide the structure to spread into other countries all the things AIA had learned and perfected in Venezuela and Brazil.

Camp and Jamieson felt that the information program was the ripest for proliferation. Through CIDEA and CBR in Venezuela, many techniques had been developed, many hard facts had been driven home, and certainly the need had been defined. In Brazil, where no definite or exclusive information program had been developed, the frustration of lack of communications told not only in the operations themselves but also in the tempers of the people directing them.

120

As a possibility Camp thought of the Inter-American Institute of Agricultural Sciences, whose director, Dr. Allee, was still unhappy about the non-fulfillment of the 1947 scholarship agreement.

Late in 1957 Bradt attended a conference in Lima of information specialists from all countries of South America (there were some thirty delegates in all). With his characteristic candor Bradt quickly recognized that the program AIA had developed in Venezuela was more professional and more effective than any of the others. CIDEA had already been transferred and was flourishing under the aegis of the National Nutrition Institute. Bradt had a going program, resting between CBR and the Extension Service—resting a bit uneasily, to be sure, because of political tensions in Venezuela—but destined to weather the storms with flying colors. Among the delegates at Lima were representatives of the Institute who expressed wistful interest in the exciting things that had been and were being done in Venezuela.

Back in Caracas, Bradt and Camp huddled, worked out broad details of program content on a hemisphere-wide basis and, in the spring of 1958, proceeded to Turrialba.

Allee was enthusiastic, particularly since the Institute was about to embark on an extension information project with funds provided by ICA (International Cooperation Administration, the predecessor of AID). Both the AIA people and Allee recognized that what was needed was training. Until a body of men and women trained in modern techniques of communications was available to head programs in other countries of the continent, these projects could never become truly effective as educational efforts but were, more likely, to become implements for the politically ambitious.

An agreement setting up a mass communications program—destined to be the first of three historic accords between AIA, the small private foundation, and the Institute, the large international organization, representing twenty-one individualistic and independent republics—was signed on May 27, 1958. It was called Programa Interamericana de Información Popular, or Inter-American Popular Information Program, and known as PIIP, happily pronounced "peep" in both languages.

Bradt was named AIA's representative in Costa Rica, in addition to having responsibility for the mass communications program. In the course of the next few months he, Allee, and Camp jointly worked out details of other areas of cooperation. Allee, keenly alert to the advantages of the flexibility that little AIA had, was eager to extend AIA's approach to rural youth work and credit and extension programs to other areas of the hemisphere.

In 1960 Camp and Allee signed an agreement setting up the Inter-American Rural Youth Program (called PIJR from its name in Spanish). And in 1962, by which time Armando Samper had succeeded Allee as director and Camp had become executive vice-president of AIA, an accord setting up the Inter-American Rural Development Program (PIDR) became official. In 1966 the three agreements were incorporated into one master agreement.

Incidentally, the 1947 agreement with the Institute concerning scholarships in vocational agriculture for aspiring Venezuelan farmers was amended in 1954 to provide advanced technical training in agriculture for Venezuelans, and then further revised in 1961 to provide scholarship aid to qualified young people of *any* Latin American country and in *any* field relating to rural development. The three

Schuyler Bradt, center, supervises PIIP students as they make records
for an information program.

joint programs in the course of the next eight years made good use of these scholarships.

Although Camp's primary responsibility had been in Venezuela, the breadth of his experience and the quiet philosophical cast of his mind, had had a profound effect on all AIA's operations. He was known and welcomed in all parts of the hemisphere—over a cup of heavily-sugared coffee in a thatched hut in the depths of the Goiás jungle or over a crystal martini glass in the presidential palace in Caracas.

Camp had devised the basic pattern of the international agreements that he and Samper signed, and their execution was his responsibility. The end result of his stewardship and the relationship between the Institute and AIA is described by Samper with simple directness as "a great success."

Samper, a Colombian, educated at Cornell and as completely at home in English as in his native Spanish, is not a blind optimist, for he freely spells out some of the mistakes both organizations made. Some of these mistakes were those of personalities: the wrong person chosen for the right job or the right person for the wrong job. In many cases it was the difficulty of a large international organization to keep step with the more free-wheeling outfit. And in other cases it was an error in program design.

"The plusses far outweigh the minuses," reminisces Samper. "AIA brought some real advantages to our joint programs. Perhaps its real secret weapon was Nelson Rockefeller. His wartime work, his imagination, and his very real devotion to the cause of the developing countries of Latin America had long endeared him to our people.

"Some of the other advantages AIA brought was its smallness and the fact that it sent down competent people, all of whom spoke or quickly learned the language and stayed long enough in a country to know it intimately. But perhaps its greatest asset was the fact that it was *not* an agency of the U.S. government. It had great freedom of action and was not affected by political motivations nor by changing relationships between governments."

To AIA the affiliation with the Institute has given it a prestige that it would never have had otherwise, the security of a massive and respected partner, and a very real working relationship with hundreds of able and devoted experts from all countries of the hemisphere who make up the Institute's staff.

Today Camp evaluates these international programs as "operations based on the practical experience we had gained in Venezuela and Brazil. The agreements were pretty hard-nosed and there was very little theory. But they complemented the Institute's goals and brought to the Institute a much needed affiliation with an organization that had freedom of movement.

"At the same time, while all of us of AIA thought we were pretty good, in all honesty I have to admit that we never could have accomplished our objectives alone. Without the academic qualifications of a Samper, combined with his down-to-earth appreciation of the farmers' problems; without the intimate knowledge of individual countries by all Institute workers; and without the advanced research techniques of the graduate school at Turrialba, AIA would never have been able to multiply its activities as effectively as it has."

Chapter 1

PIIP

Both the agricultural extension people and the information specialists had by this time recognized that the tools then in use were inadequate to close the tremendous gap between knowledge and use. It was estimated that there were no more than 2,500 professional extension workers in agriculture and home economics in Latin America, about one to every 45,000 rural people.

All agreed that a major remedy lay in the use of mass communications techniques better adapted to, and hence more effective in, the customs and cultures of the Latin American countries.

In addition, educational levels varied widely among the different countries. Lack of accurate or in some instances of any census data made most vital statistics subject to suspicion. There are ranges from the 92% literate populations of Uruguay and Argentina to the almost 90% illiterate populations in remote areas of Bolivia, Peru and Haiti.

The very use of the word "illiterate" is misleading. A man is called illiterate because he cannot read and write Spanish—a foreign language to him. Is he truly illiterate who speaks only some Indian dialect that has existed for thousands of years without ever developing the symbols of a written language?

These are among the problems which faced both AIA and the Institute. They were not all solved, but at least a start was made.

Organizing from Scratch

As we have seen, Bradt, Camp and Allee met in the tropical setting of Turrialba in the spring of 1958 and hammered out the agreement that created PIIP.

It was to be directed by AIA and administered in cooperation with the Institute. In this way the extensive experience of AIA in the development of mass information methods in Venezuela during the

125

previous ten years was to be combined with the administrative facilities of the Institute to supplement the activities of its own Scientific Communications Service.

"In Venezuela," reminisces Bradt, "I walked on to the set, so to speak, with the cast fully assembled, and was backed by technical advisors in agriculture and in local mores. In Costa Rica, when I arrived in September as director of the new program, there was no set or cast and on turning around I found nobody behind me.

"The physical facilities were not hard to come by. Even the most difficult item, a telephone, was arranged for through the joint efforts of the then U.S. Ambassador and the President of the Republic whom I had met in the casual fashion of Costa Rican VIP's at the bar of the Union Club. Personnel is something else again, but fortune held and Nina Feoli (later replaced by Flora Bedoya) became PIIP's secretary and Ernesto Maduro its accountant-comptroller."

The first step the new organization embarked on was to provide a basic course in communications for the heads of information and other members of information staffs of ministries of agriculture, public health and education. Some of these people came to their jobs with a smattering of newspaper writing or radio announcing, but most came with no experience at all in the field.

Rogelio Coto, the Costa Rican head of the Institute's Scientific Communications Service, and Calvert Anderson, U.S. newspaperman with experience in a land-grant college extension information program, recently arrived to head up the Institute's communications training program, agreed to furnish teaching facilities and instructors while PIIP agreed to supply training equipment and student scholarships.

These three—Anderson, Bradt and Coto—were the self-designated "ABC's of Communications."

AIA had agreed to equip the desperately needed classroom if the Institute would build it. After a long period of negotiation but no action, Coto one day walked into Allee's office and laid two papers on his desk, saying, "With all due respect, sir, sign one or the other."

One paper was authorization to build the classroom, the other Coto's resignation. Allee signed the authorization.

"Coto and Anderson formed what was virtually their own construction company," recalls Bradt, "in order to transform a dilapidated rubber plantation godown into a campus, including art shop, visual aids center, printing plant, radio studio, classroom, executive offices and canteen. They ordered sand, cement, roofing material and lumber. As an example of the sophistication of the planning of these two, they set the classroom windows to such a height that students would not be distracted by passersby."

At one point the entire project threatened to come to a halt through lack of money to buy nails. Anderson and Coto located two kegs of used nails and spent days straightening them, passing them directly to the carpenters.

Catalogues were mutilated in the search for equipment—slide projectors, opaque projectors, overhead projectors, moving picture projectors, tape recorders, disc recorders and the indispensable urn for the indispensable coffee break.

In San José, PIIP was printing prospectuses for distribution to U.S. AID personnel in every country in Latin America and straining with the nightmare of proofreading English copy set by enthusiastic Latinos. Spanish versions were distributed to all government ministries. Curriculum was drafted, redrafted and equipment ordered by cable. There was no telephone connection between San José and Turrialba, so conferences had to be held in person and the PIIP Baby Austin literally began what was to be its death rattle, pounding through the potholes of the connecting mountain road.

"Through patience and diplomacy," says Bradt, "Coto and Anderson thrashed out the curriculum to a satisfactory conclusion. From the beginning they tried to introduce the principles of learning and processes of social change to broaden the students' horizons and understanding of their role in a developing society, but at the same time to develop the very practical skills of written, visual and oral presentations including press, radio, television, publications and the planning and execution of promotional campaigns.

"Four weeks before the course was to begin there were only three confirmed students. Like many troupers we got stage fright. We cabled urging cancellation of the course.

"No!"

So the course was given—for three months and for three students.

127

Preparing visual materials in the Basic Communications course at Turrialba.

That first course almost came to a close a few days after it opened. Anderson took the entire student body (all three) in a decrepit station wagon to Turrialba. The wagon stalled on the railroad tracks directly in front of an on-coming express. Brakes screamed, sparks flew, people shrieked as the train engineer slammed on his brakes and brought the train to a halt just five feet from the car where the four occupants were frozen in terror.

At the end of the first course enthusiasm was high, on the part of both sponsors and students. So plans, based on the initial experience, were made for the next course.

Subsequent courses were set for five months, to hit a happy medium between the minimum teaching time and the maximum length of time students could be away without losing their jobs.

Curriculum

The second course was planned for eight, but response to the announcement turned up fifty applicants from sixteen countries. Ultimately fourteen of the best qualified were chosen.

The five-month curriculum covered:

Orientation—History, theory and basic problems of communications (1 week).

Rural Sociology—Composition of human communities, how opinion is molded, and problems in the acceptance of new ideas (1 week).

Philosophy of Extension—A study of the methods of transmitting research results to farm families and helping put these results to practical use (1 week).

Putting Information to Work—Discussion of the idea or course of action to be sold. Audience characteristics and what information techniques should be used to communicate with them (1 week).

Printed Materials—The communications problems which can be solved through use of printed materials. Forms of printed matter and methods of reproduction. Actual work in the Institute's printing plant. Preparation of copy, essentials of pictorial composition, layouts, typography, dummies, seeing the material through the press. Distribution, records and evaluation (4 weeks).

Visual Aids—Production and demonstrations by each student of flannelgraphs, flip charts, chalk talks, slides, demonstrations on the use of puppets (2 weeks).

Motion Pictures—Problems which motion pictures can and cannot solve. Techniques, planning the films and writing shooting scripts. Use of motion pictures in an educational program. Production, distribution and evaluation (2 weeks).

Slide Films—Use and preparation of slide film material for photography. Projection, distribution and evaluation (1 week).

Radio and Television—Problems radio and television can and cannot solve. Introduction to tape recording, record cutting and other studio operations. Production and broadcast of students' radio scripts. Production of television scripts. Distribution and evaluation (3 weeks).

Meetings, Exhibitions, etc.—The conduct of public meetings and exhibtions. The use of mobile units (1 week).

Press—Proper use of newspaper and magazine facilities. Preparation by students of articles, columns, and agricultural and public health pages. Visits to newspapers. Distribution and records (2 weeks).

Organization and Administration—The organization and administration of various types of information services and offices. Sampling methods for general evaluation surveys (1 week).

Review and Examination—All work reviewed, oral examinations given, and, where qualified, diplomas awarded (1 week).

In all, five basic courses and ten short courses and seminars were given to a total of 450 students during a period of seven years.

This was not accomplished without some headaches and heartaches. One of the minor factors was the culture shock some of the students experienced, even though in most cases there were no language barriers. For example, Mexicans and Peruvians did not cotton to the bland food of Costa Rica. And one Brazilian from the Northeast of Brazil, not only was unable to understand Spanish, but could not understand the Portuguese spoken in Rio, and finally had to quit the course.

Southern Office

But things progressed and it was decided to open a regional office in the southern part of South America—in Montevideo. This would take care of candidates from the southern part of the hemisphere who were numerous and hard pressed to find the transportation costs to Costa Rica. Anderson left his post with the Institute in 1960 to take charge of this operation for PIIP.

Under his tireless and enthusiastic direction, not only were the basic communications courses given, but a variety of special ones that seemed to be called for: a four-month training course in Written Communication with twenty-one participants; a two-week seminar in

Chile on the Role of Communications in Agricultural Development with forty-five participants from all ten South American countries; training for agricultural information people in Peru in basic communications; similar courses for staff people in Colombia, Paraguay and Chile.

In 1964 a move for self-determination on the part of the beneficiaries of the PIIP program improved the whole course of the program. At a meeting in Santiago the heads of the information services of ten South American countries recommended that international courses be de-emphasized and that the program devote itself to support of national courses and assistance in development of national programs.

Bradt and Anderson enthusiastically embarked on a new program. AIA conditioned its participation on several factors: it would provide instructors but not scholarships; it would assist in planning and presentation but would not handle local arrangements; and it would assist in evaluation and planned follow-up but the responsibility was with the local agency.

Cal Anderson, fourth from the left, proudly joins members of a seminar on Communications and Economic Development held in Santiago, Chile.

131

Under these arrangements, courses in agricultural information were presented for the entire staff of OTIA (Technical Office of Agrarian Information) of Peru, for the staff of INCORA (Colombian Institute for Agrarian Reform), for regional extension workers in Paraguay and Chile, and for extension workers and agricultural editors in the state of Rio Grande do Sul of Brazil. Contributions were also made to the on-going training program of information workers conducted by INTA (National Technical Agricultural Institute) of Argentina.

One of the interesting phenomena that was encountered was the increasing importance of radio, due to the arrival of the small, low-cost transistor radio. Anderson reports: "On one field trip I talked with a farmer on the altiplano of Bolivia—dressed just as were his Inca ancestors, ploughing with a team of oxen and a wooden plough, and tucked into a fold of his poncho was a transistor radio. This man spoke only Aimará as his language of confidence. If we are to reach him with educational messages, they must be in the dialect of his farm, the tongue he trusts."

Technical Guidance

During this period both Bradt and Anderson were scurrying all over the hemisphere providing technical guidance to individuals, groups, governments. A blueprint for a rural radio information program was set up in Brazil, where the latest in farm techniques is still being broadcast all over the country. A 16-mm. motion picture production and distribution plan was also prepared for Brazil.

One of the real success stories of this program is in Peru. Anderson first went to Peru in 1960 to help plan for an office of information. He submitted a preliminary program and was asked back in 1961 to do a more detailed job. On this trip he met a young Peruvian who was technical editor of the research department of the Ministry of Agriculture, Carlos Prato Blume.

In spite of the fact that Prato had only twelve words of English and Anderson only 120 of Spanish, the two developed a friendship and a working relationship that has affected agricultural information development not only in Peru but all over the hemisphere.

The plan for an information service for the Ministry of Agriculture that they designed was approved and put into effect, although its execution and development took seven years and are not yet complete. Prato rose to be Under-Secretary of Agriculture of Peru, but always with responsibility for information. Anderson was named official advisor to the government and was honored with the Peruvian Medal of Honor in Agriculture, the "Orden del Mérito Agrícola."

During these seven years of work Prato learned English and Anderson learned Spanish, but neither lost track of their objective— to get information from the research laboratory down to the last *campesino* at the end of the road in a form in which he can use it.

Because it had no axe to grind, this team was called upon for help in all parts of the continent. Anderson and Prato were invited to Chile and submitted the plan on which the agricultural information service of that country is based; they advised the Ministry of Agriculture of Bolivia on its needs for establishment of an office of information; they outlined the information service for the Uruguayan agricultural experiment station at La Estanzuela; they outlined the needs for an office of information in Paraguay; and they advised the Colombian government on some of its information problems.

Comprehensive studies and directories of the rural press in both Uruguay and Argentina have proven to be bonanzas in helping the dissemination of agricultural news to the areas most in need. The surveys have aroused the interest of rural editors in the whole program of communications. They have subsequently given constantly increasing coverage to agricultural news in both countries.

In addition to Peru, blueprints—carefully documented and tailored to the individual country's need—have been prepared for offices of information in Chile, Paraguay, Uruguay, Bolivia and Brazil.

Perhaps one of the most encouraging products of these years of work has been a phenomenon entirely new in Latin America—the cooperation between countries in their attack on mutual problems. An interchange of information staff members, for training and broadened experience, has already taken place between Peru and Colombia, while Bolivia and Peru, Argentina and Chile, Paraguay and Uruguay have programs in formation.

Did the program give results? Since it was a program of training people, perhaps one measure might be to look at a few of the participants and see what happened to them:

José Vargas, Peru—former shipping clerk, now head of the Department of Personnel and Administration in the Ministry of Agriculture.

Maria Auxiliadora Galvão, Brazil—former secretary, now head of the Office of Information in the Ministry of Health.

Miguel DiLorenzo, Argentina—former commercial artist, now head of Extension Information Services, National Institute of Agricultural Technology.

Sergio Dacak, Paraguay—former publications editor in the Agricultural Ministry's Office of Information, now owner and operator of one of the most influential radio stations in the country.

Mario Villarroel, Bolivia—former visual aids specialist, now head of Rural Youth and Information Programs for the Ministry of Agriculture.

Eduardo Pereira Brum, Uruguay—former newspaperman, now head of Information for the Agricultural Experiment Station at La Estanzuela.

Graduate Training

There had been some form of sporadic communications training in Latin America since the early '50s, when various international organizations and certain North American universities, responding to calls for help, developed various programs, working together and sometimes independently.

Through these efforts, more than a thousand communications technicians and five thousand field agents received some sort of very brief, basic communications training. This, added to the more sophisticated or still more practical AIA program, was simply a first step. Permanent academic facilities were needed to train communications specialists in Latin America.

Every year hundreds of new agriculturalists leave Latin American campuses with considerable knowledge of plants, animals, soil and water, but with little or no understanding of how human interaction occurs and how human behavior can be influenced to help people employ new knowledge.

134

A realization of this deficiency caused several international organizations to join efforts to develop professional training in communications without totally abandoning their efforts at the non-professional level.

Several agricultural colleges wanted to give this type of training also but there were no teachers.

Thus there was established a need for graduate training leading to a Master's degree in Developmental Communication.

One solution has been to send B.S. degree holders to North American or European universities for postgraduate training. This approach has been and is being used, but it is not satisfactory. One factor is language. The ability to speak a second language is not a good predictor of professional competence in Latin America. Another is culture. Many of the problems of communications and development

When the roads are too tough information specialists take to pack mules.

in Latin America can best be studied in Latin America. Much of the training in foreign institutions is non-relevant, and much that is needed is not provided. Also, the relative cost of postgraduate study within and outside Latin America is self-evident.

For these reasons it was clear that a graduate training facility was needed in Latin America itself. The Agrarian University at La Molina, Peru, was chosen.

This university is one of the two or three most advanced institutions of higher agricultural education in Latin America. It is the only agricultural education center that has a school of social sciences and the only one that has offered some training in communications.

In 1966 AIA and Michigan State University joined with the Inter-American Institute of Agricultural Sciences and La Molina university to launch the project. Instruction began in September, 1967, and includes the following subjects:

Introductory Courses—Social psychology, general sociology, methodology of social sciences, statistical methods for the social sciences.

Major Courses—Communication theory, mass communications, communications in formal organizations, advanced rural sociology, communication of innovations in the process of change.

In mid-1968 AIA's commitment to the program at La Molina was completed. It had designed a course of study and trained faculty members. The course is now a part of the graduate school and hopefully will continue to turn out Masters of Information.

Publications

In the course of its life PIIP was responsible for some publications that have made history in the field of communications. *A Manual of Communications,* in Spanish, resulted from the series of basic courses. It is the only thing like it in the hemisphere and is used even in Spain, where normally there is considerable prejudice against the Spanish written and spoken in the former colonies. Another manual, also in Spanish, that has proven very popular is one containing the hows and whys and wherefores of setting up an information office. Others include: *Planning and Presentation of Short Courses in Communica-*

tions (Spanish and English), *Communications in Agrarian Reform* (Spanish and English). In addition, a monthly newsletter, *Comuniquémonos* (Let's Communicate), has been published for and by communications personnel throughout Latin America. This latter, which has a distribution of over 500, is being continued by OTIA of Peru with Prato assuming Anderson's duties as editor.

Early in its career PIIP participated in a program called ADECO, from its Spanish initials. It was the first uncertain attempt to translate, adapt and prepare a mass of available training materials to see what could be created for a "Train the Trainer" program. The first international presentation was put on in San José, Costa Rica, and the second, the following year in Tucumán, Argentina.

Both these courses had considerable impact on teaching and training methods throughout the hemisphere. Some problems were encountered in Tucumán, primarily because of its isolation, but many people feel that its very remoteness was one of the most important factors contributing to the success of the program. There were no distractions.

Communications Research Program

AIA's experience in Venezuela and Brazil indicated that there was a lot to be learned about the communication of ideas in Latin America.

For instance, too little was known about the target audience. A corollary to that was the fact that nobody really knew whether or not techniques developed in the United States were applicable to other cultures. The examples of resistance to change in all parts of the world are as numerous as they are grimly humorous.

Long-handled shovels were once supplied in quantity to the Egyptians to replace short-handled ones which were thought to be the cause of a prevalent back ailment. A subsequent check showed that all the long handles had been sawed down. The Egyptians were too accustomed to the short handles to change. As part of an anti-rat campaign in the Middle East, a moving picture was shown on U.S. rat-control methods. Close-ups of rats on a twenty-foot screen were interpreted by the audience to indicate that U.S. rats were twenty feet long, so a collection was taken in behalf of the U.S. technicians whose country obviously faced problems more monstrous than their own. A special white chicken was introduced into a Latin American

137

country in an effort to increase dietary protein intake. A year later it was discovered that not a chicken had been killed as white birds were sacred to that area.

In 1957, spurred by AIA, communicators began to try to resolve some of these anomalies. One man's empirical experience was pitted against another's. The consensus was: let's try to establish a creditable scientific base from which a body of theory can be developed resulting in more effective communications techniques and efficient campaigns.

One of the foremost institutions in the communications field and in foreign studies was Michigan State University. Bradt set up a working relationship with Dr. Glen Taggart, Dean of Foreign Programs, and Dr. David Berlo, head of the Department of Communication of the College of Communication Arts.

Meanwhile, *A Study of the Human and Institutional Resources in the Social Sciences and Communications Research in Selected Coun-*

A PIIP field researcher gets data in the highlands of Guatemala.

tries in Latin America was undertaken in 1961. It was carried out for PIIP by Dr. Antonio M. Arce of the Institute. The countries surveyed were Mexico, Guatemala, Colombia, Ecuador, Peru, Bolivia, Argentina and Chile. Its objectives were to find out what research was being done in the social sciences and in mass communications, and to locate possible collaborators for future research.

In a further attempt to establish guide lines to indicate directions for useful PIIP research, *Three Preliminary Bibliographies of Works Related to the Social Sciences in Latin America* was prepared.

The evolution of a study generally followed these lines. It was conceived by PIIP either alone or, more often, in collaboration with another agency. If it was decided that the study contributed to PIIP's objectives, a design was drawn, followed by a questionnaire which was pre-tested on a group of about thirty individuals. Meanwhile, a random probability sample was devised. If the study was to be nation-wide in scope for a country the size of Costa Rica (population: 1,400,000), for example, interviews with 1,500 individuals sufficed. Interviewers, usually university students, were trained and put into the field. The data they collected were coded on IBM cards and analyzed, sometimes by computer. Results were written up and distributed as widely as possible to pertinent people and agencies throughout Latin America.

Responsibility rested with PIIP's directors of research, Dr. Paul Deutschmann and Dr. Frederick Waisanen, assisted by Dr. John McNelly, Dr. William Lassey, Dr. Jerome Durlak and Dr. Alfredo Méndez.

Collaborators included: Dr. Orlando Fals-Borda (National University of Colombia), Dr. Méndez before he joined AIA (Nutrition Institute of Central America and Panama), Dr. Arce and Dr. Juan Díaz Bordenave (Inter-American Institute of Agricultural Sciences), Dr. Gonzalo Adis Castro and Dr. Rodrigo Sánchez (University of Costa Rica). Sponsors included: Michigan State University, UNESCO, USAID, the Milbank Memorial Fund, the National University of Chile, the University of Buenos Aires, the University of Costa Rica.

In all, thirty-six studies were made in fourteen countries. Eight thousand copies of the findings were distributed to institutions and change agents in thirty-five countries.

PIIP studies confirm that early innovators in the adoption of new practices are young literates having a relatively high standard of living and, in rural communities, having contact in some form of communication with the outside world either through travel or the mass media. They also indicated ways of identifying opinion leaders. The thought here was that expensive mass communications might be obviated by working directly with these leaders. As yet this has not been conclusively proved out.

In general, more data was gathered than there was time for a proper analysis of it. Momentum was lost, too, by the untimely death of Paul Deutschmann, PIIP's first research director.

PIIP has made the results of its studies widely available throughout Latin America and, as a consequence, there is now much information which will serve as a foundation for action programs undertaken by Latin Americans themselves. This is an innovation, since in the past many North American researchers after having gathered data in various parts of the hemisphere have taken all the material home, with the result that Latin American collaborators and other interested professionals have not had the full benefit of this work.

Chapter 2

RURAL YOUTH

Latin America is a land of young people. In fact it has a greater percentage of young men and women than any area of the world except Africa. Forty-three percent of its population is under fourteen years old and 61% is under twenty-five.

Latin America is also an agricultural land. Fifty percent of the people live on farms and, of these, 50,000,000 are between the ages of ten and twenty.

For most of these youngsters the future is dim indeed. Their education is minimal or non-existent. Their health is always in jeopardy from inadequate nutrition or disease. And their potential is severely restricted.

It is to this group that the rural youth program, sponsored jointly by AIA and the Institute, is directed.

The brutal dictum "Catch 'em young" has served many evil purposes in modern history. But fortunately it can also serve good ones. The 4-H club movement in the United States is proof of that. From a small beginning at the turn of the century, this movement has spread until today there are 3,250,000 members in 95,000 clubs. This is 8.5% of the U.S. population that is eligible for membership. Compare this with 250,000 Latin American youngsters enrolled in rural youth clubs—only .5% of the eligibles.

Howard Law received his first real confrontation with the fact that the youth of the continent was the hope of the future back in Venezuela when he was directing the tractor-driving school for CBR. At first he tried to recruit people under thirty-five. Each month he lowered the ideal age until the school was taking them as young as eighteen.

"For some reason, the older people always seemed to have two left feet—which didn't fit on a tractor brake," says Law.

141

He also discovered that the extension work had to be very intensive. The old ones were apt to agree to do what the agent asked because they were polite. But the minute the agent's back was turned most of them returned to the old ways. The younger ones were interested, more alert, and more receptive to new ideas.

Law began his first work with youth clubs in Venezuela, where the 5-V club system had been set up in 1938. There were 154 clubs in the country, with 3,500 members. They were set up on the classical line—attached to the school, subject to the discipline of the teacher, and a compulsory part of the school curriculum.

In effect these were "agricultural clubs," not 5-V clubs as Law conceived them. Law listed the disadvantages of these clubs succinctly:

1. The teachers lack technical know-how in agriculture and home economics.

2. Clubs operate only during the school season.

3. Parents are critical because children are put to work on gardens at school and the product is consumed in the school.

4. Teachers serve as leaders because the ministry authorities require them to do so, not because they have a vocation or personal dedication for the work.

5. Club work is a compulsory part of the curriculum.

The U.S. pattern of rural youth clubs, and the one that Law subscribed to, was to separate the clubs from the schools—make them independent and membership a purely voluntary action. Another basic rule was to have the young people grow their crops, rear their animals, or make their furniture at their own homes. Thus there was a year-round continuity and a permanent showcase was always on hand for family and friends to admire.

By the time CBR set up the two demonstration centers in San Francisco and Palo Negro in Venezuela for training extension workers, the club program had been transferred from the Ministry of Education to the Ministry of Agriculture. Law, who headed up the work at both centers, decided to bring the 5-V program into the mainstream of extension training.

One of the first things Law did was to organize thirteen clubs with more than 250 members in the two local communities, put a farm and a home demonstration agent in charge of each, and use them as training grounds for the neophyte extension workers. Club work was to be an integral part of the extension agent's job.

The clubs were an instant success. There was such a rush of would-be members among the youngsters that the communities could easily have supported fifty clubs. Every time a club held a meeting, there was a mob of kids clustered around the windows watching what went on and hoping to get in.

The first Achievement Day held at Palo Negro was an EVENT. This was the day when each youngster was to get recognition (maybe nothing more than a commendatory word, perhaps even a pin) for something he had accomplished—a fine rabbit hutch constructed, a good stand of corn planted, a savory batch of beans canned.

Law recalls that the young leader of the club had labored long over his speech, writing it himself and practicing far into the night. When the great day came, the fact that he stumbled a bit over his own handwriting did not diminish the glory in which he basked.

The proud parents who watched the proceedings were perhaps for the first time made aware of some of the new farm and home practices which could lead them to a richer, fuller and healthier life.

The Andrés Tarazona Story

Parents didn't always see it this way, as the story of Andrés Tarazona, an early member of the 5-V club of San Francisco, will illustrate.

San Francisco is a town of some 5,000 people near Lake Valencia. In the center of a sugar cane and cotton region, perhaps its greatest claim to fame is that it was the site of a stud farm owned by the late Ali Khan. Agrarian reform has turned over the acreage to small farmers who work the land for less glamorous but more useful purposes. A stately mansion on a hill top is the only reminder of the bygone days of opulence.

Andrés joined the 5-V club when he was twelve, and Evelio Tovar, who is today executive secretary of the National Association for 5-V Clubs, tells the story:

An enterprising and intelligent youngster, he rose rapidly and soon became president of the club. He developed several projects, including bee-keeping and raising rabbits. With the full cooperation of two rabbits he had won in a competition, Andrés parlayed them into a thriving business.

The club held an annual "Achievement Day" when prizes were awarded to the winners of different categories. In 1956 Andrés was given the prize for vegetable gardening. In 1957 he again won first prize—this time for his rabbits. But his supreme triumph came in 1958 when his skill in constructing beehives earned him an electric saw.

Andrés lived with his family in a mud-and-cane house, and when an "aided-self-help" housing program was announced by the Ministry of Health, CBR, and the Mendoza Foundation, he persuaded his father and brothers to apply for a long-term construction loan of Bs. 5,700 ($1,700) and all of them went to work.

The house was finished in record time, and a fine symbolic ceremony was planned. We were going to bring in a bulldozer, push down the old Tarazona house with one whoosh, and then present the keys to the new one to Andrés' father.

But on the great day the father faltered. He had lived in the old house all his life; his children had all been born there; and, furthermore, if he moved into the new house, it would set him off too much from all his old friends.

Andrés, though disappointed, bowed to his father's will and used the new house as a carpentry workshop. He recalls that he made more than fifty beehives with his electric saw.

Andrés wanted to become an agronomist, but it cost money, which he did not have after helping to support his family.

But in 1960 his old 5-V club gave him a loan of Bs. 1,500 (about $450) with which he enrolled in the school of agriculture.

After his graduation three years later he got a job selling agricultural supplies for a commercial firm; then he became an extension agent for the Ministry of Agriculture; and now he is with the government-sponsored Cotton Development Fund where his work takes him among the people he knows and understands best—the farmers. Today Andrés is an influential leader in the community.

During all this time Andrés has never lost touch with the local 5-V club. He has worked with the boys and girls at every turn and is always available to give a helping hand.

The house? The one his father wouldn't move into? Andrés married sister lives in it today.

By 1968 the total number of clubs in Venezuela had grown from the 154 to more than 800 with 13,000 members. And like Andrés the youngsters that were members of the early clubs in San Francisco and Palo Negro are now farm and home demonstration agents, farmers of substance, and officials of government agricultural offices. An interesting development in Venezuela, also, is that both schools and colleges of agriculture give priority to applicants who have had 5-V club experience.

The Achievement Days of those early days in the state of Aragua have today grown into a national program of District, State, National and even International ceremonies. An annual encampment at Acarigua, with bunks for 150 youngsters, is one of the important outgrowths of this program.

In Brazil

Meantime, in Brazil, Apodaca was learning about the youth of Minas Gerais by starting the new-style 4-S clubs (*Saude*—health; *Saber*—knowledge; *Sentir*—feeling; *Servir*—service).

Apodaca organized the first club in the little town of Rio Pomba in Minas Gerais on July 15, 1952. This date is still honored today as the National 4-S Club Day. On the fifteenth anniversary in 1967 a special 4-S club stamp was issued by the Brazilian government to commemorate the event. President da Costa e Silva affixed the first cancellation at a special ceremony. The President praised his young neighbors for having obtained corn harvests four and five times greater than the average for the region.

"Perhaps the most important part of the work," he said, "of the 4-S club movement is the practice of democracy as it is carried out in club meetings, the sense of cooperation and aid to the works of community betterment, and the creation of responsible leadership among young people."

Apodaca admits he did not have a hard job selling the rural youth club idea:

This program is the easiest thing in the world to sell. Everybody

President da Costa e Silva of Brazil cancels the first 4-S stamp at a
ceremony in the country's new capital Brasília.

loves children and even those who have doubts are quickly won
over when they see the influence the program has on the kids.

It is after you have sold it that the difficult part starts. Because
you have to be *right* with young people. They won't take any
shoddy thinking or half-right solutions. Lots of people get cold
feet when they realize they are forming future citizens. I have
known both professional and volunteer leaders to get scared.
They feel the responsibility is too great.

By 1954 there were only thirty-four clubs in the state with 731
members, but many anxious youngsters were waiting to get in. Apodaca, who by then was director of ACAR, faced the problem that
he had no trained leaders to take on the job. So he asked a young lady,
Aurea Helena Andrade, who had had six years' experience in extension work in Brazil, to go to the United States for some specialized
training in youth work.

She came back fired with ambition for the club program in Brazil
and wrote a voluminous and meticulous report, to which nobody paid
any attention.

146

"It was a great report," says Apodaca, "but there was just too much of it. Nobody could digest all of it."

He recommended that she reduce it to three pages, with three basic steps: (1) Training of volunteer leaders, (2) Preparation of project literature, and (3) Administrative procedures for setting up clubs.

This the board of ACAR in Minas Gerais adopted and put Miss Andrade in charge of all club work in the state. She later became National 4-S Club Leader of ABCAR, went to Turrialba where she earned her Master's degree, and today rejoices in the title of Executive Director of Social and Cultural Projects for ABCAR.

From time to time Aurea Helena's initial report came out of the file, and certain additional recommendations were adopted until today that report is a very practical and universal guide for all states and groups that wish to set up rural youth clubs.

As each state, beginning with the Northeastern group and finally the national organization, ABCAR, came along, Apodaca saw to it that a youth club program was incorporated into the extension and credit plans.

Although he believes firmly that the social and cultural activities are a valid and important part of the youth club program, Apodaca rode herd on the newly emerging clubs, insisting that they start realistically with the goal of increasing agricultural production.

"The social activities and the awards and recognitions can come later," he said. "But first get going on better agricultural practices and a healthier home life. Then the fun things can become the frosting on the cake."

And in 1957, when Apodaca moved to Rio de Janeiro to become technical advisor to the president of the newly formed ABCAR, he brought with him all the philosophy that had worked in Minas Gerais.

How PIJR Started

When Camp signed the agreement with the Institute in 1960 setting up the PIJR, or rural youth program, he had in Law and Apodaca two staff members ready-made to push the new program with singular energy.

Law moved to Costa Rica, Apodaca remained in Brazil to cover the entire southern part of the hemisphere—quite an undertaking, as you will see if you consult a map.

Soon after he arrived Law recruited two talented Cost Ricans—Edgar Arias and Edgar Mata—henceforth always to be known as "the Edgars." Arias had been national supervisor of the 4-S club movement in Costa Rica, and Mata had been head of the Costa Rican Extension Service.

Law deployed his staff to coincide with the zones of operations of the Institute—the southern (Apodaca), the northern (Arias), and the Andean (Mata).

Their assignment: to spread the gospel throughout the western hemisphere.

These four men brought a wide variety of talents, different personalities and diversified experiences to the job. Perhaps their success is due to their very divergences. Law, a big, blonde man with a crew cut who speaks fluent Spanish with a strictly Utah accent, inspires endless confidence. Apodaca, who is equally fluent in English, Spanish and Portuguese, is the son of Mexican immigrants to the United States southwest and has a compassionate understanding of people trying to achieve some of the good things of life. Arias, short and cherubic, with boundless energy and enthusiasm, always has some new project in hand. And Mata, calm, dispassionate, with a cool approach to each aspect of his job, keeps all the administrative ends tidied up.

Law's dictum from the beginning of PIJR had been: encourage the development of support entities, train voluntary leaders with the same vigor that is put into developing club systems themselves, and try to get some political muscle behind the movement in each country. These aspects can help insure the implantation of rural youth work deep in the consciousness of the average citizen. Through the involvement of the businessman, the teacher, the farmer, the doctor, the parent, support and permanence of the club movement is better insured.

International Committees

Law wasted no time after the organization of PIJR in setting up two

148

international committees: one made up of some of the hemisphere's most prominent VIP's, including four ex-presidents, under the chairmanship of Dr. José A. Mora, then Secretary General of the Organization of American States. The other was one of technical advisors to the VIP's and also to the PIJR.

In December of 1961 the Technical Committee held its first meeting in Costa Rica. Every two years since then the group has met in different countries, usually in connection with a national or international gathering of rural club members and leaders. And every year the meetings have become more animated and meatier as each technical worker reports progress from his particular area.

National Support Entities

Law was particular about the make-up of national entities (committees, foundations, associations, societies, call them what you will). While he welcomed a modest number of government officials and teachers, he much preferred that each group be dominated by businessmen or other local leaders. The greatest difficulty in getting the National Association for 5-V Clubs set up in Venezuela had been presented by a tug-of-war between different government officials ever who was going to run the organization. Law resisted all such pressure, even though the creation of the association was delayed until after he left the country. Today he is happy knowing that the organization is completely independent and made up 90% of businessmen.

AIA is also convinced that the rural youth club movement in each Latin American country needs a lobbyist or a pressure group behind it.

"In the United States," Law explains, "there were the Farm Bureau, the Grange and other private organizations as well as county and state groups, including the State University, that cooperated with the 4-H club movement. They were powerful groups and they put some political muscle into the youth movement. They constantly needled the Extension Service—and they were very effective with Congress.

"There is nothing of this sort in Latin America. Hopefully these national committees may eventually provide the political power that the club movements require."

Galo Plaza, former President of Ecuador, a large landowner in his own country, president of the National Foundation of Ecuador, a civic committee to support the 4-F clubs, and today Secretary General of the OAS, is one of the earliest and strongest supporters of the civic support program. One of his daughters was active for many years as a club leader, but Galo Plaza refuses to give her entire credit for his interest.

In 1961, he commented, "Whether local or national, these committees are partners of the government agency under which the rural youth extension program is conducted. Between them, they unite all forces, public and private, in support of a common goal. . . . The partnership of government and civic committee is a strong democratic force for the betterment of rural life in Latin America."

Law is particularly pleased with the growth of the support entities in the individual countries—from seven in 1961 to twenty-three in 1968. Some of course are better than others; some are fairly new and just getting going; some represent large and prosperous countries, others small and poor countries. But, within their limitations, they are doing all they can.

For example, the group in Peru, with the important financial assistance of the North American Committee, made up of North American businessmen in Peru, started a loan program in 1963 to

Galo Plaza, former president of Ecuador and present Secretary General of the OAS, (center facing camera) takes time out to organize the National 4-F Club Foundation of Ecuador.

150

assist youthful potential chicken farmers. This project has already given a tremendous boost to both chicken and egg production in the areas where the loans have been made. The original revolving loan fund of the North American Committee of 254,600 soles ($12,730 at 20 soles to the dollar) has generated almost 5,000 poultry projects of rural youth members worth 5,695,000 soles ($284,750) or 22 times the original contribution. This is a rate the average Wall Street investor would not mind having.

This enterprising Peruvian support entity also publishes an *Agricultural Youth Club* calendar, which carries advertising, is sold all over the country, and is bringing in a tidy little income.

The membership list of the Association for 4-A Clubs in Argentina sounds like a Who's Who of Industry. It publishes a quarterly, which carries advertising and which has a circulation of 15,000. The income not only pays the professional editor but also a large part of the executive secretary's salary. The Association also sponsors a weekly half-hour television farm program, which gives particular emphasis to youth club work.

In Panama the enterprising committee persuaded the government to share the proceeds of the national lottery, with the result that every year some $10,000 from this source is available for loans to promising Panamanian agriculturists.

And Guatemala, with funds from the local office of Esso and management by the Bank of America, has set up a 4-S Club Bank. Over the past two years these funds have amounted to $6,000, have provided loans to 172 youngsters of whom only two have been in default, and have generated the incredible gross income of $30,000.

Full-Time Executive Secretaries

By 1967 nine of the support entities had full-time paid executive secretaries and in August representatives of all national entities met in Bogotá, guests of the Colombian Association for 4-S Clubs. It was a seminar on the functions and responsibilities of both the secretaries and their organizations. Every aspect of the work was covered: increased club membership, fund raising, information. The report of the seminar was published in the form of a manual or guide for youth program officials, both current and future.

151

The staff of PIJR was delighted to see the enthusiasm and interest that these men and women (there was just one of the latter, and a pretty one at that) displayed. They were very new to the work since most of them had come from business or agriculture and had had little experience in youth work. One was head of a large print shop, another was a retired professional agriculturist. The young lady was a graduate agricultural technician. But they were all devoted to their jobs.

Law, in his opening remarks to the group, urged that the increase of membership in the clubs be the first order of business.

> The development of the human and agricultural resources of Latin America and the Caribbean is a vital and urgent necessity. In the future we will need better prepared farmers, housewives and rural leaders in all these countries. The youngsters, through the rural youth clubs, can and must lead the way to rural development in all its aspects, particularly in increased food production through the introduction of better and more modern agricultural practices, the use of fertilizers, pesticides, insecticides, machinery, as well as improved marketing systems.

The PIJR staff has noticed a general improvement in the organization and functioning of all these committees as a result of the opportunity to share problems as well as successes that the Bogotá meeting offered the executive secretaries.

Volunteer Leaders

The use of volunteer leaders not only saves money but is one other method of bringing the community, both local and national, closer in touch with the youth clubs and their projects.

From the very beginning PIJR has sponsored frequent seminars on the subject of selection, identification, use and training of volunteers, and has published several handbooks and guides to help club leaders in making maximum use of these leaders.

Volunteer leaders can be young mothers who give a couple of mornings a week to helping the girls in their sewing classes, a farmer who devotes an afternoon a week leading young boys through the mysteries of proper seed selection, or a local banker who helps both boys and girls on keeping records of their projects.

152

Another activity that occupied the PIJR staff during its first year of existence was the reorganization of a program in which AIA had been cooperating with the National 4-H Club Foundation of the United States. This was the so-called IFYE (pronounced in the truly Rooseveltian manner "iffy,") the International Farm Youth Exchange.

The program, which had been started by the 4-H Club Foundation back in 1948 as one of its first tentative steps toward an international movement, provides for the interchange of approximately 200 young men and women who travel abroad and share the work of home and farm, as well as the social life of the community where they live, for six months. Of the foreign countries that participated in the 1967 program, eleven were in Latin America, receiving a total of twenty-six youngsters *from* the United States and sending twenty-five *to* the United States. From the beginning of the exchange twenty years ago, a total of nineteen Latin American countries have participated, with 406 North Americans going south and 391 Latinos coming to the farms of the U.S.

Peace Corps Volunteers and IFYE exchange students man the four-language welcome sign at the Inter-American Rural Youth Club Congress in Rio de Janeiro.

Each exchangee is required to have a camera and take colored slides as well as pictures in black and white. He is also required to prepare a speech to give to groups all over his own country. One young American who had spent six months in Venezuela gave his speech, with slides, over one hundred times, and his Congressman inserted it in the *Congressional Record.*

For several years before the AIA operation moved to Costa Rica, CBR had cooperated with the 4-H Foundation in Venezuela by helping to select the young Venezuelans, by orienting and keeping a fatherly eye on the U.S. exchangees who came to Venezuela, and generally assisting in making the whole experience as meaningful and rewarding as possible.

The Foundation learned that sometimes the returning Latin Americans had a hard time getting jobs.

They were frequently heard to say, "But this isn't the way they raise pigs in Iowa," or "You should cook the vegetables this way— it leaves in more nutrients," or "You should plow *around* not *up* the hill." Such admonitions were not designed to endear the returned travelers to their family and neighbors.

The Foundation felt that the youngsters needed some practical help in putting their U.S. experience into focus, in adapting North American methods to local conditions.

So Grant A. Shrum, director of the Foundation, asked Law if his organization could take on the job. Law, who saw in this an opportunity of even further refinement of training of rural youth leaders, agreed readily and, every year since 1960, has conducted a ten-day seminar for seventeen to twenty-five young men and women. The students return from the United States by way of Costa Rica where the seminars are held.

Awards and Exchanges

Everybody likes to be recognized for what he thinks is a good job. Everybody likes to get an award of some kind or to be selected to represent his group at a national or international meeting. PIJR has capitalized on this only too human desire for approval and has encouraged all local clubs, as well as the national support groups, to sponsor national club days or weeks, national and international meetings, contests of all sorts, achievement and recognition days, exchanges such as IFYE, scholarships, etc.

The PIJR staff has also tried to instill the principle that everybody should get a recognition of some kind. Then those who don't get the blue ribbon have some consolation. If a Queen of the National Rural Youth Day is selected, she always has a retinue of lovely ladies who share in the limelight.

PIJR has always encouraged exchanges, both national and international. It started the inter-American exchanges back in 1961 when it made possible twenty-two exchanges of young people among the countries of Central America. The national clubs themselves have picked up the idea—both on a national and an inter-American basis. Today an average of 5,000 young people every year go some place—to a state meeting, to a national encampment or abroad for brief, sometimes long, stays with their counterparts in neighboring countries.

Corn Production Contest

One of the most successful contests held so far in the hemisphere has been the Corn Production Contest, made possible by a grant from

A young contestant demonstrates a method of weaving a hammock.

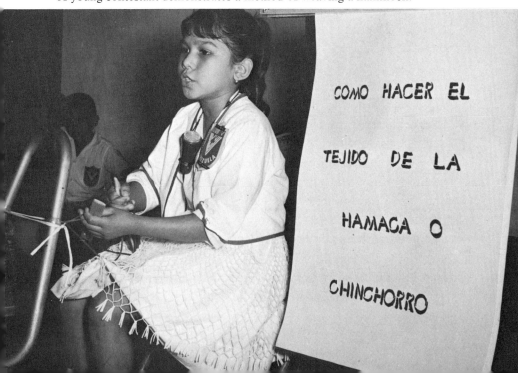

COMO HACER EL

TEJIDO DE LA

HAMACA O

CHINCHORRO

the International Minerals & Chemical Corporation. This is a closely-supervised contest in which boys (and a surprising number of girls also) select and plant seed corn, nurture it with all the latest approved practices and keep detailed records of every step of the process, including the final yield. The field trials are under the supervision of youth club leaders in each competing community.

The first year, 1966, 1,700 youngsters from eight countries—in six financing was by International Minerals and in two by the countries themselves—enrolled in the contest and about 500 completed their records, which is considered a high percentage in view of the fact that the whole program was trying to teach the fundamentals of farm management, as well as how to grow corn. In 1967, 2,700 enrolled, of whom more than a third completed the course. In addition to those countries that have had PIJR support for this project, several other countries have entered the contest on their own. The 1968 figure of entrants pushed 5,000 and represented a total of fifteen countries, eight of which International Minerals financed.

Dissemination of the Good News

PIJR has always encouraged local club units to seek the fullest publicity for the club activities. Stories in the local weeklies, on the local radio stations and through any other channel possible about club projects serve to bring the community more and more into the rural youth picture.

One of PIJR's first publications was a manual for Latin American rural youth programs and clubs, *Your Publicity Program,* containing very down-to-earth advice on how to prepare press releases, how to take newsworthy pictures, and how to take advantage of any radio and television outlets.

PIJR has published a quarterly bulletin containing a judicious mixture of news of all countries' activities, plus some "how-to-do-it" and "how-to-do-it-better" advice. From an initial run of 2,500 copies. the bulletin, edited by Eduardo Andrade, now has a circulation of 7,000 throughout the Western Hemisphere as well as in many other countries.

In addition, it has published and distributed throughout the hemisphere a series of manuals for leaders, both voluntary and pro-

Contest winners from Venezuela observe corn cultivation at the
University of Florida.

fessional, on different aspects of conducting rural youth clubs successfully. Some of these have been translations of U.S. 4-H club documents that have already proven to be valuable.

Progress

Success in this field can be told in a dozen different ways—the growth of Dominican 5-D club membership from 650 members to 3,250 in two years; the increase from a few thousand dollars available for loans to members throughout the hemisphere to over a million; the decision by Paraguay to set aside for youth loans 1% of a $6,000,000 loan from the Inter-American Development Bank.

For Law there will be no final success until the rural youth of Latin America is enrolled 100% in youth clubs.

"In this case quantity is almost more important than quality," he says. "We must reach the saturation point to show real results. And with each additional member the movement gets some more support from the community, so that bringing in the next member is not quite so difficult."

But perhaps stories such as that of little San Gabriel in Ecuador, as told by Augusto Torres, information officer of SCIA (Inter-American Cooperative Agricultural Service) in the summer, 1962, issue of

A 4-S club member from Guatemala presents a demonstration on the nutritional value of milk and bananas at an international meeting.

A Peruvian illustrates to his colleagues at the Rio meeting how to vaccinate cattle against undulant fever.

Juventud Rural, a publication then put out by the Ford Motor Company, do better than any amount of statistics.

In the San Gabriel zone on the northern border of Ecuador, the land is a dramatic panorama of mountains and valleys dotted with small adobe huts with straw roofs. Family income is low and the comforts of life few. The altitude is 8,000 feet and the climate is generally cold and rainy.

Most of the farmers work on *haciendas* and raise a few sheep for their personal use, but until recently the poor native sheep of the region have yielded no more than four pounds of wool per shearing. For the people of this mountainous canton, life has been without hope.

Today there is a new spirit in San Gabriel. Farmers are raising fine purebred sheep yielding heavy clips of wool. Small home weaving industries are under way. San Gabriel sheep are winning blue ribbons at the fairs and wool clothing produced in the homes is in wide demand. In addition, many homes now have thriving flocks and herds of heifers, pigs, rabbits, poultry and goats. Family income is increasing and diets are improving. Today in San Gabriel there is progress and hope for tomorrow. In this great revival, the four 4-F clubs of the zone are playing a leading part.

Three agencies have cooperated to bring about the change. The animals are the gift of Heifer Project, Inc., the interdenominational church organization that supplies a steady stream of animals to the hungry regions of the world. The club projects are supervised by the Agricultural Extension Service of the Ecuadorean Ministry of Promotion, with the help of SCIA.

By February, 1962, the boys and girls of the four 4-F clubs in the zone owned 200 purebred sheep and had made 400 crosses with native sheep to upgrade wool production. The purebred sheep and the crosses yield between ten and twenty-five pounds of wool per shearing, as against the native average of four pounds or less. One sheep recorded fifteen pounds from its first shearing at seven months of age!

Many individual stories of success, added together, make vivid San Gabriel's new spirit of progress:

. . . With money earned from his sheep Sergio González was able to go 300 kilometers to enter the College of Agriculture.

(1) Number of rural youth clubs

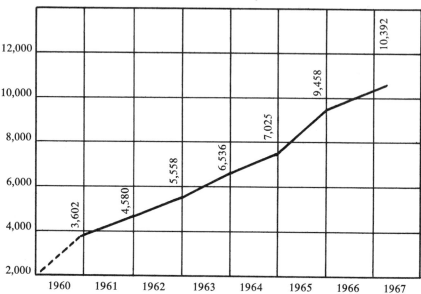

(2) Number of club members

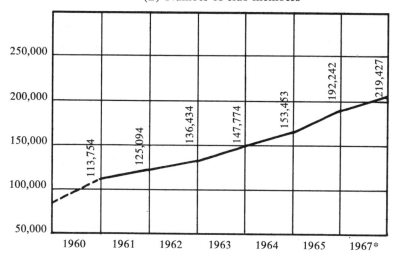

* No data available for 1966

. . . Segundo Quintanchala is an orphan, but with his wool income he supports himself and pays all his school expenses. He is the owner of the lamb that gave fifteen pounds in its first shearing.

. . . Carlos Andrade has ten sheep and has sold several. He has formed a partnership with his father, and at sixteen years is a full-fledged farmer with his own capital.

Then there is Gerold Krambeck, who is fifteen years old. He lives on a small farm with his family in the state of Santa Catarina in Brazil. His family is quite average as far as Santa Catarina farm families go—not wealthy, not poor, fairly well educated and eager for progress.

Gerold has been a member of the 4-S club of Santa Catarina for several years and in 1967 entered the club's competition for growing corn. With the cooperation of a local producer of high-quality seed, the club members were urged to use the best seed and were instructed in the best methods of cultivation.

Gerold's record-breaking yield of 10,060 kilos per hectare was some 400 kilos greater than his nearest competitor, but was six times that of the state average of 1,750 kilos.

Meanwhile, in Venezuela, young José Esperragoza of the state of Aragua, who wasn't quite fifteen, produced 9,780 kilos per hectare. His fellow club members, while they didn't quite meet José's record, were, nevertheless, showing phenomenal results, sufficiently high to impress their elders. The established farmers of the state were watching the youngsters use good seeds, fertilizers and other recommended methods of cultivation, and even before the national contest was over, were beginning to adopt some of these practices.

Pitfalls

All AIA staff members are painfully aware of the pitfalls in connection with youth work—painfully because they have all dropped into them at one time or another.

They agree that the first requisite is to instill self-confidence in the young folk—to give them a feeling that some of the good things of life are within their reach. But in doing this great care must be taken that the goals are not too remote. These youngsters don't even know about Cloud One, much less Cloud Nine.

Arias tells the sad little story of a club near Limón in Costa Rica. There were some fifty to sixty enthusiastic members, with eager support from their parents and community.

"Everybody thought this was going to be the greatest," recounts Arias. "The leader started the kids off with manual training and home crafts with the idea they would make a fortune selling the products, all in demand. A local congressman gave the club $1,000 (his Christmas bonus from a grateful government). The club bought sewing machines, an oven and an electric saw. When these were all delivered it was discovered there was no power. So the club got a loan to purchase a generator. But they didn't know how to make the generator work.

"By the time somebody figured out an answer, frustration had set in. The club slowly dissolved. This was an almost fatal blow to the club movement in that area. It was a case of going too fast."

There are clubs that have stumbled by overemphasizing certain activities so that their shelves are loaded with a great oversupply of towel racks, tea cozies or hand-embroidered doilies. Others have been bedazzled by the dream of making money—like the club in Central America that was sweet-talked by a promotor into growing tomatoes for the market in the Canal Zone. The first year everything was great: the promotor provided a weekly plane, the club membership grew by leaps and bounds, and there was even a waiting list. The second year the club had to go into the business of building boxes for shipping, and delivering them to the plane for shipment. And then, all of a sudden, wham! The promotor complained that the tomatoes were not up to the desired quality and went elsewhere for his supply.

"The club leader who had sponsored this project wanted to commit suicide," said Law. "But he didn't. He salvaged something from the effort, since he had learned a great deal about growing tomatoes. This area, which had formerly been entirely a one-crop region, dependent upon tobacco, is now growing tomatoes and a whole array of other vegetables for their own use. So something has been salvaged."

There are certain built-in hazards in developing a program of

162

this sort in Latin America. Political instability is one important factor, as it is in all development programs. A new government in one country wants to make the club movement an arm of the political party. Another feels that it is a waste of time—the farmers themselves can do all that's needed.

Another factor is the inefficiency of moving information from the field to areas where it might do some good. This is not an exclusively Latin American trait but is particularly frustrating to the U.S. technician. For example, some important fertilizer field trials were conducted on a high scientific level in Guatemala and the results were of real significance. But no report was made—not for two years, and then only in a brief technical paragraph aimed at the technician and not at the farmer who needed it.

Finally, the needs of agriculture are always last on a country's budget, and youth work is only a small part of that. To remedy this there must be an ever-continuing educational job at all levels.

Chapter 3

RURAL DEVELOPMENT

Practically within days after the 1962 signing of the agreement with the Institute, the so-called rural development program (in effect agrarian reform) was operating in high gear in Costa Rica.

Louis Heaton, who had been appointed regional representative, went to work in his hotel room with a portable typewriter, not bothering to wait for an office to be rented or a secretary and telephone to be acquired.

His first job with the new setup was to continue the cooperation with CBR, which meant putting the finishing touches on a presentation from the Agricultural Bank of Venezuela for a $10,000,000 loan from USAID for a supervised credit program in Venezuela.

The loan was approved and the $10,000,000 was matched by the Agricultural Bank of Venezuela, making the total operating fund $20,000,000. In addition, USAID provided technical services at a cost of $200,000 and the Agricultural Bank paid for training services provided by CBR for an additional $200,000. All of these loans and contributions were for four years—from 1962 to 1966. Beyond that the Agricultural Bank committed itself to an additional $5,500,000 a year for supervised credit loans from 1967 on. AIA continued its cooperation with CBR by helping to train bank and CBR officials in the techniques of supervising loans.

The program has been an outstanding success: at the end of three and a half years, 7,377 loans for a total of over $33,000,000 had been made. The repayment rate of loans due was 81%, which compared favorably with the collection record of less than 50% on other loans made by the Bank including its commercial farm production loans. It is significant that over half of these supervised credit funds were for permanent farm improvements and capital purchases, for establishing permanent crops, for livestock facilities, for machinery and

164

L to R—Louis E. Heaton of AIA coordinates the work of Bertram Ellenbogen, rural sociologist, Roberto Lizarralde, geographer and Milton L. Barnett, anthropologist.

equipment purchases. Credit for basic farm structure adjustments is usually lacking in Latin America. This lack is a serious obstacle to increased farm efficiency. The other half of the credit was used for annual loans for production costs, largely for field crops.

During the same period, food production in Venezuela of thirty-three basic food commodities rose 30%, although even the most enthusiastic supporters of the credit program don't claim that it was solely responsible.

In Brazil

Meanwhile, in Brazil, Crawford, after bowing himself and AIA out of all the CAR organizations, was looking for new worlds to conquer. His first step toward this was the preparation of a comprehensive report, *Agriculture in Brazil*. It contained an analysis of the country's human and agricultural resources, and concluded that there must be migration from the troubled northeast area which could never produce enough food to support its population.

This report, which has been one of AIA's publications most widely in demand, came to these conclusions:

Agriculture is of major importance to Brazil because:

(1) it provides food for the people and raw materials for important industries that produce essential products;

(2) it is the principal source of foreign exchange, thus assuring further means for the country's development;

(3) it provides the consumer market for varied and important industries;

(4) it constitutes the principal occupation of nearly 60% of the population; [based on 1950 figures]

(5) it contributes toward the gradual integration of the national territory.

In spite of this,

(1) it receives only 26% of the national income; [based on 1950 figures]

Preparing cartographic material to illustrate a special study.

(2) it is held down by uneconomic and unproductive methods that provide relatively little purchasing power and a totally unsatisfactory standard of existence;

(3) more than half (55%) of the total farm labor force either has no land or not enough;

(4) it is heavily concentrated in coastal areas which, because of either low rainfall, poor topography or soil exhaustion from long use, are no longer productive.

Thus it services poorly the people who engage in it and those who depend upon it for sustenance.

To solve these problems, many corrective measures are called for, the principal ones being:

(1) Relocation of a portion of the rural population, especially those with little or no land resources, from the more densely populated and least productive areas, onto new lands subject to mechanization and the application of scientific methods. The best hope of doing this is to utilize the vast sparsely settled areas of the high plateau region in the west-central portion of Brazil.

(2) Intensification of technological, economic and social research in both the new and the old areas, to discover and improve crops and animals, practices and management systems which are harmonious with the soil and ecological conditions of the various regions. This is a critical need in the northeast and other troubled areas.

(3) Institution of land-use planning and zoning techniques, together with credit for the consolidation of uneconomic sized units and recapitalization, in areas from which population is drawn.

(4) Expansion and improvement of educational programs which directly assist rural people.

Crawford has a less exalted way of describing the Brazilians as agriculturists.

"They are not born farmers. They are descended from the Portuguese who were famous explorers and traders, not men of the land."

He cites the story of the Portuguese explorer, Pedro Alvares

Cabral, who discovered Brazil. After sampling the delights of the new land he wrote to King Manuel the Fortunate in Lisbon:

"Plantando, da."—Plant, and it will grow.

His successors have generally had the same idea—the soil is so fertile that agriculture can take care of itself.

In recent years, however, some perceptive Brazilians have had their doubts and have added a sentence to Cabral's opinion, "Mas ninguen planta,"—but no one plants.

"Actually neither assertion is correct today," concedes Crawford. "For more and more of the country's leaders are recognizing that worn-out soils must be replenished and that the pressure of increasing population requires the exploitation of undeveloped lands."

Governor Magalhães Pinto of the state of Minas Gerais, later Foreign Minister, and his Secretary of Agriculture (Paulo Salvo, who had been ACAR's first president), read the report and conceived an ambitious project for which they asked AIA's assistance.

The Jaíba Project

The proposal was to set up a colonization program on a tract of nearly a million acres of state-owned land in the São Francisco river valley in an area called Jaíba. The region is potentially rich but dry and isolated. Crawford and Heaton rounded up a group of technicians and prepared a detailed proposal for a $7,500,00 project to settle approximately 1,000 families in the area. Of the proposed total the state was to put up 30% and, hopefully, the Inter-American Development Bank was to lend the rest. The plan provided estimates of the self-liquidating costs for five years.

However, although the people most involved, including the Bank in Washington, were enthusiastic, a variety of political pulls and hauls intervened. So the three-volume report, called *Plan for Colonization of Jaíba,* one of which was three-inches thick, complete with detailed maps, mathematical calculations, and basic soil, agronomic and economic data, was reluctantly put on the shelf by Governor Magalhães Pinto.

But by 1966 political tensions had eased. The successor to Magalhães Pinto created a new state-controlled organization, the Rural Foundation, to cope with colonization problems in all parts of the

168

state. Its first assignment was to revise and bring up to date Crawford's and Heaton's report. Work has now started on the project, and the only major deviation that has been made from the original recommendation was to introduce irrigation practices in the first phase of the development instead of in the second.

The Central Plateau

Another project that Crawford initiated in 1961 was the proposed development project for the so-called *Planalto Central* (the central plateau).

Way back in 1946 Rockefeller had endeared himself to a Brazilian audience with this story:

> I shall never forget the day when I had luncheon with President Roosevelt at his desk shortly after returning in 1942 from a trip to Brazil. When I had finished making my report and the plates had been taken away, he relaxed, lit his cigarette, pulled out a big map of Brazil and said: "You know, Brazil is a most wonderful country. If I were a young man starting out in the world I would go there."
>
> Then pointing to the great plains of the central plateau, Mr. Roosevelt added: "Some day thas will be the most important area of development in the world, the whole history of our West will be repeated. Never forget one thing, when this war is over the hope for the future is going to rest in the new world."

In the spring of 1960 Brazil's brand-new capital, Brasília, rising flamboyantly out of the bright red earth of the central plateau, was inaugurated by its creator, President Kubitschek. The new capital was far from centers of population, and living quarters of legislators and government workers were the last edifices to go up. So roads had to be built connecting Brasilia with its predecessor, Rio de Janeiro (where most of the government personnel still lived), São Paulo where flows the economic life-blood of the country, Belo Horizonte and other important state capitals.

While government officials watched the fabulous new architecture taking shape, they suddenly became aware that it was rising in the midst of one of the world's few remaining tracts of open, unpopulated level lands. With roads and planes now giving access to these *campos cerrados* (a name given to scrub brush areas of low natural fertility), interest was centered on development possibilities. Ibec Research Institute, formerly a part of AIA, had already provided evidence that this land could be made productive, with proper treatment.

The campos cerrados of the central plateau of Brazil, on the left, yield to improved agricultural practices and produce good pasture land, on the right.

PIDR was asked by the Ministry of Agriculture and USAID to make a study of the agricultural potential of the area. Crawford again collected a group of technicians and for two months the group drove, rode and walked all over the area, taking soil samples, making topographical surveys and interviewing the few struggling farmers eking out their existence in deepest isolation. The preparation and publication of the report consumed another four months.

The result was the most comprehensive report ever done on the whole region. The findings, in general, indicated many favorable characteristics of the area:

Good climate
Good rainfall
Good topography
Good physical characteristics of soil
Low population density
Ready accessibility

Isolated patches of *terra roxa* (soil of a dark reddish-purple color found along river banks) which is very rich.

BUT the single limiting factor is the low fertility of most of the soil.

The report excited considerable interest, both in Brazil and in the United States. A consortium of four U.S. land-grant colleges (the Universities of Wisconsin, Illinois and Indiana and Michigan State University) cooperated wth the Brazilian National Research Council to form a joint entity to coordinate research and carry out pilot development projects. Unfortunately, due to difficulties over assignment of authority for various segments of the project, it became dormant.

However, like the Jaíba project, this too came to life. In 1967 the National Research Council revived it and has suggested that the first steps be financed out of a $10,000,000 loan proposed to USAID.

The Campos Project

A third project that PIDR developed in 1964 was a regional approach to agricultural problems. This centers around a city called Campos, in the state of Rio de Janeiro, in the delta of the Paraíba river. This area has been devoted to sugar cane for over 300 years. In recent years, due to a decline in sugar prices and also to the exhaustion of the land, the whole area has reached a state of economic crisis.

A progressive sugar grower in the area, Edmundo Barbosa da Silva, a long-time friend of AIA and head of the Antunes Foundation, one of the few private non-profit foundations in Brazil devoted to agricultural betterment, talked over the problem with Crawford.

"Diversify," came Crawford's prompt response.

Barbosa da Silva promoted a proposal in the local Cooperative Bank of Sugar Producers, located in Campos, which formally requested the Antunes Foundation and PIDR to make a survey of the agricultural potential of the area.

The report included a brief resource survey, a recommendation that all the problems be considered on a regional basis, and, specifically, a proposal to set up a milk cooperative immediately.

Again nothing happened until about three years later when the Brazilian Bank for Cooperatives, from funds made available to it by the Inter-American Development Bank, turned over $100,000 to the milk cooperative. A building was promptly started and equipment ordered.

It looks as though a regional office were going to be established at Campos and through the technical assistance program of the OAS, a group of six Italian technicians will start to work on developing other crops, such as pineapples, pigs, poultry, small fruits, mandioca, soy beans as possible lines of diversification for the area.

"If you just wait long enough," says the philosophical Crawford, "things happen."

The Antunes Foundation, in addition to its support of the work in Campos, has set up a regional Development Institute operating in the territory of Amapá. Amapá lies directly on the Equator, on the north side of the mouth of the Amazon, and they say that a girl and a boy can walk down a street of the capital, Macapá, hand in hand, one in the Northern Hemisphere and the other in the Southern.

Recent discoveries of manganese deposits have brought a measure of prosperity to the region, but there is great need for the development of agricultural resources. The Antunes group is sponsoring experiments in crop and livestock production and exploring future possibilities of fisheries, forestry and small business to service the mining enterprises.

Crawford, who had started his professional career in the Farm Security Administration in Arkansas in the early '30s, reflects that his work in the distressed Campos area has brought him a full circle.

"Physically and psychologically eastern Arkansas during the '30s and Campos today are very much alike. They look alike—black soil, lots of mud, bad roads, sad little shacks for homes, even sadder little shacks for schools, little or no health or sanitation services. And both with a one-crop economy—cotton in Arkansas and sugar cane in Campos.

"Arkansas has changed and I have hope that Campos will also."

Studies, Training, Technical Guidance

1962, the first full year of operation of the program working out of Costa Rica, also saw an impressive list of operations started: a special study of retail marketing in Caracas by CBR; organization of a supply and demand study of agricultural products in Venezuela; preparation

172

of a proposal to the Inter-American Development Bank for loans for two significant colonization programs in Bolivia.

The next year saw the agreement of the Inter-American Development Bank of a $1,600,000 loan to Costa Rica for a colonization project in Bataan, to provide farms and technical assistance, as well as cash, to some 600 farm families.

The Bank also came through in 1963 with $3,500,000 for the development of two large virgin areas in Bolivia as colonization projects. The loan was accompanied by an indication that additional loans of some $10,000,000 would be available in following years.

While all this was going on, Heaton, the one-man team, was preparing curricula and giving courses of instruction in the subtleties of agrarian reform in San José, at a large irrigation project in northern Peru, and at the newly established Inter-American Center for Agrarian Reform at Bogotá, Colombia.

All of this adds up to much more than the $31,000,000 in cold cash that he helped procure for working capital. The intangible multiplying effect of all these projects in attracting more capital and more devoted work in agricultural development will probably account, in the long run, for many times more than the direct investments.

Surveying the terrain for an agricultural study in Venezuela.

173

For example, Heaton worked closely with the Costa Rican agency responsible for the country's colonization program not only in framing the proposal for the Inter-American Development Bank, but perhaps more importantly, in many less tangible ways. Informal association with technicians of the country and consultation on methods permitted the program to get off to a good start, with fewer of the hazards and risks which usually face such newborn programs.

Heaton stressed the need for basic resource studies before outlining the specifics of an agrarian reform program. He set up an interdisciplinary study group, from various government agencies, to make a resource study in the Upala region of Costa Rica. The study provided basic information on soils, land use, forests, geology, hydrology, and the local economy.

Although the responsible agency had already made theoretical plans for the development of the area without having made field studdies, it quickly changed its mind when the results of the survey showed that all of the land slated for productive use was already fully and productively being used.

Thus the government was saved from a costly mistake and was able to develop a sound procedure for all future land reform actions. Perhaps the most important result of this one small operation was the training it gave to technicians in various government departments, laying the groundwork for a successful future operation.

Basic guides on how to select farm families for resettlement, on how to parcel out land, and how to determine the size of a farm so that it is an economically workable unit were developed specifically for the governments of Costa Rica and Panama. These guides have been instrumental in changing the thinking of many colonization planners and project administrators, with the result that these two countries were not plagued by some of the mistakes made in other countries. One of the most frequent problems had been in the size of farms, making them too small to provide an adequate income for the family. These how-to-do guides are now being prepared by various international agricultural agencies for the use in other countries.

Another technical aid that AIA was responsible for in this field was a research guide for CBR to use in its campaign to increase and improve the fruit crop of Venezuela. The program eventually resulted in an increase of 232% in plantain production and 128% in other fruits over a period of five years.

With AIA assistance, CBR completed a study of the supply and demand for agricultural and livestock products in Venezuela, financed by the U.S. Department of Agriculture. This study has had a profound effect on plans and programs in Venezuela in connection with the products analyzed. The consumer survey part of the study has provided, for the first time in Venezuela, a national base for calculating the relationship of demand to prices and supply, indicated by both urban and rural populations.

This study was one of several similar studies commissioned by the U.S. Department of Agriculture in Latin American countries. The Venezuelan one was the first finished and has served as a model for most of the subsequent ones. It has already proven its value in formulating future agricultural development.

A colonization survey party landing in the jungles of Costa Rica.

Heaton was also the study director of a benchmark study, *Present Status and Possibilities of Agricultural Development in Venezuela,* commissioned by the Ford Foundation and completed by CBR in March, 1967.

The findings included such reassuring facts as that crop production is rising at a rate about double the 3.5% annual rate of population increase. Net agricultural product consumption is around 115% of domestic production, compared to 130-140% during the preceding decade, thus indicating an approach to self-sufficiency. Approximately one-third of the country's farmers who account for about 13% of the nation's agricultural production have been established in settlement projects under the agrarian reform laws, and acreage in crops is increasing about 4.8% annually due largely to public reclamation, irrigation and drainage projects.

Crawford has, at the request of the Ministry of Agriculture of Paraguay, prepared a study of agricultural credit for that country and also made a study and analysis of Paraguay's colonization work and formulated basic recommendations for a large colonization project.

Because of their mobility, both Heaton and Crawford have been most effective in sparking interchanges between countries. For example, Crawford has been instrumental in having several students sent from Paraguay to study in Brazil, and Heaton has seen to it that many of the advances made in Venezuela have been adapted in Costa Rica. This has been an informal operation, almost a by-product of the main course of their jobs. But it could very well prove to be of great importance.

Perhaps the greatest handicap to the rural development program was the absence of a corporate contracting agency. Both AIA and the Institute had wanted to set up such an organization, with the idea that it could undertake experimental and demonstration projects in rural development to be financed by USAID, the Inter-American Development Bank or other international institutions. However, after trying for more than a year, this plan had to be given up because approval could not be obtained from all members of the board of the Institute.

Not all was beer and skittles, and not all programs worked out successfully. Some failed for lack of proper support within the indi-

176

vidual countries, some because they were wrongly conceived, some because they were ahead of their time, and some because of the vagaries of politics.

In 1963 a detailed plan for establishing a new supervised credit program in the Dominican Republic was halted before it got started by the overthrow of the Bosch government, and assistance to the agrarian reform program in Panama was terminated at the death of its primary mover and supporter in the government.

In summary, although the program has operated without the advantage of a corporate entity, it has achieved a maximum of success with a minimum of personnel. Its effect will long be felt among the hundreds of technicians who have been taught to have a clearer, more realistic attitude toward the agricultural economic facts of life.

But the need is still there. During the past eight years, twelve countries have enacted agrarian reform legislation and have set up special agencies to carry it out. As these programs flourish and other countries follow suit, the need for qualified planners and project managers will rise. But the countries themselves, or already established international agencies, now have the technical competence to carry out development and training programs. Now the development of administrative skills and the appreciation of established procedures, in both the public and private sectors, remain the most critical needs in Latin America.

Chapter 4

PLAN VICTORIA

In winter in southern Chile (June, July and August) it rains constantly, is always cold, and gray clouds hang low. The roads become almost impassable to motor vehicles, and the rural communities, never very conspicuous, seem to disappear into the dripping landscape.

The children, most of them ragged and barefoot, protected from the cold only by threadbare ponchos, walk sometimes four miles to school—when there is one available. There they sit and shiver, listening passively to lessons which have no relationship to the lives they lead. The teachers, lacking both adequate training and teaching materials, take refuge in a deadly rote system of teaching. This is no more inspiring to the student than to the teacher.

So every year more and more children quit. The educators of Chile, noted among Latin American countries for its advanced educational system, became alarmed at the drop-out rate among rural children—some 85% in the first six years of school. There were economic factors: poor families need every pair of hands they can get to make a precarious living from their reluctant acres. But the basic reason is the fact that the learning process is so dull and the result so far afield from their daily lives that the youngsters have no incentive to remain.

It was into this situation that AIA, armed with a generous grant from the Rockefeller Brothers Fund, moved early in 1962.

The Fund, a private philanthropic organization, whose trustees have many close ties to Latin America, was deeply concerned at the destruction that the 1960 earthquake had caused in Chile. Hardest hit had been the rural areas, with thousands left homeless and hundreds of schools and other public buildings destroyed.

Following a survey and recommendation by Galo Plaza, former President of Ecuador and international trouble-shooter, the Fund

178

made a grant of $500,000 to construct model rural schools and to modernize and reorganize the whole rural educational pattern.

Ernest Maes, who had carried out the vocational education program in Venezuela, was chosen to represent AIA in the development of the program.

He sought the cooperation of the Development Corporation (CORFO) and the Ministry of Education; a Special Commission for Rural Education was set up; the Department of Victorja was chosen as the location; AIA agreed to contribute $315,000 for school construction, $135,000 for curriculum development; the Ministry of Education would contribute land, furniture for the schools and all the permanent personnel; and the Development Corporation would contribute the administrative and accounting services.

An executive secretary was chosen, Enrique Salinas, a brilliant young teacher in one of the country's leading normal schools. When

L to R—Enrique Salinas, former executive secretary of the Special Commission for Rural Education, Ernest Maes, of AIA and Juan Guirao, of the Chilean Ministry of Education.

he reported for work in June, 1962, he had instructions to build eight rural schools, in communities not yet designated, and to enlist the aid of local residents—an unheard of idea. In addition, he was to preside over teacher workshops which would design the new curriculum and prepare all the teaching materials needed.

His first task was to determine the eight locations. Word got around fast and applications flooded in, making the final selection a delicate job of diplomacy. But finally they were chosen, the buildings designed, workshops under way, and local committees in each community organized.

From this last activity has developed what might be viewed as a by-product—but a by-product that almost overshadowed the original purpose—for, by enlisting the cooperation of parents, community leaders and just people, the instigators of the program turned up a sense of community responsibility and creativeness that is rare in Latin America.

The Special Commission, working in close cooperation with the local committees, decided, with some trepidation, to try out a do-it-yourself school building program rather than contracting out the construction. The planners of the project reasoned that if this worked not only would costs be held down, but perhaps it might lead to other projects in which neighbors worked together democratically on a common project in a way reminiscent of the North American frontier tradition.

The experiment worked—the amount of community cooperation exceeded even the hoped-for goals—with the result that most of the schools actually cost only 30 to 40% of what contractors' figures would have been. Through the contribution of their own labor in the evenings, on weekends and holidays, the contribution of materials (bricks, lumber, paint) and transport, and a careful eye on prices, these local committees kept costs down to the point where the program was able to build four additional schools with the same budget.

New leaders emerged: a lady who ran the meat store in Quino mobilized every able-bodied man, woman and child. Under her severe supervision every weekend they hauled rock, sand, bricks and other materials to the school site in trucks, wheelbarrows, ox carts, and sometimes in their arms. In Colo, one of the five large farm owners

180

A first-day student shares his teacher's pride in the new school at Colo.

Youngsters at Las Lilas experimenting with educational blocks.

contributed the land for the school and provided the vehicles to haul the materials. One of the laborers of his farm was elected president of the local committee, and the landowner now cheerfully serves on the committee, following the leadership of his employee.

The application of another community for a school was turned down because there was no road over which supplies could be transported. This lack of a road, incidentally, had isolated the community from more than education. The traditional leader of the community failed in his appeal to the governor of the state, whereupon a soft-spoken, shy Indian peasant farmer came up with the suggestion that the able-bodied members of the community build the road themselves. Under his leadership they did it—eight kilometers, all with hand labor, even to the crushing of rock—and the village got a school.

Soon the buildings became realities and in due time all twelve were inaugurated, each with an all-out gala celebration.

Splendid though the new physical facilities were, the real test of the permanence and effectiveness of Plan Victoria was the development of classroom work more closely in harmony with the needs and daily life of the average rural child.

In addition to modernizing the curriculum in the three R's, the teachers' workshop developed a vocational and prevocational program.

A shop program was devised, tools and materials secured, and at least one teacher from each school had been trained in teaching shop practices by the time the first eight schools were opened. With this as the core of the new program, it was recognized that, to be functional and attractive, a rural school program needed good materials and well-trained teachers in three practical aspects of education which had previously been neglected:

1. Elementary prevocational shop

2. Health and home-life education

3. Rural youth club work and elementary prevocational agriculture

The plaque states, "The community of Colo and the Rockefeller Brothers Fund together have constructed this building. They dedicate it to the rural children of Chile."

183

The impact of even a partial practical program, involving only the prevocational shop element, was immediately reflected in the drop-out rate. The enrollment of all schools went up an average of 17%.

Perhaps the best commentary on Plan Victoria was the speech given by an almost illiterate Indian who presided at the inauguration of the school in the village of Las Lilas. The feature of the inauguration was to be the planting of a sapling from the province from which came each Chilean official who had taken part in the project.

I greet and welcome our visitors who are here to help us inaugurate our school and to plant some trees that are native to their land, and we have planted these trees that are of our land. I am old. I lament that when I was young I did not have a school to attend. I have helped build this school and it will be a blessing for our children.

One of the three types of schools built under the Plan Victoria.

We have now planted these trees. I know I shall not live to enjoy their fruit or their shade. But our children will enjoy the fruit and any traveler passing this way will be able to rest in their shade. The future will be better because we have done these things. I have spoken.

Even before the Plan Victoria was completed in 1965, it was being duplicated in the neighboring province. This program, called Plan Nuble, is copied step by step from the Victoria pattern. The U.S. Agency for International Development contributed $370,000 for the program and asked AIA to continue its association.

Maes retained the original Special Commission, adding only a representative of USAID. And with the same community spirit and effectiveness six schools have been completed.

The fame of the Chilean venture is spreading both within and without Chile's borders. Educators in other countries have heard of this plan for rationalizing rural education and feel that it perhaps offers answers to many of their own problems. There is little doubt that, if necessary financing is found, Plan Victorias will be started in many other countries in the hemisphere.

Part 6

PART VI

A JOB WELL DONE

Early in 1967 AIA, as was its wont, took a long, hard look at itself and asked, "Where are we going?" The corporate membership looked at the record as it has been outlined in this book and decided that it has been a good job, done with a minimum of mistakes, staff and money.

Staff

To the board members of AIA it seemed a minor miracle that so much had been accomplished by so few. At no time had the number of technicians on the AIA payroll exceeded twenty-one and over the years it had averaged thirteen, about half of them Latin Americans. Of course this does not include the local personnel employed in all the individual joint programs. The total of such employees ran into the hundreds.

Rockefeller had remained president of the corporation until 1953 when he resigned both as president and as a member of the board because of his appointment by President Eisenhower as Assis-

186

tant Secretary of the newly created Department of Health, Education and Welfare. He was succeeded as president by Harrison who has held the position ever since. After his resignation from the Federal Government, Rockefeller returned to the board in 1956 and again became active in the program until 1958 when he was elected Governor of New York State.

In the ten years since he has been governor, Rockefeller, although not active in the day-to-day operations of AIA, has nevertheless remained close to it, intellectually and emotionally.

"AIA from the very beginning has been only as good as its staff," says President Harrison. "In fact AIA is people—not money, not administrative organization, not a fine headquarters setup, not even all the publications we get out. It's just been people. And without John Camp it could never have been done. He slogged through the bush and made other people enjoy doing it. He sat quietly alone and outlined thoughtful programs that other people enjoyed carrying out. And he made his board of directors feel they were the greatest, the most creative group working in this field."

Another unique part of AIA's operation has been the degree of autonomy given to the people in the field. Occasionally the board showed its displeasure, even made a suggestion now and then. But, on the whole, its principal reaction to program development was benign and grateful approval. With a small board and a handful of operators there was unusual opportunity for personal relationships. Members of the board traveled occasionally, but more frequently asked the field staff to come to New York for meetings and general refreshment. While some envious colleagues from other organizations felt AIA staffers were pretty freewheeling in their operations, actually these men and women were singularly responsive to the feelings of board members but happily free of petty restrictions.

For a few years there was no New York office as such. Camp directed the whole operation from Venezuela. In 1964 he moved to New York, setting up a centralized headquarters. Always a field man at heart, however, Camp has spent almost as much time in the back country of Latin America as he has in mid-town Manhattan. His trips throughout the hemisphere have served as a unifying force among members of the field staff.

Mrs. Boyer, a member of the board since 1954, vice president and a member of the executive committee, has been a constant factor in AIA's life. Her knowledge of Venezuela in the early days and her close professional association with Rockefeller over the years have made her of singular usefulness to the organization.

Mrs. Brennan who, after the early days in Venezuela, joined Rockefeller in Washington in his wartime job, and later took part in all his postwar activities, became corporate secretary of AIA in 1962. Since then, as a backstop for Camp, she has been the indispensable den mother for the whole operation.

Lawrence H. Levy, again an associate of Rockefeller's from the wartime Coordinator days, has been another constant factor in AIA. As corporate secretary, 1948-62, Treasurer 1957-62 and a member of the board since 1962, he has been an ever-vigilant watchdog over the legal and financial matters of the Association.

Louise A. Boyer, AIA board member.

Flor P. Brennan, Secretary of AIA.

Contributors

A few but very special contributors have made possible the work of AIA. Rockefeller has been a steady contributor of money as well as of time, enthusiasm and wisdom. Other individual members of the Rockefeller family have also been most generous in support of the program.

Another consistent supporter in recent years has been the Rockefeller Brothers Fund, which was set up in 1940 by Rockefeller and his four brothers and sister to make philanthropic contributions to causes of mutual interest. Since 1962 when it asked for AIA's help on the Chile project, its support of the general program of AIA has been consistent and generous.

Other important contributors, of course, were the oil companies in Venezuela in the early days. Many local companies, subsidiaries of United States companies with large foreign operations, have also contributed to individual programs, particularly individual rural youth nationl committees. Local branches of United States banks have also been liberal in making sums available for loans to rural youth.

A complete list of contributors will be found in the appendix.

Chapter 1

DECISION TO TERMINATE

In answer to the question, "Where are we going?" members of the board came up with another question, "Why should we be going anywhere? Maybe we've reached where we want to be?"

The final decision was difficult, for there were many alternatives and much still needed to be done. Also there was much emotion, because nobody who ever worked for AIA approached his job with dispassion or disinterest. He was personally involved, completely immersed in the joy and the anguish of helping people help themselves.

By this time almost all the individual country programs were in the hands of local governments or organizations. Brazil's ABCAR had flourished until it covered the country. The vocational education programs in Venezuela and Chile were in the hands of the teachers that AIA had trained. All the myriad programs that CBR had spawned were still being carried on either by CBR itself, of which AIA had no part except as consultant, or by other state or federal groups. The umbilical cord tying AIA to the information program in Venezuela had long, long since been severed and that youngster was a thriving teen-ager.

In other words AIA had almost achieved its primary goal—to turn going programs over to the beneficiaries. There remained only the international programs being carried out in conjunction with the Inter-American Institute of Agricultural Sciences. These were strong and healthy and could easily survive transplantation to other and more permanent sponsorship.

So perhaps it was time to push the last of the fledglings over the edge of the nest?

The decision was made at meetings held in March, 1967. The field staff was summoned to New York for discussions about the best methods for insuring the future of the three international programs.

There were some regrets—nobody likes to see his young depart, no matter how mature and competent those young might be.

But regrets soon disappeared in the intoxicating contemplation of the quiet but effective revolution that all had had a part of during the past twenty-two years. Each AIA staff member of course had his own personal evaluation of what he had done, but, even better, was the increasing outside, impartial appraisal of the effects of this revolution in Latin America.

Felipe Herrera, president of the Inter-American Development Bank, a hardheaded man of money, reports that "Latin America today is at the threshold of its economic take-off."

And speaking of the agricultural development of the continent he comments:

> In the agricultural sector it is clear that Latin America understands more than ever the need to improve productivity and effectively to incorporate the rural population into the area's economic structure so that it can improve its role as supplier of foodstuffs and raw materials to meet expanding domestic and world needs, as purchaser of manufactured foods and as a generator of domestic savings for investment.

He cites the fact that agricultural output, including domestic foodstuffs and export commodities, has risen in volume by 70% since 1950. There has been a growing consciousness of social needs, and an ever increasing mobilization of international resources backed by foreign assistance has resulted in notable improvements since the adoption of the Alliance for Progress, particularly in such fields as education, health and housing. Improvements in the field of health, such as sanitation, have resulted in a dramatic reduction in mortality rates.

And the United States Ambassador to the Organization of American States, Sol M. Linowitz, reports with some pride that of all the expenditures of the Alliance for Progress, the United States supplies a small portion.

"The fact is that 90% of what is being done under the Alliance for Progress," he says, "is being done by the Latin American countries themselves. This is a cooperative undertaking in which we are a very minor partner. During the last six or seven years we have put in a

191

little over $7,000,000,000 from all sources in this country, private and public. This includes some pretty heavy industrial investments.

"I think there is a growing feeling among the Latin American countries that this has to be their own future, which is going to be worked out in their own way—with our assistance, but under their leadership.

"Looking back over the years of the Alliance for Progress, we can see what has happened. To mention just a few things, more teachers have been trained under the Alliance for Progress than in the previous twenty-five years. More schools have been built, more institutions created, more doctors have been trained and more agrarian reform has been realized than in the previous twenty-five years."

Venezuela is getting ever nearer to self-sufficiency in food, according to the Agricultural Bank in Caracas. The bank reported that agricultural production, apart from that consumed by farmers themselves, reached a record value of Bs. 2,977,000,000 ($662,000,000) in 1968.

The Venezuelan farmer is earning ten times more today than he did twenty-two years ago, when AIA first began its ministrations there. And the small farmers are getting the lion's share of agricultural loans and new housing. And in Brazil the whole CAR structure remains as a unique monument to AIA's work.

So members of the staff returned to the field, each determined to do his very best by his own program. And instead of doing it in two and a half years, they did it in one year. By the end of 1968 all programs were either turned over to their new sponsors or phased out and completed.

Chapter 2

THE FUTURE

Like a couple of shy lovers, PIJR and the United States National 4-H Club Foundation first eyed one another, back in 1950, then tentatively set up an experimental cooperative program, and finally in the course of the years reached a functioning and effective working relationship.

The marriage was consummated on December 13, 1967 when Camp for AIA, Shrum for the National 4-H Club Foundation, and Samper for the Institute, signed an agreement in San José, Costa Rica, whereby AIA turned over its responsibility for PIJR to the Foundation. Thus the rural youth movement in Latin America reaped the advantage of active and official affiliation with the powerful U.S. group and the National Foundation was provided with a tremendous boost for its international programs.

The 4-H Foundation is a private, non-profit educational institution. It is chartered by the Cooperative Extension Service of the State Land-Grant Universities and the U.S. Department of Agriculture. Through this network of affiliations, the Foundation will be able to give the rural youth programs of the Americas a direct tie to the important educational resources of the U.S. agricultural universities and extension services which conduct the 4-H program.

One of the most enticing facets of the new association perhaps is that it will provide a broader base for economic support from the many U.S. companies and other institutions that are already helping to support 4-H club work and that are interested in expanding their assistance to Latin America. In fact, the budget for the first year's operation of the combined programs is triple that of PIJR in the past.

PIIP and PIDR ceased to exist as entities at the end of 1968, but their memory is green. The trained men and women who are working in their own countries and in turn training their successors attest to the work of that Heaton, Crawford, Bradt and Anderson have accomplished over the years.

The work of the Institute itself reflects their influence, and many individual government agencies, innumerable private groups and several international organizations have profited by the ideas and the work that AIA has brought to the southern hemisphere.

AIA has also left some very tangible contributions in addition to those already cited in this book. For example, Anderson has completed an inventory of information facilities in Latin America and a training manual on the role of information in agricultural development. Heaton has provided a blue-print for graduate study at the Inter-American Agrarian Centers in Turrialba and Bogotá and has planted the idea of integration of national agricultural development plans into a regional

L to R—Howard E. Law, Director of PIJR; Grant A. Shrum, Director of the National 4-H Club Foundation; Armando Samper, Director General of the Inter-American Institute of Agricultural Sciences and John R. Camp, Executive Vice-President of AIA conclude an agreement in which the PIJR program is transferred to the National 4-H Club Foundation.

concept for Central America, to keep pace with the economic integration that is being carried out in the area. And, although he has returned to his own country, Crawford keeps a fatherly eye on the "sistema CAR," ready to help at any moment.

Dr. Alejandro M. Osorio, Venezuelan Minister of Agriculture, in expressing "the sincere appreciation and gratitude of the Venezuelan government to the board of directors of the AIA for its outstanding cooperation," said of the future: "AIA may rest assured that its name and its achievement will remain alive in the agricultural sector of Venezuela after it discontinues direct participation in our programs."

And, evaluating the impact of AIA on the entire western hemisphere, Dr. Samper of the Institute called the ten-year association "an era of effective cooperation of mutual benefit, but above all of great value to all the hemisphere countries. The work that has been done is of great significance, particularly in the field of communications, which has accomplished the pioneering job of opening the way for postgraduate study in Latin America. The work done among rural youth has had the effect of creating an awareness in all the hemisphere countries where evidences that the movement is going forward can already be appreciated. . . . The work carried out in the field of rural development also has had characteristics of importance, particularly with regard to the support of national programs such as those in Brazil.

"It is for all these reasons the Inter-American Institute of Agricultural Sciences of the OAS, while regretting the decision taken by the directors of AIA, wants to express to them the deepest gratitude for having sponsored this cooperative relationship which, in such a short time, has produced significant benefits for the hemisphere."

APPENDIX I

Representative International Agreements Entered into by AIA

ACAR

AGREEMENT ENTERED INTO BETWEEN THE GOVERNMENT OF THE STATE OF MINAS GERAIS AND THE AMERICAN INTERNATIONAL ASSOCIATION FOR ECONOMIC AND SOCIAL DEVELOPMENT (AIA) PROVIDING FOR THE ESTABLISHMENT OF A CREDIT SYSTEM THAT WILL STIMULATE CROP AND LIVESTOCK PRODUCTION AND ADMINISTER OTHER BENEFITS TO THE RURAL COMMUNITY

On the 6th of December, 1948, in the Palácio da Liberdade (Liberty Palace), in Belo Horizonte, Capital of the State of Minas Gerais, Brazil, being present Governor Milton Soares Campos, representing the State of Minas Gerais, and, as representative of the American International Association, of New York, United States of America, Mr. Robert W. Hudgens, Director of the said Association, resident in that city, *IS CELEBRATED* the present agreement for the purpose of establishing a system of financial and technical assistance within the terms of Act n°29 of December 10th, 1947, which makes possible the development of crop and livestock production and the improvement of the economic and social conditions of rural life, *BY WHICH ACT IF ORGANIZED,* on this date, the Associação de Crédito e Assistência Rural (ACAR), according to the following clauses which form an integrate part of this agreement:

FIRST—The Association will be known as Associação de Crédito e Assistência Rural (ACAR); its domicile will be Belo Horizonte, Minas Gerais, but it may also establish agencies and offices in either parts of the State or any other place which may be helpful in the accomplishment of its plan.

SECOND—In order to second the purposes and efforts of the state government directed toward the economic and social progress of Minas Gerais and of Brazil, and having in view the various mutual plans of the Government and of the AIA in this respect, the Association, that is hereby constituted, will have as its fundamental objective the increasing of crop and livestock production and

197

the improvement of economic and social conditions of rural life. This objective will be accomplished through the application of a dual assistance, technical as well as financial. This dual assistance will facilitate the adoption of an adequate credit system for small crop and livestock producers and a plan of supervision that guarantees the efficient use of credit. Such plan will adhere to the following general policies:

1) The types of loans should cover, in an adequate manner, the agricultural and domestic needs of rural people. In general terms, the loans will be divided into three groups:

   a) Loans for improving living conditions of the family and for increasing the production of crops and livestock;

   b) Loans for the purchase of essential implements, repairs, and for acquiring workstock, foundation herds and sires;

   c) Loans for the purchase or development of land, and for constructions and necessary instalations.

2) Loans will be based on carefully prepared farm and home management plans in which is verified the productive possibilities and guarantees of the borrower, as well as the details of execution and liquidation of the plan of operations.

3) Interest rates should be moderate and the amortization schedule will be determined by the type of loan and repayment possibilities of the borrower, according to the development of the pre-established farm and home management plan.

4) Loans will be secured by chattel mortgages, real state mortgages or both.

5) The conditions and details of execution of the operations will be established between ACAR and the financing entity or entities.

6) The Association will direct its attention, in collaboration with the competent departments of the Minas Government, toward the improvement of rural life, along the following lines:

   a) Improvement of physical conditions, especially those related to health, sanitation and living quarters;

   b) Education of the rural population with special attention to agricultural instruction, domestic industries, nutrition, alphabetization and development of community spirit;

   c) The promotion of social services in the rural community, such as pre-natal care of mothers, medical assistance, infant welfare and recreation;

   d) The carrying out of studies and demonstrations of certain types of residences and other rural constructions of minimum cost which are adapted to the environment and which make use of the materials native to the regions.

THIRD—The Association will have a duration of three years, from the 1st day of January, 1949, and may be extended by mutual agreement of the parties.

FOURTH—The capital of ACAR will be determined by mutual agreement of the parties, and in the same manner increased. The initial capital of ACAR will be equivalent to U.S. $450,000.00, transformed into cruzeiros, which the State of Minas Gerais and the American International Association will contribute in equal quotas in the following manner:

State of Minas Gerais	*American International Association*
1949—U.S. $ 25,000	U.S. $ 75,000
1950— 75,000	75,000
1951— 125,000	75,000
Total U.S. $225,000	U.S. $225,000

The capital mentioned will be used to cover:

1) The expenses of conducting field operations of the program, during a period of 3 years in a maximum of 12 areas, and;

2) The operations of a central office for ACAR in Belo Horizonte during the same period.

In January, 1949, the State of Minas Gerais will deposit to the account of ACAR the sum in cruzeiros which corresponds to U.S. $25,000 and the AIA will deposite the equivalent in cruzeiros of U.S. $75,000 deducting, however, the approximate cost of salaries and expenses of personnel employed by AIA and placed at the service of ACAR.

The sums corresponding to the following fiscal years will be deposited by the parties in the same month adopted for the first year according to the specifications of this clause.

FIFTH—The Association will be directed by an Administrative Board composed of five members, two of which will be designated by the Government of Minas and two by AIA; the fifth member will be a person proposed by AIA who merits the approval of the Minas Government and who will also occupy the position of Director of ACAR. The President will be elected from the members of the Administrative Board indicated by the Government. The Administrative Board will hold at least one meeting each month and may be called into extraordinary sessions by its President, by the Director of ACAR, or by any of its members in case it is considered necessary for furthering the activities of the Association. The members of the Administrative Board are obligated to attend ordinary and extraordinary sessions and their failure, either temporary or permanent, will be substituted by persons designated by the parties to this agreement. The decisions of the Administrative Board will require the affirmative vote of at least four of its members, and the same number will constitute a quorum for any meeting.

SIXTH—The attributions of the Administrative Board are:

1) Approve the general plan of work of ACAR;

2) Approve the selection of municipalities or zones in which the ACAR will function;

3) Approve or disapprove the total budget of expenses for each fiscal year according to the general plan of work;

4) Approve or disapprove budgetary modifications;

5) Present to the State Government an annual report that contains a detailed account of the operations of each fiscal year;

6) Adopt any other means or resolutions necessary or convenient to achieve the objectives of the Association;

7) Consider the report that the Director must furnish each trimester regarding the activities of the Association and the plans that have been formulated, notwithstanding the fact that the Board may also solicit at any other time any information that it considers necessary.

SEVENTH—The attributions of the Director of ACAR are:

1) Execute the plans of ACAR;

2) Propose to the Administrative Board the names of essential technical personnel and appoint them, once approval of the Board has been attained;

3) Appoint and remove subordinate personnel on his own responsibility and submit such actions to the post-approval of the Board;

4) Fix salaries, expenses and working conditions of employees upon approval of the Administrative Board;

5) Deposit and withdraw the funds of the subsidiary bank account;

6) Submit to the approval of the Administrative Board any budgetary modifications which he considers convenient;

7) Develop and present to the Administrative Board for its consideration, a general annual plan of work, and also such other plans of work as he considers convenient;

8) Furnish the Administrative Board with the information necessary for the trimestral and annual report;

9) Represent the Association in all acts, public and private, in which it is interested and appoint legal counsel to defend the rights of the Association, judicially or extrajudicially, with previous authorization of the Administrative Board;

10) Delegate to subordinate personnel such powers and responsibilities as are necessary for the proper administration of the activities of the ACAR;

11) Execute all the decisions of the Administrative Board and direct the activities of the Association.

EIGHTH—In no case may the Association contract obligations or make commitments in excess of the amount of its available capital.

NINTH—The funds of the ACAR will be handled by means of two bank accounts, called *PRINCIPAL ACCOUNT* and *SUBSIDIARY ACCOUNT*.

The Principal Account will be drawn upon by checks signed by two of its members, one selected from those named by the Government and the other from those named by the AIA. The sums corresponding to the contributions of the two parties will be deposited in the Principal Account, and from it will be transferred to the Subsidiary Account the sums necessary to cover budgeted expenses according to the decisions of the Administrative Board. The Subsidiary Account will be drawn upon by checks signed by the Director and one employee designated by the Board.

TENTH—The Association is completely non-profit and its objectives are clearly defined. Whatever grants, gifts, profits, or other benefits that may be obtained by ACAR will be totally invested in the application or execution of the general plan of work of the Association. At the termination of this agreement all of the property, whatever it may be, belonging to the Association, will be transferred to the State of Minas Gerais or to any other organization or institution designated by the Government of the State.

ELEVENTH—By indication of the Government, Dr. José de Almeida Barbosa Melo and Dr. Paulo Salvo, and by indication of the AIA, Dr. John B. Griffing and Mr. William H. Alton, have been appointed members of the Administrative Board. The fifth member and Director who has been proposed by the AIA and approved by the Government, is Mr. Walter L. Crawford.

TWELFTH—Doubts and controversies, of whatever nature, that may arise in relation to this agreement and which cannot be resolved in an amicable manner by the parties will be decided by the competent courts of Brazil, according to its laws.

Given this the 6th day of December, 1948, in the Palácio da Liberdade, in Belo Horizonte.

s/ MILTON SOARES CAMPOS
Governor, State of Minas Gerais

s/ ROBERT W. HUDGENS
Director, American International
Association for Economic and
Social Development

ABCAR

DECLARATION

The organization signing below, the AMERICAN INTERNATIONAL ASSOCIATION FOR ECONOMIC AND SOCIAL DEVELOPMENT, represented by its Director and holder of its power of attorney, Walter L. Crawford, in the capacity of founding member of the ASSOCIAÇÃO BRASILEIRA DE CRÉDITO E ASSISTÊNCIA RURAL (ABCAR), hereby declares, for all legal effects and purposes in carrying out the dispositions of Article 8, paragraphs 4 and 16, of the ABCAR statutes, the following:

1)—The representative of the declaring party, AMERICAN INTERNATIONAL ASSOCIATION FOR ECONOMIC AND SOCIAL DEVELOPMENT, in the Governing Board of the ASSOCIAÇÃO BRASILEIRA DE CRÉDITO E ASSISTÊNCIA RURAL (ABCAR) will be Walter L. Crawford, who, by the present, designates as his substitute Henry W. Bagley, Director of the declarer in Brazil.

201

2)—The contribution of the declarer to the ASSOCIAÇÃO BRASILEIRA DE CRÉDITO E ASSISTÊNCIA RURAL (ABCAR), corresponding to the first fiscal period closing December 31, 1956, will consist of:

a)—The amount of US $35,000 (thirty-five thousand dollars) in cash, which will be placed at the disposal of ABCAR and which can be received by it either in dollars or in cruzeiros at the exchange rate of the day on which the operation is made, in accordance with the instructions of the Governing Board;

b)—Technical services to be provided by technicians and administrative personnel as well as the travel expenses that may be incurred in the service of ABCAR, in the total estimated sum of US $25,000 (twenty-five thousand dollars).

c)—In addition to the above-mentioned amounts, the declarer will expend the amount of US $6,000 (six thousand dollars) to defray expenses that indirectly benefit the program of ABCAR, such as recruiting, contracting, maintaining and transporting employees and technicians from abroad to Brazil and from Brazil to abroad, as well as maintaining its activities that are of interest to the ABCAR program and its associated members.

3)—For the 1957 fiscal year, the declarer commits himself to the following contribution:

a)—US $30,000 (thirty thousand dollars) in cash to be placed at the disposal of ABCAR, which may be received either in dollars or in cruzeiros at the exchange rate on the day that remittance is made, in accordance with the instructions of the Governing Board;

b)—Technical services to be provided by technical and administrative personnel as well as necessary traveling expenses incurred in the services of ABCAR, the total cost of which is estimated at US $55,000 (fifty-five thousand dollars).

c)—In addition to the above-mentioned amounts, the declarer will expend, in benefit of the ABCAR program, the amount of US $15,000 (fifteen thousand dollars) in payment of expenses that will indirectly benefit the ABCAR program, such as recruiting, contracting, maintaining and transporting technicians from abroad to Brazil and from Brazil to abroad, and the maintenance of its activities in the country.

4)—The contributions for following fiscal periods will be declared in accordance with the dispositions of the Footnote of Article 16 of the statutes of ABCAR.

Rio de Janeiro, June 21, 1956

AMERICAN INTERNATIONAL ASSOCIATION
FOR ECONOMIC AND SOCIAL DEVELOPMENT

s/ WALTER L. CRAWFORD,
Director

STATUTES OF ASSOCIAÇÃO BRASILEIRA DE CRÉDITO E ASSISTÊNCIA RURAL

TITLE I

Name, Domicile, Objectives and Duration

Art. 1—By this Act is founded the Associação Brasileira de Crédito e Assistência Rural (ABCAR), a private civil society, non-profit in character, with headquarters in the Capital of the Republic and area of action throughout the national territory.

Art. 2—The objectives of ABCAR are to coordinate and stimulate:

a) Programs of Rural Extension in an effort to bring to rural families, through educational means, the knowledge necessary for improvement of agricultural and home management practices, thereby modifying their habits and attitudes as a means of attaining better social, cultural and economic standards of living.

b) Programs of Supervised Rural Credit in an effort to institute a system of credit based on the integral planning of the agricultural and home activities of rural families, as well as adequate supervision of agricultural development, in order to assure that the credit fulfills the function of assisting, technically and economically, small and medium-sized farmers to improve their standard of living.

Art. 3—In order to carry out its objectives, ABCAR will:

a) Obtain financial and technical resources from international, inter-regional, inter-governmental and national organizations for specific application in programs of Rural Extension and Supervised Credit in Brazil.

b) Distribute the above mentioned resources among the various regional and state member organizations that are carrying out, or plan to carry out, these activities.

c) Promote the coordination of regional and state programs in an effort to establish uniform regulations and standards of performance and safeguard the fundamental principles of Rural Extension and Rural Supervised Credit, in accordance with the characteristics of the systems now in use, but allowing for normal development and necessary local adaptations.

d) Orientate the implantation and accompany the development of organizations that propose to execute programs of Rural Extension and Rural Supervised Credit, assisting them technically and financially.

e) Cooperate in the training of technical and administrative personnel of associated member organizations.

f) Establish and intensify the exchange of information and techniques among the various regional and state organizations that are engaged in the execution of programs of Rural Extension and Supervised Credit.

g) Document and disseminate the results of the various programs.

Art. 4—The duration of ABCAR is indefinite, the fiscal year coinciding with the calendar year.

Membership

Art. 5—The members of ABCAR are:

I—*Cooperators:* Public or private organizations with which ABCAR celebrates agreements that provide substantial financial, technical or material aid to carry out its objectives.

II—*Beneficiaries:* Organizations of Rural Extension and Rural Supervised Credit that are associated with it in order to receive the advantages and assistance specified in Art. 2 of these statutes.

Footnote: The Founding Members of ABCAR are the following organizations which sign the articles of incorporation:

1. The Associação de Crédito e Assistência Rural (ACAR)
2. The Associação Nordestina de Crédito e Assistência Rural (ANCAR)
3. The Associação Sulina de Crédito e Assistência Rural (ASCAR)
4. The Confederação Rural Brasileira (C.R.B.)
5. The American International Association for Economic and Social Development (AIA)
6. The Escritorio Técnico de Agricultura (E.T.A.)

Art. 6—The members of ABCAR are not responsible, individually or collectively, for the obligations assumed by it.

TITLE III

Organization and Responsibilities

Chapter I

Organs

Art. 7—The organs of ABCAR are:

I—The Governing Board

II—The Executive Direction

Chapter II

Governing Board

Art. 8—The Governing Board, the organ of final authority, will be composed of one representative of each member of ABCAR and presided over by a President elected by it, from its members, for a period of three years.

Footnote 1—The President of the Governing Board shall be the President of ABCAR.

Footnote 2—In addition to the President, there shall be elected a Vice President for an equal term, who will substitute the President in his absences.

Footnote 3—For election of the President and Vice President, a quorum of at least two-thirds of the members is necessary.

Footnote 4—Each representative on the Governing Board will have a substitute, to be designated by the respective member of ABCAR.

Art. 9—The Governing Board will meet regularly once each three months, and in special meetings when called by the President or by a majority of its members.

Footnote 1—The Board can only make decisions with the presence of more than half of its members.

Footnote 2—Decisions of the Board, not specifically excepted in the Statutes, will be made by majority vote of those present.

Footnote 3—The Executive Director may attend the meetings of the Governing Board and take part in discussions but without the right to vote.

Art. 10—Members of the Governing Board may be reimbursed for normal travel expenses incurred in the service of ABCAR.

Art. 11—The functions of the Governing Board are to:

a) Elect a President, a Vice President and an Executive Director;

b) Approve the plans of work, annual budgets and the annual reports prepared by the Executive Director;

c) Establish the criteria for distribution of resources to beneficiary members and fix the amounts to be designated to each, keeping in mind, among other factors, those of technical structure of the organization, and size and characteristics of the area of operation;

d) Decide on the admission of new organizations as members of ABCAR, in accordance with the criterion to be established by it;

e) Decide on the agreements to be celebrated by ABCAR to carry out its objectives;

f) Accompany the development of regional and state programs in an effort to remove any deficiencies;

g) Decide number and type of employees as well as personnel policies and practices to be followed by ABCAR;

h) Establish the salary of the Executive Director, or gratification in case he is a government employee placed at the disposition of ABCAR;

i) Approve the operating budget of administrative and technical services of ABCAR, adhering to the minimum indispensable for its proper maintenance;

j) Present to the members of ABCAR an annual report of the activities of each period, with an accounting of how resources were applied;

k) Solicit collaboration of organizations, and specialists of recognized competence to advise in its work;

l) Adopt such other measures, or solutions necessary or convenient to carrying out the objectives of ABCAR.

Art. 12—The functions of the President of ABCAR are to:

a) Call and preside over the meetings of the Governing Board as mentioned in Art. 8;

b) Sign agreements of interest to ABCAR which are approved by the Governing Board;

c) Represent ABCAR legally in or out of court;

d) Establish the Executive Director in his position;

e) Represent or name a representative of ABCAR on the governing boards of the regional or state organization of Rural Extension and of Rural Supervised Credit which are associated with it.

Chapter III

Executive Director

Art. 13—The Executive Direction will be exercised by an Executive Director, selected by vote of the absolute majority of the members of ABCAR among technicians of recognized competence in Extension and Supervised Credit, preferably an agronomist or rural economist, for a period of four years.

Footnote—The Executive Director will be substituted for in his absence by a person chosen by the Governing Board from among its components that satisfies the same technical requirements specified for the Executive Director.

Art. 14—The responsibilities of the Executive Director are:

a) Prepare and submit to the Governing Board the annual plans of work and budgets of ABCAR, and execute them after having been approved;

b) Submit to the Governing Board any modification of the budgets or plans of work deemed convenient;

c) Prepare and submit to the Governing Board the annual reports accompanied by respective documentation;

d) Execute the resolutions of the Governing Board;

e) Disburse funds as mentioned in Art. 18;

f) Name, transfer, dismiss and apply disciplinary measures to personnel, in accordance with the policies approved by the Governing Board;

g) Delegate to the personnel subject to his direction responsibilities and powers necessary for the proper functioning of ABCAR.

TITLE IV

Resources

Art. 15—The resources of ABCAR will be derived from the following sources:

a) Contributions from the founding organizations fixed for one year or greater period;

b) Contributions from contracts and agreements entered into with international, inter-regional, inter-governmental and national organizations, either public or private;

c) Donations voted by the National Congress;

d) Assets and rights that may be transferred to it by donation or legacy that are acceptable to the Governing Board.

Footnote—Apart from contributions in cash, either in national or foreign currency, the organizations mentioned above may contribute materials and technical services to ABCAR.

Art. 16—The founding members of ABCAR will declare, at the time of signing this Statute, the financial or technical resources that they will contribute for the first fiscal year.

Footnote—Annually thereafter, during the month of October, the members of ABCAR will inform it of the resources that they wish to place at its disposal during the following fiscal year.

Art. 17—The financial resources of ABCAR will be deposited in the Banco do Brasil, S.A. in a common fund.

Art. 18—The common fund of ABCAR will be deposited in two bank accounts to be opened in the Banco do Brasil, S.A. and called *Principal* Account and *Subsidiary* Account.

Footnote 1—Funds in the Principal Account will be activated by checks signed by the President and Executive Director, or in his absence by his legal substitute. All contributions in cash received by ABCAR will be deposited in it and from it all transfers of cash to beneficiary members and the Subsidiary Account will be made.

Footnote 2—Funds in the Subsidiary Account will be activated by checks signed jointly by the Executive Director, and in his absence by the statutory substitute, and an official designated by the Governing Board, and will be earmarked to cover the administrative expenses of ABCAR.

TITLE V

General Dispositions

Art. 19—In order to achieve greater development of the respective programs and realization of their objectives, the members of ABCAR may celebrate contracts and agreements that provide them additional financial or technical resources.

Art. 20—The present Statutes can only be revised by two-thirds vote of the members of the Governing Board, at a special meeting called for that purpose.

Art. 21—In case a member wishes to disassociate himself from ABCAR, it must notify the Governing Board in writing, at least three months in advance of the date of withdrawal. In such case, the financial (cash) contribution for the remainder of the fiscal year cannot be withdrawn.

Art. 22—The dissolution of ABCAR can only take place by a vote of two-thirds of the members of the Governing Board at a special meeting called together for that purpose.

Art. 23—In the event of dissolution, the existing assets, once all financial responsibilities have been attended to, will be equitably distributed among the various programs in progress at the time by organizations associated with ABCAR.

Art. 24—To the Banco do Brasil, S.A. is reserved the right to participate, at any time, in ABCAR as a Cooperating Member under equal conditions with those of the Founding Members signing this Statute

Rio de Janeiro, June 21, 1956

s/ João Napoleão de Andrade
Associação de Crédito e Assistência Rural (ACAR)

s/ Kurt Weissheimer
Associação Sulina de Crédito e Assistência Rural (ASCAR)

s/ José Irineu Cabral
Associação Nordestina de Crédito e Assistência Rural (ANCAR)

s/ Ben Hur Raposa
Confederação Rural Brasileira (CRB)

s/ Walter L. Crawford
American International Association for Economic and Social Development (AIA)

s/ Ralph E. Hansen
Escritorio Técnico de Agricultura (ETA)
Diretor Americano Interino

s/ R. de Oliveira Motta Filho
Escritorio Técnico de Agricultura (ETA)
Diretor Brasileiro

CBR

AGREEMENT BETWEEN THE AMERICAN INTERNATIONAL ASSOCIATION FOR ECONOMIC AND SOCIAL DEVELOPMENT AND THE INSTITUTO TECNICO DE INMIGRACIÓN Y COLONIZACIÓN

WE, the undersigned, Julio Grooscors, Venezuelan Citizen of legal age, resident of Caracas, acting in the Capacity of Director of the Instituto Técnico de Inmigración y Colonización, hereinafter called "ITIC", sufficiently authorized by the National Executive, as per official letter No. 2424 of the Ministerio de Agricultura y Cría, dated June 29, 1948, as party of the first part; and as party of the second part, Mr. John R. Camp, North American Citizen, of legal age, residing in Caracas, acting in his capacity as Venezuelan Director of the American International Association (Asociación Internacional Americana) for Economic and Social Development, hereinafter called "AIA", a non-profit organization constituted under the laws of the State of New York, United States of America, domiciled in Caracas and inscribed in the Subaltern Office of the

First Registry Circuit of the Department of Libertador, under No. 14, folio 23, of Protocol 1, Volume IV, 2nd quarter of the year 1948, whose power of attorney is recorded by document registered in the same Office under date of May, 1947, No. 67, folio 116 of Protocol 3:

DECLARE: that by previous agreement we have met on this date and have agreed to constitute and do so constitute in this act, a Venezuelan civil association according to the following articles:

FIRST: The Association will be called CONSEJO DE BIENESTAR RURAL (CBR) (Council for Rural Welfare); its domicile and principal place of business will be Caracas, but it may establish such agencies and offices in any other part of the Republic or abroad, as may be necessary or convenient to the execution of its projects.

SECOND: For the purpose of promoting the ideals and efforts of the National Government directed toward fulfilling the economic and social aspirations of the Venezuelan people, and for which ITIC and AIA have various plans in common, the Association constituted today will have the following fundamental objectives:

A. Development of agriculture, of rural industry, and the distribution of their products, with the object of increasing production and improving living conditions. This objective will be accomplished by means of technical as well as economic assistance.

B. Collaboration with authorized organisms of the National Government to attain:

1. Improvement in the physical environment, including those related to health, sanitation and housing.
2. Training and education of the rural population, with special emphasis being given to agricultural instruction, home industries, improved nutrition, literacy and home management.
3. Promotion of community social services, such as maternal and infant care, medical services, child welfare, and recreation.

C. The creation and development of a system of supervised credit, adequate to meet the needs of each community or zone in which CBR operates and along the following general lines:

1. The CBR, after each individual loan application or collective project for agricultural development or rural welfare has been considered and studied, will take steps to obtain from the Banco Agrícola y Pecuario, the Corporación Venezolana de Fomento, or other credit agency, the loans needed for its complete execution. In each case CBR will present the relevant report, and will make whatever recommendations may be in order, all according to previous agreements with the said institutes or with whomever a definite agreement for loan funds is made, according to whatever is decided upon by ITIC and its higher administrator, the Ministerio de Agricultura y Cría.

It is understood that the said credits will be supplied and administered directly by the granting entities, but under the technical guidance and supervision of CBR, without the latter assuming any responsibility whatsoever as regards compliance with or fulfillment or obligations on the part of the beneficiaries.

2. The CBR will give advice and technical assistance to the farmers and livestock producers through inspection, orientation and supervision for their agricultural and livestock raising activities, including advice on rotations, intensifications, insect and disease control, and any other technical assistance that may be practicable and feasible considering the characteristics of the zone, available work materials and human element involved.

THIRD: The Association will have a duration of three years from the date of its registration, which time may be extended by mutual agreement between both parties.

FOURTH:

A. The capital of CBR will be determined periodically by mutual agreement of the parties, and it may be increased in the same manner. The initial capital of the Association will be three million, three hundred thirty thousand bolívares (Bs3,330,000), equivalent to one million dollars (US$1,000,000) which both parties will contribute in equal shares in accordance with the following formula:

	Contribution from ITIC	Contribution from AIA	Total
Fiscal year 1948/1949	Bs 369,996.30	Bs 740,005.92	Bs 1,110,002.22
Fiscal year 1949/1950	" 554,997.78	" 554,997.78	" 1,109,995.56
Fiscal year 1950/1951	" 740,005.92	" 369,996.30	" 1,110,002.22
	Bs 1,665,000.00	Bs 1,665,000.00	Bs 3,330,000.00

The initial capital of Bs 3,330,000 is expected to cover:

1. The total cost of running a central office in Caracas, during the indicated period of three years, if the operations do not exceed ten areas or communities; and

2. The field operations during the same period in three communities. The services and functions of CBR may be extended to new areas or communities at any time, in which case the financing of the field operations between ITIC and AIA will be computed in the proportion indicated in the following formula:

Area No.	AIA	ITIC	Area No.	AIA	ITIC	Area No.	AIA	ITIC
4	1 :	3	8	1 :	7	12	1 :	11
5	1 :	4	9	1 :	8	13	1 :	12
6	1 :	5	10	1 :	9	14	1 :	13
7	1 :	6	11	1 :	10	15	1 :	14

3. The first contributions of capital for fiscal year 1948/49 will be made in the following manner: ITIC will contribute BS 369,996.30 during the month of August of the present year and AIA will contribute its respective amount, excepting the cost of technical personnel and services referred to in paragraph 4) of this Article during the course of the thirty days following the signing of this contract. The contributions for the following fiscal years will be deposited by both parties in annual payments, in the same manner as that adopted for the first year.

4. The salaries and expenses of the technical and administrative personnel that AIA places at the service of CBR will be included in the AIA contributions specified in this Article. The list and details of cost of this personnel, as well as the technical personnel supplied by ITIC, will be previously approved by the Administrative Board in accordance with the Sixth Article.

FIFTH: The Association will be directed by an Administrative Board composed of five members, two of whom will be designated by ITIC and two by AIA; the fifth member will be the person proposed by AIA, who merits the approval of the ITIC, and who will, in addition to becoming a member of the Board, have the character of Director of CBR. The President will be elected from among the members of the Board. The Board will hold regular quarterly meetings, but special meetings may be called by the President of the Board or the Director of CBR whenever it is considered necessary or desirable for the well being of the Association. There may also be special meetings held when ITIC and AIA jointly call them. The members of the Board will be obligated to attend the regular or special meetings and their temporary or complete absence will be substituted by persons representing the parties in the same manner as the principal members.

The decisions of the Board will be made by majority vote and a quorum will consist of three members.

SIXTH: The duties of the Administrative Board will be: 1) to consider the general plan of work of CBR and submit it for approval to the Minister of Agriculture. 2) Consider the report on the activities of the Association and plans that have been made that the Director must present quarterly to the Minister of Agriculture, notwithstanding the fact that the Minister may request whatever information he may consider necessary at any moment. 3) Approve or disapprove the overall budget for each fiscal year in accordance with the general plan of work. 4) Approve or disapprove budgetary changes. 5) Present to the Minister of Agriculture an annual report containing in detail the activities of each fiscal year. 6) Adopt any further measures and resolutions that may be necessary or desirable to attain the objectives of the Association.

SEVENTH: The duties of the Director of CBR are:

1. To execute and put into practice the plans of CBR.
2. Present the Board with a list of the technical personnel, and upon its approval effect appointments of technicians.

3. Appoint and discharge freely administrative and subordinate personnel under his direction.
4. Fix salaries, expenses and working conditions of employees.
5. Control the funds within the auxiliary bank account in the manner determined in Article 9.
6. Submit to the Board of Directors all budgetary modifications that he may consider necessary to make.
7. Draw up and present to the Administrative Board the general plan of work of CBR and also the projects of work that he may judge appropriate.
8. Submit to the Board the necessary information for the quarterly and annual reports referred to in the sixth Article.
9. Represent the Association in all public or private acts in which it might be interested and appoint attorneys to defend the rights of the Association judicially or extra judicially, with the previous authorization of the Administrative Board.
10. Delegate to subordinate personnel such responsibilities and powers as may be necessary for the proper functioning of CBR.
11. Execute all of the decisions of the Administrative Board and direct all of the activities of the Association.

EIGHTH: In no case may the obligations or commitments contracted by the Association exceed the amount of its capital.

NINTH: The Management of the organization's funds will be by means of two bank accounts, called the principal account and the auxiliary account. The principal account will be drawn on by checks signed by two of the directors, one selected from those appointed by ITIC and the other from those appointed by AIA. The subscription of capital will be deposited in this account, and checks will be drawn on it in favor of the auxiliary account to cover expenses provided for in the budget in the manner to be decided upon by the Administrative Board. The auxiliary account will be drawn upon by checks signed by the Director and the Cashier or Accountant of the Association, and all expenses will be paid from it, with the exception of those that, because of their size or importance, it is decided by the Board should be taken directly from the principal account.

TENTH: The Association does not seek to make a profit and its objectives are clearly defined. Therefore, any gain that might be obtained by CBR in its operations, will be totally invested in the amplification or execution of the general plan of work of the Association. At the termination of the contract, all of the assets, of every kind, that belong to the Association, will remain the property of the ITIC or whatever other agency or institution the Minister of Agriculture and Animal Husbandry might designate.

ELEVENTH: The following have been appointed members of the Administrative Board by ITIC: Messrs. Dr. Daniel Uzcátegui Ramírez and Ildegar Pérez

Segnini; and by AIA members: Messrs. John R. Camp and Bernardo Jofre. The AIA has proposed Mr. Dale B. Jacques as the fifth member and Director, and ITIC has approved the designation. All of the above are of legal age, domiciled in Caracas, and have agreed to accept their respective duties.

TWELFTH: Doubts and controversies of any nature whatsoever that might arise with reference to this contract, and which cannot be resolved in a friendly manner by the contracting parties, will be decided on by the competent Courts of Venezuela, in conformity with its laws, and which for no reason or cause may give rise to foreign claims.

This contract has been approved by the Comptroller General of the Nation as vouched for by official letter No. 11332 dated June 26, 1948.

Caracas: July 2, 1948

> s/ Julio Grooscors
> Director, Instituto Técnico de
> Inmigración y Colonización
>
> s/ John R. Camp
> Director en Venezuela,
> American International Association
> for Economic and Social Development

IICA

AGREEMENT OF COOPERATION BETWEEN THE INTER-AMERICAN INSTITUTE OF AGRICULTURAL SCIENCES (IICA) AND THE AMERICAN INTERNATIONAL ASSOCIATION FOR ECONOMIC AND SOCIAL DEVELOPMENT (AIA)

The Inter-American Institute of Agricultural Sciences, San José, Costa Rica, a specialized agency of the Organization of American States, hereinafter called the "INSTITUTE," represented by the Director General, Armando Samper, as party of the first part; and as party of the second part the American International Association for Economic and Social Development, a philanthropic organization constituted under the laws of the State of New York, U.S.A., hereinafter called the "ASSOCIATION," represented by its executive vice president John R. Camp, subscribe to the following agreement:

FIRST: The parties recognize that the objectives of the programs known as the Inter-American Popular Information Program, Inter-American Rural Youth Program, and Inter-American Rural Development Program, hereinafter called "Programs," which have been carried out under joint sponsorship, are of great value to the member States of the Organization of American States, because they have contributed in an effective way to the improvement of com-

213

munications in the fields of agriculture and health, to the organization and development of the rural youth movement and to the basic studies, planning and agrarian reform that are necessary to give impetus to rural development.

SECOND: The parties consider that this association has also been beneficial to both institutions and consequently they agree to extend it from January 1, 1966 to December 31, 1970, under the conditions which are explained in the following articles.

THIRD: The "Institute" and the "Association" will maintain full responsibility and independence in the conduct, financing and administration of the programs pertaining to each institution. The "Association" within its own budget will contribute to the "Programs" the salaries of the directors and technical and administrative personnel, as well as necessary travel expenses and allowances; it will furnish funds for training, for secretarial and office expenses and for the necessary supplies, materials and equipment. The total of these contributions for the "Programs," calculated on the basis of an annual average for the period 1966-1970, is estimated as follows: $140,000 for mass communications; $140,000 for development of the rural youth movement; and $79,000 for rural development.

FOURTH: On its part the "Institute" will earmark within its own program-budget and in accordance with its own administrative policies, for activities related to the "Programs" developed by the "Association," on the basis of annual average for the period 1966-1970, sums that are estimated to be $234,000 in the field of communications; $235,000 in the fields of extension and agricultural education, including activities relating to rural youth; and $800,000 in the field of agrarian reform and rural development. Such estimated amounts are subject to continuation of the programs anticipated and approval by the Board of Directors of IICA. In addition, the "Institute" will assist the "Association" in the conduct of its mass communication, rural youth and rural development "Programs," by putting at the disposal of the "Association" its bases of operation and technical contacts and official relationships, developed in the member States during long years of experience as an inter-American organization dependent on the Organization of the American States; also the aid of its personnel for the carrying out, jointly, of specific activities.

FIFTH: When deemed of mutual advantage, the parties will develop jointly specific activities in any of the fields encompassed by the "Programs." This joint action in specific activities will be agreed to in each case by an exchange of letters between the Director General or Assistant Director, representing the "Institute," and the Executive Vice President or his designee, representing the "Association." In these letters there will be indicated the period of duration of the joint activity, the cost, quantity and quality of the resources that each of the parties will contribute, including the responsibilities of the personnel; also mentioned will be the form of publication of the works that might originate from the joint project, taking into account what is established in number 7 of Policy and Procedures of the "Institute" regarding "Publications and documents."

214

SIXTH: The Executive Vice President of the "Association," and the Regional Representatives and Directors of the three "Programs" will receive an appointment letter as personnel associated with the "Institute." When the "Institute" issues these letters of appointment, they will receive the benefits enjoyed by members of the Regular Professional Personnel of the "Institute" in accordance with the privileges and immunities granted to the "Institute" by member States and will be able to use the "Official Travel Document of the OAS," in accordance with the regulations of the "Institute." These privileges shall not be extended to their successors nor to other staff members of the "Association," except in the specific cases indicated in paragraph five. It is understood that the benefits which the countries grant and the use of the "Official Travel Document of the OAS" may be withdrawn at any time if the Governments or the General Secretariat of the OAS so decide and in this regard the "Institute" assumes no responsibility whatsoever. The technicians participating in joint activities specifically agreed to receive appointments as Professors or Resident Scientists during the period in which they directly participate in said joint activities. Consequently, they will enjoy the benefits mentioned only during the periods in which they were attending to said joint activities.

SEVENTH: The characteristics and objectives of the "Programs" are specifically indicated in the annex to this agreement, as an integral part of the same and entitled "Characteristics and Objectives" of the Inter-American Popular Information Program, Inter-American Rural Youth Program and Inter-American Rural Development Program.

EIGHTH: Any revision or amendment made to this agreement will be effectuated through an exchange of letters between the parties.

NINTH: This agreement will terminate on December 31, 1970 without need to state it expressly nor to fulfill any requirement for such purpose. In case of extension, this will have to be executed at least three months before the expiration date.[1]

In witness whereof the undersigned, duly authorized for the purpose, sign this agreement in quadruplicate in the city of San José, Costa Rica, on the 10th day of the month of December 1965.

For the: INTER-AMERICAN INSTITUTE
OF AGRICULTURAL SCIENCES

s/ Armando Samper G.
Director General

For the: AMERICAN INTERNATIONAL
ASSOCIATION FOR ECONOMIC
AND SOCIAL DEVELOPMENT

John R. Camp
Executive Vice President

---

[1] This agreement was terminated effective December 31, 1968 by an exchange of letters between the parties.

Characteristics and Objectives

Inter-American Popular Information Program

In the field of mass communications the Inter-American Popular Information Program is concerned with ways and means of putting basic knowledge in usable form into the hands of Latin Americans. Such knowledge covering all developmental areas, but mainly in the form of practical information on better farming methods, and health and sanitation practices, is already available but lack of an ability to communicate this knowledge is a fundamental barrier to economic and social progress.

In the 1966-70 period the Inter-American Popular Information Program will endeavor to assist member nations of the Organization of American States:

a) In establishing training programs in fundamental and immediately applicable communications techniques.

b) By providing follow-up advisory and consultation service in communications methods.

c) By offering intermediate level training for persons now active in communications work, who for various reasons cannot aspire to formal graduate training.

d) By assisting selected Latin American universities to establish graduate training programs in communications.

e) By completing the present communications research program and adapting its results for field use; at the same time planning, introducing and integrating long-term communications research into selected Latin American government agencies, universities and other educational institutions.

Inter-American Rural Youth Program

The basic concept of the Inter-American Rural Youth Program is that the rural youth of Latin America represent the most neglected segment of the population, and at the same time offer the largest potential for assisting Latin American development. Agricultural production is lagging behind population growth in Latin America, and it is believed that an expanding rural youth club program can help significantly to increase agricultural production by introducing improved farm and home practices. The Inter-American Rural Youth Program during the period 1966-70 will endeavor to assist member nations of the Organization of American States in the following ways:

a) Encourage the organization of national rural youth program committees, foundations or associations to promote and stimulate the expansion of rural youth club work.

b) Organize award, recognition and exchange projects in cooperation with national rural youth club programs and national committees to stimulate greater public interest and support in rural youth club work.

c) Cooperate in organizing special training courses to prepare professional and voluntary club leaders in rural youth work.

d) Encourage increased publicity for activities and accomplishments in rural youth club work.

Inter-American Rural Development Program

The Inter-American Rural Development Program is mainly concerned with the most serious challenge to Latin American countries today, agrarian reform. Agrarian reform is not merely a problem of opening up new lands for settlement and increasing productivity on the 25% of the land area now devoted to agriculture. It is also concerned with the welfare of the peasant farmers, farm workers and their families which make up 56% of the total population. The crux of the problem is the present imbalance in land ownership where 48% of peasant farm plots are less than 5 hectares in size and make up only 1% of the total farm land, while a little over 1% of the farm owners control 64% of the total farm land.

Agrarian reform is concerned with the basic problem of establishing an equitable system of rural property ownership, so that with adequate credit, technical assistance, and marketing services, such land will become the economic base of the man who works it and will assure him of a decent living.

During the 1966-70 period when many Latin American countries will be applying recently enacted agrarian reform legislation, the Inter-American Rural Development Program will endeavor to assist the member nations of the Organization of American States with the following:

a) technical assistance and training in organizing and conducting basic resource surveys;

b) research and training in selected agricultural economic fields;

c) planning, training and otherwise helping to establish sound agricultural credit, extension and marketing practices;

d) planning and training personnel in the organization of specific land development or colonization projects and assisting in obtaining international financing for such projects.

PLAN VICTORIA

AGREEMENT ON A SPECIAL PROGRAM FOR RURAL PRIMARY EDUCATION IN CHILE SUBSCRIBED TO ON DECEMBER 21, 1961 BY THE AMERICAN INTERNATIONAL ASSOCIATION FOR ECONOMIC AND SOCIAL DEVELOPMENT, THE MINISTRY OF PUBLIC EDUCATION AND THE CHILEAN DEVELOPMENT CORPORATION

On the basis of the exchange of letters between Mr. Laurance S. Rockefeller, president of the Rockefeller Brothers Fund, and His Excellency don Jorge Alessandri, President of the Republic of Chile, dated June 8, 1961 and

July 17, 1961, respectively, the American International Association for Economic and Social Development, a private non-profit organization with headquarters in the City of New York, United States of America, hereinafter called "AIA," represented by Mr. John R. Camp, its Executive Vice President, as party of the first part, and as party of the second part the Ministry of Public Education, hereinafter called "Ministry," represented by the Minister of Education, don Patricio Barros Alemparte, and as party of the third part the Corporación de Fomento de la Producción, hereinafter called "CORFO," represented by its Executive Vice President, don Arturo Mackenna, all duly authorized, have agreed to enter into the following agreement:

Clause I

The contracting parties will carry out a special program of rural school construction and of technical development of rural education during a period of two (2) years, beginning the 1st of January, 1962, and terminating on December 31, 1963. The program will be carried out in the area devastated by earthquakes in 1960, and it is agreed by the parties hereto that such a program could contribute effectively not only to the reconstruction of the stricken area, but also to the economic development of the country. It will be understood that the area referred to is that designated by Law 14.171.

Clause II

To administer this special program, the contracting parties hereby establish a Special Commission for Rural Education to be made up of a representative of each. The members of the Special Commission will serve on a part-time basis and their function will be to prepare, in collaboration with the technical personnel of the Ministry, of CORFO and other appropriate governmental organizations, as for example the Ministry of Agriculture, an Annual Plan of Work for each year of the life of the agreement, which, when approved by AIA, the Ministry and CORFO, will constitute the basis for the program for that year. In addition, the Special Commission will have the function of establishing and maintaining contact with the program carried out in the field for the purposes of technical supervision and evaluation. (The representative of AIA on the Special Commission will also be AIA's Special Representative in Chile for all matters related to this Agreement.)

The Special Commission will function as an ad hoc division of CORFO.

Clause III

The program that the Special Commission for Rural Education will carry out will have two components, as follows:

1. The component of rural school construction, including the construction of some rural school buildings that can serve as models as to the building techniques and materials used and as to the way in which they reflect the needs of a functional rural education program. This phase of the program will also include some experiments to determine the type and amount of contribution that may be obtained from Chilean rural communities for the construction of schools.

2. The component of technical development of rural education through an experimental program that the Ministry, in collaboration with the Commission, will organize to develop functional plans and study programs for rural schools that will reflect the real needs of the rural population of Chile. This program will also include the training of teaching and supervisory personnel needed to initiate application of the new program in rural schools, beginning in a selected area of the disaster zone. In addition, the program will include the preparation and reproduction of teaching materials for rural schools as required by the new program.

Clause IV

To implement this agreement the contracting parties will contribute material and administrative resources, as follows:

1. AIA, on the basis of a financial contribution of the Rockefeller Brothers Fund, will place at the disposal of the Special Commission for Rural Education the following sums for the two components of the program indicated in Clause III of this agreement:

a. For model rural school construction	$315,000
b. For technical development of rural education	$135,000
TOTAL	$450,000

In addition AIA will contribute the services of its representative on the Special Commission on a part-time basis and other technical and administrative services required by the program in Chile to fulfill the legal requirements of evaluation and accounting of the Rockefeller Brothers Fund.

2. CORFO, for its part, will contribute the service of its representative on the Special Commission on a part-time basis and the administrative and accounting services required for the controlled disbursement of the funds made available to the Commission. In addition, CORFO will provide office space and secretarial services for the Commission.

3. The Ministry will contribute the buildings of an experimental rural normal school and the salaries of the permanent teaching personnel needed to carry out the experimental program in rural education and also the salaries of the permanent teaching personnel of the rural schools where the experimental program will be applied. This program, upon termination of the agreement and provided it is feasible, will remain as a permanent entity within the administrative and budgetary structure of the Ministry.

The Ministry will assume responsibility for obtaining the land where the school buildings provided for in this program will be constructed. These will remain as the property of said Ministry.

Clause V

The disbursement of funds made available to the Commission by AIA will be made in accordance with the stipulations of the Annual Plans of Work. These Plans will include a budget indicating expenditures for each of the two phases of the program and will also indicate if the expenditures are to be made

219

in Chile or in the United States for materials and equipment. Expenditures made in the United States will be credited against AIA's contribution at the then prevailing rate of exchange.

The funds required for expenditures in Chile will be deposited in a special bank account established for this purpose by CORFO, and will be disbursed in accordance with administrative rules and procedures established by the Commission.

Clause VI

The materials and equipment and the buildings acquired with funds provided by AIA will remain the property of the Ministry of Education and after termination of this agreement will continue to be used exclusively for the purposes of rural education.

Clause VII

The contracting parties designate the city of Santiago, Chile, as headquarters for all matters related to this agreement and those that may derive from same.

Signed in the city of Santiago, on the 21st day of December, 1961.

s/ JOHN R. CAMP
American International Association
for Economic and Social Development

s/ PATRICIO BARROS ALEMPARTE
Ministry of Public Education

s/ ARTURO MACKENNA
Corporación de Fomento
de la Producción

APPENDIX II

List of Cooperating Organizations

Following are the principal organizations with which AIA and the programs it has sponsored have cooperated. Initials are used as follows: Information Program, PIIP, Rural Youth Program, PIJR, Rural Development Program, PIDR, Vocational Education Program—Venezuela, VE, and Rural Education Program—Chile, RE. Years shown indicate the period of cooperation.

ARGENTINA

Asociación de la Prensa. Buenos Aires,
PIIP, 1966-67.
Asociación Nacional Pro-Clubes 4-S.
Buenos Aires,
PIJR, 1964-67.
Comité Intergubernamental para las Migraciones Europeas. Buenos Aires,
PIIP, 1966-67
Instituto Nacional de Tecnología Agropecuaria. Buenos Aires,
PIJR, 1962-67.
PIIP, 1961-67.
Universidad de Buenos Aires. Buenos Aires,
PIIP, 1964-67.
Universidad de Tucumán. San Miguel de Tucumán,
PIIP, 1961.

BARBADOS

Ministry of Agriculture and Fisheries. Bridgetown,
PIJR, 1963-67.

BOLIVIA

Ministerio de Agricultura, Ganadería y Colonización. La Paz,
PIIP, 1961-67
PIJR, 1962-67

BRAZIL

Fundação Antunes. (in formation) Rio de Janeiro,
PIDR, 1963-67.
Associação da Imprensa Rural do Rio Grande do Sul. Pôrto Alegre,
PIIP, 1967.
Associação Brasileira de Crédito e Assistência Rural. Rio de Janeiro,
AIA, 1956-61.
PIIP, 1961-66.
PIJR, 1962-67.
Associação Nordestina de Crédito e Assistência Rural. Recife,
AIA, 1953-56.
Banco Lar Brasileiro. Rio de Janeiro,
PIJR, 1966.
Comitê Nacional de Clubes 4-S. Rio de Janeiro,
PIJR, 1964-67.
Companhia Industrial e Comercial Brasileira de Produtos Alimentícios (Nestlé). São Paulo,
AIA, 1950-54.
Conselho Nacional de Pesquisas. Rio de Janeiro,
PIDR, 1966.
Departamento de Correios e Telégrafos. Rio de Janeiro,
PIJR, 1966.

221

Estado da Guanabara. Rio de Janeiro,
PIJR, 1966.
—————. Secretaria de Turismo.
Rio de Janeiro,
PIJR, 1966.
Estado de Minas Gerais. Belo Horizonte,
PIJR, 1966.
—————. Associação de Crédito e
Assistência Rural. Belo Horizonte,
AIA, 1949-61.
PIIP, 1961-66.
PIJR, 1966.
—————. Secretaria da Agricultura.
Belo Horizonte,
AIA, 1952-55.
PIDR, 1962.
—————. Secretaria da Saúde. Belo
Horizonte,
AIA, 1951-61.
—————. Universidade Rural de
Minas Gerais. Viçosa,
AIA, 1952-61.
Estado de Pará. Secretaria de Turismo.
Belem,
PIJR, 1966.
Estado do Rio Grande do Sul. Associação Sulina de Crédito e Assistência Rural. Pôrto Alegre,
AIA, 1950, 1960-63.
PIIP, 1965-67.
Estado de São Paulo. Secretaria da
Agricultura. São Paulo,
AIA, 1948-54.
PIDR, 1966-67.
—————. Secretaria da Saúde. São
Paulo,
AIA, 1948-54.
Instituto Brasileiro do Café. Rio de
Janeiro, São Paulo, Brasília,
PIJR, 1966.
Instituto Interamericano de Ciências
Agrícolas da OEA. Rio de Janeiro,
PIJR, 1960-68.
PIDR, 1962-68.

Instituto Nacional do Desenvolvimento
Agrário. Rio de Janeiro,
PIJR, 1966.
Instituto Nacional do Mate. Rio de Janeiro,
PIJR, 1966.
Ministério da Agricultura. Rio de Janeiro,
PIDR, 1962-63.
PIJR, 1966.
—————. Serviço de Informação
Agrícola. Rio de Janeiro,
PIJR, 1966.
Ministério da Educação e Cultura. Rio
de Janeiro,
PIJR, 1966.
Ministério de Relações Exteriores. Rio
de Janeiro.
PIJR, 1966.
Organização Internacional de Congressos. Rio de Janeiro,
PIJR, 1966.
Pantour Pampulha Turismo S.A. Rio
de Janeiro,
PIJR, 1966.
Prefeitura de Belo Horizonte. Belo
Horizonte, Minas Gerais,
PIJR, 1966.
Prefeitura de Juiz de Fora. Juiz de
Fora, Minas Gerais,
PIJR, 1966.
Remington, S.A. São Paulo,
PIJR, 1966.
United States. Agency for International
Development. Rio de Janeiro,
PIIP, 1958-59.
PIDR, 1962-63.
PIJR, 1966.
Varig—Viação Aérea Riograndense.
Rio de Janeiro,
PIJR, 1966.

BRITISH HONDURAS
Ministry of Agriculture.
Belize,
PIIP, 1959.

CHILE

Corporación de Fomento de la Producción. Santiago,
RE, 1961-66.
Corporación de Reforma Agraria. Santiago,
PIIP, 1966-67.
Instituto de Educación Rural. Santiago,
PIIP, 1961-67.
Junta Nacional Pro-Desarrollo de la Juventud Agrícola de Chile. Santiago.
PIJR, 1960-67.
Ministerio de Agricultura. Santiago.
PIIP, 1961-67.
PIJR, 1962-67.
Ministerio de Educación Pública. Santiago,
RE, 1961-66.
United States. Agency for International Development. Santiago,
PIIP, 1961-65.
RE, 1964-66.
Universidad Católica de Chile. Santiago,
PIIP, 1961-67.
Universidad de Chile. Santiago,
PIIP, 1962-67.

COLOMBIA

Asociación de Cafeteros. Bogotá,
PIIP, 1966.
Asociación Nacional Pro-Clubes 4-S. Bogotá,
PIJR, 1964-67.
Centro Interamericano de Desarrollo Rural y Reforma Agraria. Bogotá,
PIDR, 1965-68.
Corporación Autónoma Regional de Valle del Cauca. Cali,
PIJR, 1962-67.
Federación Nacional de Cafeteros. Bogotá,
PIJR, 1962-67.

Instituto Colombiano de Reforma Agraria. Bogotá,
PIIP, 1966.
Instituto de Fomento Algodonero. Bogotá,
PIJR, 1962-67.
Instituto de Fomento Tabacalero. Bogotá,
PIJR, 1962-67.
Instituto Geográfico Agustín Codazzi. Bogotá,
PIDR, 1962.
Instituto Interamericano de Ciencias Agrícolas de la OEA. Bogotá,
PIJR, 1967.
Ministerio de Agricultura. Bogotá.
PIJR, 1962-67.
PIIP, 1966.
United States. Agency for International Development. Bogotá,
PIJR, 1967.
Universidad Nacional de Colombia. Bogotá,
PIIP, 1962-67.

COSTA RICA

Asociación Demográfica Costarricense. San José,
PIIP, 1966-68.
Centro de Orientación Familiar, Archidiócesis, Centroamericana. San José,
PIIP, 1967-68.
Fundación Nacional de Clubes 4-S. San José,
PIJR, 1964-67.
Instituto de Tierras y Colonización. San José,
PIDR, 1963-67.
Instituto Interamericano de Ciencias Agrícolas de la OEA. San José,
PIIP, 1958-68.
PIJR, 1960-68.
PIDR, 1962-68.
Ministerio de Agricultura y Ganadería. San José,
PIJR, 1962-67.

Ministerio de Salubridad Pública. San José,
PIIP, 1966-68.
Universidad de Costa Rica. San José,
PIIP, 1962-68.
United States. Agency for International Development. San José,
PIIP, 1966-68.

DOMINICAN REPUBLIC

Comité Pro-Desarrollo de la Juventud 5-D. Santo Domingo,
PIJR, 1963-67.
Ministerio de Agricultura. Santo Domingo,
PIJR, 1963-67.

ECUADOR

Centro Internacional de Estudios Superiores de Periodismo para América Latina. Quito,
PIIP, 1961-67.
Fundación Nacional de Clubes 4-F. Quito,
PIJR, 1967.
Ministerio de Agricultura y Ganadería. Quito,
PIJR, 1962-67.

EL SALVADOR

Asociación Demográfica Salvadoreña. San Salvador,
PIIP, 1968.
Comité Nacional de Clubes 4-C. San Salvador,
PIJR, 1960-67.
Dirección General de Salud Pública. San Salvador,
PIIP, 1968.
Ministerio de Agricultura y Ganadería. Santa Tecla,
PIJR, 1962-67.
United States. Agency for International Development. San Salvador,
PIIP, 1960-68.

GUATEMALA

Asociación Pro-Bienestar de la Familia de Guatemala. Guatemala,
PIIP, 1968.
Consejo Nacional de los Clubes Agrícolas 4-S. La Aurora,
PIJR, 1967.
Dirección General de Investigación y Extensión Agrícola. La Aurora,
PIJR, 1962-67.
Instituto Interamericano de Ciencias Agrícolas de la OEA. Zona Norte. Guatemala,
PIJR, 1960-68.
PIDR, 1962-68.
Instituto para la Transformación Agraria. Guatemala,
PIDR, 1966-67.
Ministerio de Salud Pública. Guatemala,
PIIP, 1968.
United States. Agency for International Development. Guatemala,
PIIP, 1967-68.

GUYANA

Ministry of Agriculture and Natural Resources. Georgetown,
PIJR, 1962-67.

HAITI

Secrétairerie d'Etat de l'Agriculture, des Ressources Naturelles et du Développement Rural. Port-au-Prince,
PIIP, 1960.
PIJR, 1962-67.

HONDURAS

Asociación Hondureña de Planificación de Familia. Tegucigalpa,
PIIP, 1968.
Ministerio de Salud Pública y Asistencia Social. Tegucigalpa,
PIIP, 1968.

224

Servicio Técnico Interamericano de Cooperación Agrícola. Departamento de Extensión Agrícola. Tegucigalpa,
PIJR, 1962-64.
United States. Agency for International Development. Tegucigalpa,
PIIP, 1967-68.

JAMAICA

Department of Agriculture, Extension, 4-H Clubs. Kingston,
PIJR, 1962-67.
4-H Club Council. Kingston,
PIJR, 1960-67.

MARTINIQUE

Mouvement Rural de la Jeunesse Catholique. Fort-de-France,
PIJR, 1962-67.

MEXICO

Comité de Ayuda a la Juventud Rural. México, D.F.,
PIJR, 1960-67.
Fundación Ford. México, D.F.,
PIIP, 1967-68.
Secretaría de Agricultura y Ganadería. México, D.F.,
PIIP, 1959-60.
PIJR, 1962-67.
Secretaría de Educación Pública. México, D.F.,
PIJR, 1962-67.

NICARAGUA

Comité Nacional de Clubes 4-S. Managua,
PIJR, 1967.
Instituto Agrario Nacional. Managua,
PIDR, 1966-67.

Ministerio de Agricultura y Ganadería. Managua,
PIJR, 1962-67.
Ministerio de Salud Pública. Programa Pro-Bienestar de la Familia. Managua,
PIIP, 1968.
United States. Agency for International Development. Managua,
PIIP, 1967-68

PANAMA

Asociación Panameña para la Planificación Familiar. Panamá,
PIIP, 1968.
Comisión de Reforma Agraria. Panamá,
PIDR, 1964-66.
Instituto Interamericano de Ciencias Agrícolas de la OEA. Panamá,
PIJR, 1967.
Ministerio de Agricultura, Comercio e Industria. Panamá,
PIIP, 1960-68.
PIJR, 1962-67.
Ministerio de Sanidad Pública. Panamá,
PIIP, 1968.
Ministerio de Trabajo. Panamá,
PIIP, 1968.
Patronato Nacional de Clubes 4-S de Panamá. Panamá,
PIJR, 1967.
United States. Agency for International Development. Panamá,
PIJR, 1967.
PIIP, 1967-68.
United States. Southern Command. Canal Zone,
PIJR, 1967.

PARAGUAY

Asociación Pro-Desarrollo de los Clubes Agrarios Juveniles del Paraguay. Asunción,
PIJR, 1964-67.

Instituto Interamericano de Ciencias Agrícolas de la OEA. Asunción,
PIJR, 1967.

Ministerio de Agricultura y Ganadería. Asunción,
PIIP, 1961-67.
PIJR, 1962-67.
PIDR, 1963-67.

Servicio Técnico Interamericano de Cooperación Agrícola. Asunción,
PIIP, 1961-66.
PIDR, 1963-67.

United States. Agency for International Development. Asunción,
PIDR, 1963-67.
PIJR, 1967.

PERU

Asociación Nacional de Clubes Agrícolas Juveniles Perú. Lima,
PIJR, 1960-67.

Corporación de Abastecimiento. Lima,
PIIP, 1965-68.

Instituto Interamericano de Ciencias Agrícolas de la OEA. Zona Andina. Lima,
PIIP, 1958-68.
PIJR, 1960-68.
PIDR, 1962-68.

Ministerio de Agricultura y Ganadería. Oficina Técnica de Información Agraria. Lima,
PIIP, 1961-68.

—————. Servicio de Investigación y Promoción Agraria. Lima,
PIJR, 1962-67.

Ministerio de Salud Pública. Lima,
PIIP, 1965.

Universidad Agraria del Perú. La Molina,
PIIP, 1961-68.

Universidad de San Marcos. Lima,
PIIP, 1965.

PHILIPPINES

University of the Philippines. College of Agriculture. Los Baños,
PIIP, 1965-67.

ST. KITTS

Agricultural Extension Service. Basseterre,
PIJR, 1962-67.

ST. VINCENT

Department of Agriculture, Forestry and Fisheries. Kingstown,
PIJR, 1962-67.

4-H Advisory Council. Kingstown,
PIJR, 1964-67.

SOUTH AFRICA

Ministry of Agriculture. Capetown,
PIIP, 1965.

SPAIN

Oficina Nacional de Promoción. Madrid,
PIIP, 1965-67.

SURINAM

Agricultural Extension Service. Paramaribo,
PIJR, 1962-67.

TRINIDAD AND TOBAGO

Agricultural Extension Service. Port-of-Spain,
PIJR, 1962-67.

Government of Trinidad and Tobago. Port-of-Spain,
AIA, 1963.

UNITED STATES

American Association of Agricultural College Editors. Lincoln, Nebraska,
PIIP, 1961-67.

Cornell University. Ithaca, New York,
PIIP, 1961-68.

Eastman Kodak Company. Rochester, New York,
PIIP, 1965.

Florida Power Corporation. St. Petersburg,
PIJR, 1967-68.

Florida, University of. Gainesville,
PIJR, 1967-68.

Ford Foundation. New York,
PIDR, 1966-68.

Ford Motor Company. International Group. Dearborn, Michigan,
PIJR, 1964.

Illinois, University of. Urbana,
PIIP, 1964.

Inter-American Committee for Agricultural Development. Washington, D. C.,
PIDR, 1965-68.

Inter-American Development Bank. Washington, D. C.,
PIDR, 1962-63.

International Minerals & Chemical Corporation. Skokie, Illinois,
PIJR, 1966-68.

Iowa State University. Ames, Iowa,
PIIP, 1961-68.

Johnson Foundation. Racine, Wisconsin,
PIJR, 1965, 1967.

Michigan State University. East Lansing,
PIIP, 1960-68.

Milbank Memorial Fund. New York,
PIIP, 1967.

National 4-H Club Foundation. Washington, D. C.,
PIJR, 1964-68.

National 4-H Service Committee. Chicago, Illinois,
PIJR, 1964-68.

New Holland Machine Company. New Holland, Pennsylvania,
PIJR, 1964.

North Carolina State University. Raleigh,
PIIP, 1961-66.

Organization of American States. Washington, D. C.,
PIJR, 1964-68.

Rockefeller Brothers Fund. New York,
RE, 1961-66.

Sears-Roebuck Foundation. Oak Brook, Illinois,
PIJR, 1964-68.

Sigma Delta Chi. Chicago, Illinois,
PIIP, 1961-67.

Standard Brands, Inc. International Division. New York,
PIJR, 1964.

Standard Oil Company (New Jersey). New York,
PIJR, 1964, 1966-68.

United States. Agency for International Development. Washington, D. C.,
PIDR, 1963-64.
PIJR, 1964, 1966-67.

United States. Department of Agriculture. Washington, D. C.,
PIIP, 1961-68.
PIDR, 1962-68.

——————. Agricultural Extension Service. Rio Piedras, Puerto Rico,
PIJR, 1962-67.

——————. Cooperative Extension Service of the State Land-Grant Colleges and Universities. Washington, D. C.,
PIJR, 1964, 1966.

Washington State University. Pullman,
PIIP, 1961-66.

Wisconsin, University of. Madison,
PIIP, 1962-66.

URUGUAY

American Association of Uruguay. Montevideo,
PIIP, 1961-67.

Asociación Cristiana de Dirigentes de Empresas. Montevideo,
PIIP, 1965-66.

Asociación de Ingenieros Agrónomos. Montevideo,
PIIP, 1961-67.

Instituto Interamericano de Ciencias Agrícolas de la OEA. Zona Sur. Montevideo,
PIIP, 1961-68.
PIJR, 1961-68.

Ministerio de Ganadería y Agricultura. Montevideo,
PIIP, 1961-67.

——————. Centro de Investigaciones Alberto Boerger. La Estanzuela,
PIIP, 1961-67.
PIJR, 1962-67.

Ministerio de Salud Pública. Montevideo,
PIIP, 1966-67.

Movimiento de la Juventud Agraria. Montevideo,
PIJR, 1960-67.

Organización de la Prensa del Interior. Montevideo,
PIIP, 1966-67.

United States. Agency for International Development. Montevideo,
PIIP, 1961-67.

——————. Information Service,
PIIP, 1961-67.

Universidad de Uruguay. Facultad de Agronomía. Montevideo,
PIIP, 1961-65.

VENEZUELA

Asociación Civil Pro-Clubes 5-V. Caracas,
PIJR, 1960-67.

Banco Agrícola y Pecuario. Caracas,
CBR, 1948-68.
PIDR, 1962-68.

Banco Central de Venezuela. Caracas,
PIDR, 1962-66.

Centro de Estudios del Desarrollo. Caracas,
PIDR, 1965-68.

Compañía Shell de Venezuela. Caracas,
CBR, 1951-56.

Consejo de Bienestar Rural. Caracas,
AIA, 1948-68.
PIIP, 1958-68.
PIJR, 1960-67.
PIDR, 1962-68.

Corporación de Los Andes. Mérida,
PIDR, 1964-67.

Consejo Zuliano de Planificación. Maracaibo,
PIDR, 1963-64.

Corporación Venezolana de Fomento. Comisión para el Estudio del Rio Orinoco. Caracas,
CBR, 1948-56.
PIDR, 1966.

Corporación Venezolana de Guayana. Caracas,
CBR, 1959-61.

Creole Petroleum Corporation. Caracas,
CBR, 1951-56.

Escuela de Demostradoras del Hogar. Maracay,
CBR, 1955-60.

Escuela Práctica de Agricultura. Maracay,
CBR, 1955-60.

Fondo Frutícola Nacional. Caracas,
PIDR, 1962-68.

Fundación Creole. Caracas,
PIDR, 1964-68.

Fundación de Desarrollo Centro-Occidental. Barquisimeto,
PIDR, 1963-67.

Fundación Ford. Caracas,
PIDR, 1966-68.

228

Fundación Shell. Caracas,
PIDR, 1964-66.
Gobernación del Estado Aragua. Maracay,
CBR, 1949-52.
Gobernación del Estado Bolívar. Ciudad Bolívar,
CBR, 1949-52.
Gobernación del Estado Falcón. Coro,
CBR, 1949-52.
Gobernación del Estado Lara. Barquisimeto,
CBR, 1949-52.
Gobernación del Estado Mérida. Mérida,
CBR, 1949-52.
Gobernación del Estado Portuguesa. Guanare,
CBR, 1949-52.
Gobernación del Estado Táchira. San Cristóbal,
CBR, 1949-54.
Gobernación del Estado Trujillo. Trujillo,
CBR, 1949-52.
Gobernación del Estado Yaracuy. San Felipe,
CBR, 1951-54.
Gobernación del Estado Zulia. Maracaibo,
CBR, 1956-60.
Instituto Agrario Nacional. Caracas,
CIDEA, 1948-56.
CBR, 1948-68.
PIDR, 1962-68.
International Petroleum Corporation. Caracas,
CBR, 1951-54.
Mene Grande Oil Company. Caracas,
CBR, 1951-54.
Ministerio de Agricultura y Cría. Caracas,
CBR, 1948-68.
PIIP, 1960-64.
PIJR, 1962-67.
PIDR, 1962-68.

Ministerio de Educación. Caracas,
CIDEA, 1948-56.
VE, 1952-57.
Ministerio de Fomento. Oficina General de Estadística. Caracas,
PIDR, 1962-66.
Ministerio de Sanidad y Asistencia Social. Caracas,
CIDEA, 1948-56.
—————. Dirección de Malarialogía,
CBR, 1957-59.
North American Association of Venezuela. Caracas,
PIDR, 1962-68.
Oficina de la Presidencia para la Coordinación y Planificación. Caracas,
PIDR, 1962-66.
Organización de las Naciones Unidas para la Agricultura y la Alimentación. Roma, Italia,
PIDR, 1963-67.
Programa de Desarrollo de las Nacionas Unidas. Caracas,
PIDR, 1963-67.
Socony Mobil Oil Company. Caracas,
CBR, 1951-56.
United States. Agency for International Development. Caracas,
PIDR, 1963-67.
Universidad Central de Venezuela. Facultades de Agronomía y Medicina Veterinaria. Maracay,
CBR, 1955-60.

REGIONAL

Departmento Latinoamericano de Población. Bogotá, Colombia,
PIIP, 1960-68.
Federación Panamericana de Asociaciones de Facultades de Medicina. División Población. Bogotá, Colombia,
PIIP, 1967-68.
Instituto Centroamericano de Población y Familia. Guatemala,
PIIP, 1968.

Instituto de Nutrición de Centroamerica y Panamá. Guatemala,
PIIP, 1962-68.

Oficina Sanitaria Panamericana. Oficina regional. Guatemala,
PIIP, 1959-60.

United States. Agency for International Development. Regional Office for Central America and Panama. Guatemala,
PIIP, 1967-68.

APPENDIX III

List of Publications

Following are the publications issued by AIA and the programs it helped to sponsor. In some cases the publication was issued by, or in cooperation with, another organization which is so identified.

1. American International Association for Economic and Social Development (AIA), New York, New York. 1948-68.

Agriculture in Brazil. Rio de Janeiro, 1961.

Anderson, H. Calvert. *Análisis Sobre las Actividades de la Oficina Técnica de Información Agraria y Recomendaciones para su Futuro.* Lima, Perú, 1968.

Anderson, H. Calvert. *Effective Information Programs,* San José, Costa Rica. Inter-American Institute of Agricultural Sciences. 1968.

Annual Report. New York, 1956.

Bradt, H. Schuyler and Louis E. Heaton. *Analysis of the Wordless Pam-*

231

phlet on Corn Seed Selection. Caracas, Venezuela. 1957. (Also in Spanish)

Crawford, Aleta McDowell. *Alimentos Seleção e Preparo: Um guia indispensável em tôdas as boas cozinhas.* Rio de Janeiro, Brazil, 1966.

Crawford, Walter L. *Report on Village Improvement and Rural Economic Development in Trinidad and Tobago.* 1963.

Heaton, Louis E. *Reconnaissance Surveys of Agricultural and Forest Resources for Latin America.* Caracas, Venezuela: Consejo de Bienestar Rural, 1961. (Also in Spanish)

Land Reform and AIA. New York, 1965.

Lassey, William R. *Communication, Risk, and Investment Decision-Making in Costa Rica.* Ph.D. thesis submitted to Michigan State University, East Lansing, Michigan, 1967.

Maes, Ernest E. *Plan Victoria: An Experiment in Rural Education in Chile.* New York, 1967.

Mass Communications and AIA. New York, 1965. (Also in Spanish)

Progress Report. New York, 1957.

Progress Report. New York, 1960.

Progress Report. New York, 1962. (Also in Spanish)

Record #1. New York, 1949.

Record #2. New York, 1950.

Record #3. New York, 1953.

Rural Education and AIA. New York, 1965.

Rural Youth and AIA. New York, (revised) 1966.

Salvo, Paulo. *Land Development Project for the State of Minas Gerais, Brazil.* CAMIG (State-controlled, mixed capital agricultural corporation), Belo Horizonte, Brazil, 1961. (Also in Spanish.)

Seminario en Comunicaciones Sobre Demografía y Salud Pública para Centro América y Panamá. San José, Costa Rica, 1968. (Also in Spanish.)

Waisanen, Frederick B., Jerome T. Durlak, and Others. *A Survey of Attitudes Related to Costa Rican Population Dynamics.* Prepared under contract for the U.S. Agency for International Development. San José, Costa Rica, 1966. (Also in Spanish.)

2. Associação de Crédito e Assistência Rural—Belo Horizonte, Minas Gerais, Brazil, 1948-61.[1]

1° Relatório Anual da ACAR. 1949.

2° Relatório Anual da ACAR. 1950.

Relatório de Atividades da ACAR em Minas até 30 de setembro de 1951.

3° Relatório Anual da ACAR. 1951.

4° Relatório Anual da ACAR. 1952.

5° Relatório Anual da ACAR. 1953.

6° Relatório Anual da ACAR. 1954. (Portuguese and English)

7° Relatório Anual da ACAR. 1955. (Portuguese and English)

8° Relatório Anual da ACAR. 1956.

Relatório Anual 1956/57 e Programa 1957/58.

Relatório Anual 1957/58 e Programa 1958/59.

Relatório Anual 1959/60.

Relatório do Decênio. 1959. (Portuguese and English)

During the ten-year period 1949-59 ACAR's Division of Information published more than 3,000 different extension bulletins, pamphlets and posters and distributed them to farmers throughout the state.

---

[1] *Source:* Information supplied by ACAR

232

3. Associação Brasileira de Crédito e Assistência Rural, Rio de Janeiro, Brazil, 1957-61.[2]

Documentary Publications

Segunda reunião nacional de técnicos em extensão rural e crédito supervisionado: conclusões. Belo Horizonte —Minas Gerais, 1957.

Organização geral; estrutura técnico-administrativa. Rio de Janeiro, 1958.

Priméira reunião de especialistas em treinamento dos centros e das entidades filiadas. Rio de Janeiro (ETA-ABCAR) 1958.

Expressões e têrmos usados em extensão rural e crédido supervionado no Brasil. Rio de Janeiro 1958.

Terçeira reunião nacional de técnicos em extensão rural e crédito supervisionado: Conclusões. Recife, Pernambuco (ETA-ABCAR) 1959.

Priméira reunião nacional de chefes e assistentes-técnicas de economia doméstica, Rio de Janeiro (ETA-ABCAR) 1959.

Priméira reunião do pessoal de chefia administrativa do "Sistema ABCAR," Rio de Janeiro (ETA-ABCAR) 1959.

Elaboração de questionários; análise de relatórios; análise do progresso de famílias. Rio de Janeiro, 1960.

Segunda reunião nacional de líderes estaduais de Clubes 4-S. Rio de Janeiro, 1960.

Informação sôbre o Sistema brasileiro de extensão rural e crédito supervisonado. Rio de Janeiro 1960.

Cadastro de instrutores e professôres. Cursos de extensão rural e crédito supervisionado nos Centros de Treinamento. Rio de Janeiro 1960.

Reformulação da política de aplicação de crédito rural em articula-

ção com a extensão rural; conclusões e recomendações da I reunião nacional de especialistas em crédito dos Serviços de Extensão Rural e Representantes de entidades financiadoras. Rio de Janeiro 1960.

Plano diretor, quinquênio 1961-1965. Rio de Janeiro, 1961.

Trabalhos experimentais do Serviço Nacional de Pesquisas Agronômicas (SNPA) Rio de Janeiro, 1961.

Estatuto da Associação Brasileira de Crédito e Assistência Rural. Rio de Janeiro, 1961.

Extension Publications

Manual dos Clubes 4-S. Rio de Janeiro (ETA-ABCAR) 1959.

Contactos individuais. Rio de Janeiro (ETA-ABCAR) 1959.

Demonstração de resultados. Rio de Janeiro, 1959.

Planejamento de programa do escritório local. Rio de Janeiro (ETA-ABCAR) 1960.

Rádio em extensão rural. Rio de Janeiro (ETA-ABCAR) 1960.

Redação em extensão. Rio de Janeiro (ETA-ABCAR) 1960.

Supervisão nos serviços de extensão. Rio de Janeiro, 1961.

Sistema de avaliação do programa municipal. Rio de Janeiro, 1961.

Technical Publications—4-S Clubs

Avicultura para Clubes 4-S. Rio de Janeiro (ETA-ABCAR) 1959.

Clube 4-S: Projeto de Economia Doméstica, 1ª divisão. Rio de Janeiro, 1960.

Clube 4-S: Projeto de Economia Doméstica, 2ª divisão. Rio de Janeiro, 1960.

Projeto de Economia Doméstica, 3ª divisão. Rio de Janeiro, 1960.

---

[2] *Source:* Information supplied by ABCAR

Guia para projeto de Economia Doméstica, Clube 4-S, 4ª divisão. Rio de Janeiro, 1960.

Projeto Lacticínios, Clube 4-S. Rio de Janeiro, 1961.

Technical Publications—
Home Economics

Como conservar frutas e tomates. Rio de Janeiro (ETA-ABCAR) 1960.

Carnes vermelhas. Rio de Janeiro, 1960.

Vísceras (miúdos) Rio de Janeiro, 1960.

Caju: preparo, utilização. Rio de Janeiro, 1960.

Nossa família planeja um futuro melhor. Rio de Janeiro, 1961.

Miscellaneous Publications

Segunda reunião de técnicos em extensão rural e crédito supervisionado: conclusões e recomendações. Belo Horizonte, 1957 (ETA-ABCAR).

Estatuto da Associação Brasileira de Crédito e Assistência Rural. Rio de Janeiro.

Programa da 2ª reunião de técnicos em Extensão, 1957. Rio de Janeiro.

Extensão e crédito rural supervisionado. Rio de Janeiro, 1957.

Conclusões da II reunião nacional de técnicos em extensão rural e crédito supervisionado, Belo Horizonte, Minas Gerais, 1957.

Economia Doméstica, uma carreira de futuro. Rio de Janeiro, (ETA-ABCAR).

Agronomia, uma carreira de futuro Rio de Janeiro, (ETA-ABCAR).

Assistente social, uma carreira de futuro. Rio de Janeiro, (ETA-ABCAR).

Veterinária, uma carreira de futuro. Rio de Janeiro, (ETA-ABCAR).

Campanha de aumento de técnicos para a agricultura; levantamento preliminar. Rio de Janeiro, 1958.

Sugestões para uma campanha de aumento de técnicos para a agricultura (Encontro de Diretores de Agronomia, e Veterinária, Rio de Janeiro, 1958).

Campanha de aumento de técnicos para a agricultura: relação das Escolas de Agronomia, Veterinária, Economia Doméstica e Serviço Social, existentes no país (ETA-ABCAR).

Programa da 1ª reunião nacional de líderes estaduais de Clubes 4-S, Rio de Janeiro, 1958.

Conclusões do Seminário sôbre o desenvolvimento do crédito agrícola na América Latina, Paraná, 1958.

Programa da 3ª reunião nacional de técnicos em extensão e crédito rural supervisionado, Recife, 1958.

Relatório financeiro de 1958. Rio de Janeiro.

Resenha estatística das atividades de extensão rural e crédito supervisionado das Filiadas, no período de 1949-57. Rio de Janeiro 1958.

Síntese das principais atividades do Sistema Cooperativo de Extensão Rural e Crédito Supervisionado. Dados preliminares, 1959.

Tres anos de atividades (1956-1959) Um programa cooperativo a serviço do meio rural.

Tres anos de atividades: síntese das principais atividades do Sistema Cooperativo de extensão rural e crédito supervisionado. Rio de Janeiro, 1959.

Informes sôbre a execução de acôrdos e normas para o processamento de Prestação de Contas, Rio de Janeiro 1959.

Report of the Evaluation Mission for the Brazilian Extension and Supervised Credit System. Rio de Janeiro, 1959.

Informe del Centro Sudamericano de Extensión Agrícola, Belo Horizonte. Rio de Janeiro.

Síntese das atividades do Sistema Cooperativo de Extensão Rural e Crédito Supervisionado, dados preliminares Rio de Janeiro, 1959.

Expressões e têrmos usados em conservação de alimentos. 1959.

Grupo de Trabalho da Campanha de aumento de técnicos para o meio rural. Rio de Janeiro, 1959.

Plano de trabalho, Rio de Janeiro (ETA-ABCAR), 1959.

Un programa cooperativo al servício del medio agrícola; extensión agrícola y crédito supervisado: 3 años de actividades (1956-1959) Rio de Janeiro.

Sucos de frutas, Divisão de Treinamento, 1959.

Curso de capacitação inicial em extensão rural e crédito supervisionado. Aulas de conservação de alimentos por Amaury H. da Silveira, Divisão de Treinamento, 1959.

Problemas na indústria de conservas por Amaury H. da Silveira.

Demonstrações sôbre conservação de alimentos por Amaury H. da Silveira 1959.

Relatório financeiro, 1959.

Curso de extensão em habitação rural; semana de orientação. Rio de Janeiro.

Campanha de aumento de técnicos para o meio rural; Rio de Janeiro, 1959.

Campanha de aumento de técnicos para o meio rural; informação aos participantes do Encontro de Di-

rectores das Escolas de Agronomia e Veterinária, 1959.

Mejoramiento de la explotación porcina; estudio de un trabajo conducido por la ASCAR en cooperación con organizaciones oficiales y privadas. Relator: Marcos C. Pereira.

Sistema cooperativo de extensão agrícola no Brasil. Rio de Janeiro, 1959.

Reformulação da política de aplicação do crédito rural em articulação com a extensão rural; novas diretrizes e medidas propostas. Rio de Janeiro, (ETA-ABCAR), 1960.

Cursos de treinamento tecnológico especializado: plano geral. Rio de Janeiro, 1960.

Relatório da Missão de Avaliação; o sistema de extensão rural e crédito supervisionado no Brasil. Rio de Janeiro, 1960.

Report of the Evaluation Mission; the Brazilian Extension and Supervised Credit System. Rio de Janeiro, 1960.

Educação alimentar no serviço de extensão. Rio de Janeiro (ETA-ABCAR 1960.

Avaliação da IV reunião nacional de técnicos em extensão rural. Rio de Janeiro, 1960.

A boa alimentação garante a saúde do bebê. Rio de Janeiro, (ETA-ABCAR), 1960.

Crédito rural supervisionado no Brasil; reunião de trabalhos de técnicos da ABCAR e suas Filiadas. Rio de Janeiro, 1960. (SIA-ETA-ABCAR).

The Brazilian Cooperative Rural Extension System. Rio de Janeiro, 1960.

Orçamento para 1960. Rio de Janeiro, 1959.

Plano de trabalho, 1960. Rio de Janeiro Projeto 31, ETA-ABCAR 1960.

Plano diretor: quinquênio 1961-1965 (anteprojeto) Rio de Janeiro 1960.

Plano diretor: quinquênio 1961-1965: subsídios (anteprojeto) Rio de Janeiro 1960.

Economia doméstica em extensão rural. Centenário do Ministério da Agricultura. "Encontro de Economia Doméstica," 1960.

Síntese das principais atividades do Sistema Brasileiro Cooperativo de Extensão Rural ABCAR, Filiadas e Centros de Treinamento, 1° semestre de 1960. Rio de Janeiro, 1960.

Síntese das principais atividades do Sistema Cooperativo de Extensão Rural e Crédito Supervisionado. Relatório anual do Sistema ABCAR. Rio de Janeiro, 1960.

Relatório financeiro, 1960.

Problemas de habitação rural; palestras realizadas sob os auspícios do CINVA e ABCAR. Rio de Janeiro, SIA, 1960. (SIA-ETA-ABCAR).

Organização geral, estrutura técnica administrativa. Rio de Janeiro, (ETA-ABCAR) 1960.

ACAR, "Associação de Crédito e Assistência Rural", Minas Gerais, Bra-

sil, the first extension service in Brazil. 1960.

Guia para organização de uma campanha. Rio de Janeiro, 1961.

Estatuto. Rio de Janeiro 1961.

Proteínas, fontes e funções 1961.

Coma cenouras e tenha saúde. 1961.

Curso de avaliação em extensão rural. Tradução do material sôbre avaliação em extensão rural. Rio de Janeiro 1961.

Geléia de laranja, 1961.

Plano de trabalho, 1961.

Plano diretor quinquenal do Sistema ABCAR, 1961-1965; objetivos dos serviços de extensão nos Estados; atividades de coordenação a cargo da ABCAR 1961.

Relatório financeiro, 1961. Rio de Janeiro.

Relatório e demonstração das contas referentes ao ano 1961. Rio de Janeiro.

Técnicos para o desenvolvimento da agricultura: formação profissional, mercado de trabalho por J. Pinto Lima, Lincoln M. Rodrigues, Thiago Ferreira da Cunha e Yonita Assenço Torres. Rio de Janeiro, 1961.

4. Consejo de Bienestar Rural (CBR)—Caracas, Venezuela—1948-68.

Special studies, reports and other information material published or edited by the Consejo de Bienestar Rural.[3]

SPECIAL STUDIES

Before 1952

Anderson, James D. *Propuesta de Reorganización del ITIC, con Miras al Establecimiento de un Instituto*

[3] *Source: Publicaciones del Consejo de Bienestar Rural.* Caracas, Marzo, 1968.

Agrario Nacional. 1949. (Also in English.)

Informe de los Técnicos sobre un Programa de Servicios Comunales para Venezuela. 1948.

Jacques, Dale B. *Plan de Vialidad de la Isla de Margarita.* 1951. (Also in English)

Lesesne, Frank F. *Estudio de Conservación de Suelos en la Isla de Margarita.* 1948. (Also in English)

Morris, Edward E. *Caminos Vecinales en el Estado Táchira.* 1949. (Also in English.)

————— y G. Privet. *Plan de Vialidad del Estado Bolívar.* 1951. (Also in English.)

Proyecto No. 2 para la Zona de los Bancos de San Pedro. 1948. (Also in English)

Richardson, Pedro. *Estudio de la Industria de la Caña de Azúcar en el Valle de El Tocuyo.* 1950. (Also in English)

Thoms, H. W. *Recursos de Agua de la Isla de Margarita.* 1948. (Also in English.)

Wilkerson, Ogden C. *Centro de Maquinaria del ITIC en Guacara, Carabobo.* 1949. (Also in English.)

—————. *Informe en Inglés sobre Viviendas Baratas para la Zona No. 2 del ITIC en Carabobo.* 1949.

Regional Agricultural Resource Studies

Conklin, Howard E., Antonio S. de Lozada, Louis E. Heaton, y colaboradores. *Reconocimiento Agropecuario Forestal del Oriente de la Guayana Venezolana.* (Tomo I-VII) 1961.

Heaton, Louis E., Marion Striker, Miguel Almiñana, *et al. Recursos Agrícolas de los Llanos de Monagas.* 1957.

—————, —————, Edmundo Rojas, Miguel Almiñana *et al. Recursos Agrícolas del Guárico Occidental.* 1956. (Also in English)

—————, ————— Ezio Santaromita, *et al. Recursos Agrícolas y Forestales del Estado Barinas.* 1957.

Ordenación y Desarrollo de Cuencas Hidrográficas. (Cojedes Superior y Motatán)

Proyecto Venezuela 1 del Fondo Especial (UNDP) de la O.N.U. (Secciónes 1-15) 1966.

Sterling, Henry S., Milton L. Barnett, Bertram Ellenbogen, Louis E. Heaton y otros. *Problemas Económicos y Sociales de los Andes Venezo-lanos.* (Two volumes. Volume I also in English) 1956.

Striker, Marion M., Volkmar Vareschi y otros. *Recursos Agrícolas del Estado Yaracuy y Parte de los Estados Falcón y Carabobo.* (Also in English) 1955.

Studies of Agricultural Activities and Enterprises

Cardona Alvárez, Canuto. *La Caraota y Otras Leguminosas de Grano en Venezuela.* 1967.

Estrada, Hugh J. *La Ganadería en el Estado Apure. Sus Problemas y Perspectivas.* 1967.

Frye, Jr., Jennings B. *La Industria Lechera en la Zona Abastecedora de Caracas.* Vol. I & II. 1953.

Gondelles, Ricardo, Hugh Estrada, *et al. Programa Cooperativo de Investigación sobre Alimentación del Ganado de Carne en la Región de los Llanos durante la Epoca Seca.* 1962.

Heaton, Louis E. *Costo de Producción de Maíz.* 1955.

————— y Marion Striker. *Estudio Preliminar sobre las Probilidades de Incrementar la Producción del Maíz en el Valle de Barlovento, Estado Miranda.* 1952.

Herrera Klindt, Bernardo y C. Jiménez E. *La Palma Africana de Aceite —Perspectivas para su Explotación en Venezuela.* 2d. ed. 1965.

Jones, Guy L. *Estudio sobre la Clasificación del Tabaco en Venezuela, Recomendaciones sobre las Necesidades de Investigación y Extensión.* 1959. (Also in English)

Morrison, Frank B., Jorge de Alba, *et al. La Industria Ganadera en Venezuela.* 1955. (Also in English)

Sonley, Lorne T. *Estudio sobre el Almacenamiento de Granos.* 1955.

Steele, Dewey G. *La Cría de Caballos*

en *Venezuela.* 1956. (Also in English.)

Walker, Rufus K. y J. Norman Efferson. *Estudio del Plan Arrocero de la Corporación Venezolana de Fomento.* Vols. I, II, III. 1952.

Studies of Agricultural Development and Related Problems

Almiñana, Miguel, A. Grajal, J. San Martin, *et al. Proyecciones de la Oferta y la Demanda de Productos Agropecuarios en Venezuela, 1965-1970-1975.* 2d. ed. 1967. (Also in English.)

Báez Finol, V. *El Impuesto Predial Rural—Su Institución en Venezuela.* 1961.

Bourns, Charles T. *El Proyecto de Riego de El Cenizo.* 1953.

Calatrava, Alonso. *El Seguro Agrícola y su Institución en Venezuela.* 1961.

Cook, Hugh L. *Análisis de la Política Gubernamental Acerca de los Precios y Mercado de la Industria Lechera en Venezuela.* Translated by Antonio Pons. 1960. (Also in English)

Efferson, J. Norman. *Mercadeo de los Productos Agrícolas de las Colonias del IAN.* Translated by Antonio Pons. 1960.

Ellsworth, P. T. *Los Problemas del Desarrollo Industrial de Venezuela.* 1952. (Also in English)

Gondelles, Ricardo. *Lineamientos del Programa de Desarrollo y Ordenación de Cuencas Hidrográficas Nacionales.* 2d. ed. 1962.

——————. *Programa de Ordenación y Desarrollo de Cuencas Hidrográficas.* 1962.

Heaton, Louis E. *Estado Actual y Posibilidades de Uso del Frigorífico del BAP en San Fernando de Apure.* Translated by Antonio Pons. 1958.

——————, *et al. Estado Actual y Posibilidades de Desarrollo Agrícola en Venezuela.* Study financed by the Ford Foundation. Translated by Antonio Pons. 1967. (Also in English)

—————— y Miguel Almiñana. *Bases Económicas para el Establecimiento de Instalaciones de Mercado y Beneficio en la Unidad Agrícola de Turén.* 1957.

——————, —————— y Jesús Díaz Ungría. *La Opinion en el Medio Rural sobre las Actividades del BAP.* 1959.

——————, Evelio Tovar y Denise Dabrowski. *Condiciones Económicas y Sociales Prevalecientes entre Familias Campesinas Residentes en la Zona de Chirgua, Estado Carabobo.* 1956.

Jiménez, César, Walter Güdel y E. F. Seiller. *El Mercadeo de Productos Agropecuarios y Pesqueros en Maracaibo.* Translated by Antonio Pons. 1965.

Kauffman, William F., José L. Zúñiga y otros. *El Crédito Agrícola en Venezuela.* 1955. (Also in English)

Maddox, James G. *La Agricultura Venezolana y el CBR.* 1952.

Mehren, George L. *El Mercadeo de los Productos Agrícolas en Venezuela.* 2d. ed. 1965. (Also in English)

Mindiola, J. B. *El Mercadeo de Frutas en Venezuela.* 1964.

Ministerio de Agricultura y Cría. Dirección de Planificación Agropecuaria. *Atlas Agrícola de Venezuela.* 1960.

Nazario, Luis A. *Inventario de Posibilidades sobre la Organización de Cooperativas dentro de las Colonias del IAN.* 2d ed. 1961.

Shepherd, Geoffrey, *et al. El Mercadeo de los Productos Agropecuarios al Mayor y al Detal.* Translated by Antonio Pons. 2d. ed. 1963.

Veíhmeyer, Frank J. y James C. Marr. *Estudio sobre los Principios y Prácticas de Riego y Avenamiento en los Proyectos del IAN.* Translated by Antonio Pons. 1959.

Administrative Studies

Anderson, James D. *Organización Administrativa de la Corporación Venezolano de Fomento.* 1953.

Cavin, James P. *La Dirección de Economía Agrícola del MAC.* 1953.

Clawson, Marion. *Análisis General del Programa de la Administración del IAN.* Translated by Antonio Pons. 1959.

Couch, Virgil L. *Organización del MAC.* 1953.

Croy, Otto C. *La Extensión Agrícola en el MAC.* 1953. (Also in English)

Heaton, Louis E., et al. *Proposición para el Establecimiento de un Programa de Crédito Supervisado en Venezuela.* 1961. (Also in English)

Hughes, Stephen C. *Estudio Administrativo de las Actividades de Crédito del BAP.* Translated by Antonio Pons. 1959.

Loveridge, Earl W. *Estudio Administrativo de la Dirección Forestal del MAC.* 1952. (Also in English)

Magleby, Karl J. *Un Departamento de Riego en el IAN.* 1956.

Marquina, Elda. *Servicio de las Demostradoras del Hogar Campesino en las Dependencias del IAN.* 1958.

Taggart, W. C. *La Investigación Agrícola en Venezuela.* 1954. (Also in English)

EXTENSION PUBLICATIONS

Technical Bulletins

Efferson, J. Norman y Rufus Walker. *Arroz en Venezuela.* 2d. ed. 1955. (Also in English)

Frye, Jennings B. *Alimentación y Manejo del Ganado Lechero en Venezuela.* 1956.

Heaton, Louis E. *El Análisis de Explotación Agrícola.* 2d. ed. 1960. (Also in English)

Heilman, John. *El Crédito Agrícola Planeado y Supervisado.* 2d. ed. 1959. (Also in English)

Law, Howard E. *Extensión Agrícola, Principios Básicos y Metodos de Enseñanza.* 3d. ed. (revised) 1960.

Prosdocimi, Ludmilla. *El Programa de Desayuno Infantil.* 2d. ed. (revised) 1960.

Agricultural Extension Bulletins

Araque, Ricardo. *La Ciruela de Hueso.* (Serie Cultivos No. 9), 1967.

_____. *El Cultivo de la Piña en Venezuela.* 4th. ed. (Serie Cultivos No. 4) 1966.

_____. *La Guanábana.* (Serie Cultivos No. 13) 1967.

_____. *El Higo.* (Serie Cultivos) 3d. ed. 1966.

_____. *La Parcha Granadina.* (Serie Cultivos) 4th ed. 1967.

_____. *La Yuca* (Serie Cultivos No. 2) 5th ed. 1966.

Bodisco, V. y C. E. Rios. *Un Aporte al Conocimiento del Ganado en la Región de Carora, Lara.* Centro de Investigaciones Agronómicas. Boletín Técnico No. 12. 1962.

_____, et al. *Comportamiento del Ganado Criollo Lechero en Hatos Privados de la Región del Rio Limón en el Estado Zulia.* Centro de Investigaciones Agronómicas. Boletín Técnico No. 13. 1962.

La Caraota. (Serie Cultivos No. 10) 1967.

Castillo, Juan J. *El Frijol.* (Serie Cultivos No. 3) 1962.

Frye, Jennings B. *El Ganado Lechero y su Adaptabilidad a las Condiciones de Venezuela.* 1956.

El Ganado Criollo Lechero Tropical. 1956.

García Andrade, Numa y Jaime Henao Jaramillo. *El Cultivo del Café en Venezuela.* 1958.

Gondelles, Ricardo. *Los Recursos Naturales Renovables* (Guía para su Aprovechamiento y Conservación). (Manual Práctico del Campesino). 3d ed. 1967.

Herrera Aldana, Bernardo. *La Cría del Conejo.* (Manual Práctico del Campesino). 3d. ed. 1965.

Herrera Klindt, Bernardo. *El Ajonjolí, (Serie Cultivos No. 1)* 5th ed. 1966.

——————. *Cultivo del Ajonjolí* (Manual Práctico del Campesino) 2d. ed. 1965.

—————— y E. Mosquera. *Cultivo del Maíz* (Manual Práctico del Campesino) 5th ed. 1967.

——————, ——————. *Cultivo del Tomate.* (Manual Práctico del Campesino) 3d. ed. 1965.

Mondolfi, Edgardo. *Más Carne con Mayores Cosechas de Becerros.* 1957.

——————. *Pangola* (Serie Forrajes No. 3) 3d. ed. 1965.

——————. *Yaraguá Brasilera.* (Serie Forrajes No. 1). 3rd. ed. 1965.

Nuevas Variedades de Papas para la Región Central de Venezuela. 1956.

Obregón, Pedro y Hernán Oropeza. *Tres Variedades de Maíz Híbrido para Venezuela.* 1957.

Penella, José S. *El Aguacate.* (Serie Cultivos No. 11) 1967.

——————. *El Mango.* (Serie Cultivos No. 12) 1967.

——————. *El Plátano y el Cambur* (Serie Cultivos No. 8). 2d. ed. 1967.

Piñero, Luis. *La Cría de Aves.* 1957.

Ríos, Carlos E. y V. Bodisco. *Estado Actual de los Estudios de Ganado Lechero en el Centro de Investigaciones Agronómicas.* Centro de Investigaciones Agronómicas. Boletín Técnico No. 11. 1962.

Semilleros de Caña. 1958.

Stolk, Ernesto. *La Fresa* (Serie Cultivos) 3d. ed. 1966.

——————. *El Huerto Frutal Familiar.* (Manual Práctico del Campesino), 3d. ed. 1967.

Stoner, Warren N. *Los Bachacos y su Control en Venezuela* 1955.

——————. *El Huerto Familiar.* 2d. ed. (revised) 1960.

Vivas, G. y O. Peraza. *Cultivo del Algodón.* (Manual Práctico del Campesino). 2d. ed. 1967.

Zerpa, Humberto. *La Parva-Silo.* 1957.

Irrigation Bulletins—IAN-CBR

"Aguas Subterráneas para el Riego de las Cosechas." *Agricultura de las Américas.* November 1958.

Bamesberger, John G. *Nivelación de Tierras para Riego.* Translated by Antonio Pons. 1958.

Besson, Luis A. *Qué es un Plan de Conservación de Suelos?* 1959.

Marr, James C. *Preparación de Tierras para el Riego de Superficie.* Translated by Antonio Pons. 1959.

United States. Department of Agriculture. Farmers Home Administration. *Principios Prácticos para el Regante.* Translated by Antonio Pons. 2d. ed. 1963.

——————, —————— and Department of Interior. *Guía de Riego para los Agricultores.* Translated by Alfredo López. 1960.

Weir, Walter W. *Avenamiento o Drenaje del Suelo.* Translated by Antonio Pons. 1961.

Agricultural Extension Pamphlets

Las Actas de una Cooperativa Agrícola. 1961.

Asistencia Técnica y Créditos para Mecanización Menor. 1962.

Banco Agrícola y Pecuario. ¿Va Ud. a Solicitar un Crédito Agropecuario? 1959.

Britto Fernández, Clemente. Prevención de Incendios Forestales. 1961.

Conozca la Peste o Cólera Porcina. 1960.

Conozca su Tractor. 2d. ed. 1962.

Crédito Supervisado, Programa del BAP. 3d. ed. 1965.

Escuelas de Demostradoras del Hogar. 1963.

Escuelas de Peritos Agropecuarios. 1962.

Escuelas de Prácticos Agrícolas. 1962.

Escuelas de Tractoristas. 1962.

Enseñanza Práctica MAC. 1961.

Instituto Agrario Nacional. Adjudicación de Tierras al Campesinado Venezolano. 1963.

Más y Mejor Producción. 1962.

Ministerio de Agricultura y Cría. Abona tus Cafetos. 1957.

_____. Ganado Aparentemente Sano Puede Tener Tuberculosis? 1958.

_____. Más Café. 1956.

_____. Más y Mejores Cosechas con Abonos. 1957.

_____. Mejor Café Usando el Beneficio Húmedo. 1957.

_____. Vacas Mejor Alimentadas. 1957.

La Naranja Dulce. 5th ed. 1965.

Normas para el Mantenimiento de Tractores. 1959.

Oliveros, Iván J. La Guayaba. 4th ed. 1965.

Qué es el Programa de Adiestramiento Agropecuario Popular? 1960.

Rondón, Fernando. La Lechosa, un Frutal Remunerativo. 5th. ed. 1965.

Urosevich, L. Normas para Elaborar Queso Blanco Tipo Criollo Especial. 3d. ed. 1964.

Extension Leaflets

La Aftosa, Prevéngala. 1958.

Agricultor, Ama de Casa.

Agricultor! Si Desea Aumentar sus Ganancias Combata el Picudo. 1952.

Agua para tu Ganado. 1956.

Aproveche Mejor su Fuerza y la de sus Animales. 4th. ed. 1966.

El Arado, Su Uso y Cuidado. 3d. ed. 1966.

Aumente su Producción de Maíz. Mate el Cogollero. 1952.

Aumenta tus Ingresos . . . Riega. 1957.

Los Bachacos Destruyen tus Siembras, Mátalos. 1952.

Un Café, Dijo la Hormiga.

El Calor y tu Producción de Leche. 1956.

El Cerdo. 1956.

Cuidado con el Cólera o Peste Porcina. 1959.

Combata el Cogollero. 2d. ed. 1965.

Combata el Gusano del Tomate. 2d. ed. 1962.

Combate el Bachaco.

Combate la Candelilla o el Quemado de las Papas. 1958.

Cómo Plantar un Arbol. 2d. ed. 1962.

Controle la Mastitis. 1958.

Controle la Quemazón en la Cebolla. 1960.

Coseche su Tabaco. No Deje que el Cachudo se lo Coma. 1952.

Criar Terneras es un Buen Negocio. 2d. ed. 1962.

El Cultivo de la Lechosa. 1953.

Destruye la Escoba Bruja. 1956.

Elimine sus Matas de Lechosa Enfermas de Mosaico. 3d. ed. 1965.

Evite la Quema de sus Cultivos Combatiendo la Candelilla. 1952.

Hágase Apicultor. 2d. ed. 1966.

Hágase Socio de una Cooperativa Agrícola. 1961.

Injerte sus Cítricos. El Injerto de Escudete. 2d. ed. 1963.

Injerte sus Frutales. El Injerto de Púa Enchapado. 2d. ed. 1962.

La Inyectadora, Su Uso y Desinfección. 2d. ed. 1962.

Limpie su Cultivo de Cebolla con Herbicidas. 2d. ed. 1965.

Mantenga sus Aves Sanas. 3d. ed. 1966.

Más Maíz con Semilla Seleccionada.

Mejora tus Sabanas. 1956.

No Bote su Dinero Alimentando Gusanos. Acabe con el Alabama o Gusano de la Hoja del Algodón. 1952.

No Regales tu Maíz al Cogollero. 1954.

Pastos y Forrajes. 1960.

El Plan Frutícola de los Andes. 1961.

Pollos Sanos.

Prepara Mejor tu Tierra. 1956.

Prepare Bien el Semillero y Aumente sus Ganancias. 3d. ed. 1965.

I° Curso Nacional de Extensión Agrícola. 1959.

Produce Miel de Abejas. 1956.

Programa de Adiestramiento Agropecuario Popular. 1959.

Protege tu Maíz.

Protege tu Suelo. 1957.

Proteja su Maíz. 2d. ed. 1955.

Pruebe las Semillas Antes de Sembrarlas. 2d. ed. 1963.

Qué es una Cooperativa? 1960.

La Rastra de Discos, Su Uso y Mantenimiento. 2d. ed. 1963.

La Rata es tu Enemigo. 1954.

La Rinitis Atrófica del Cerdo. 3d. ed. 1966.

Va a Criar Cerdos? 3d. ed. 1966.

Extension Posters

Aumenta tus Ingresos, Riega. 1957.

Caficultor, Mata la Palomilla.

Combate el Bachaco.

Combate la Candelilla de las Papas.

Gana Más, Cría Cerdos.

Gana Más Lavando tu Café. 1957.

La Lluvia no Mata al Cogollero.

Más Maíz con Semilla Seleccionada.

Más y Mejores Cosechas con Abonos. 1957.

Mejora tus Sabanas. 1957.

Papas Sanas con Semillas Certificadas.

Protege tu Suelo. 1957.

Salud con Hortalizas. 1956.

Seca Bien tu Maíz.

Vacuna—Pollos Sanos.

Educational Comic Books

El Caso de los Cochinos Sueltos. (en colores). 1958.

La Familia Pepeguama. (en colores). 1957.

Rural Youth Publications

Apicultura—Proyecto I—Recomendaciones Sobre la Explotación Agrícola. 1963.

Ballard, V. My Life as a Venezuelan. 1965.

Cavaletto, Robert P. Mis Experiencias como Delegado IFYE 1961 en Venezuela. 1962.

Chirinos, José. Informe presentado a la II° Conferencia Internacional de Intercambio de Jóvenes Agricultores (IFYE) 1957.

Chirinos, José. Un IFYE Venezolano en Estados Unidos de Norteamérica. 1957.

Clubes Agrícolas 5-V San Francisco de Asís Nos. 1 y 2 y Palo Negro Nos. 1 y 2. Exposición del Día de Logros, 27 de Abril 1956.

Clubes 5-V, Manual de Organización y Funcionamiento. 1966.

Clubes 5-V de Venezuela. (volante)

Comisión Especial de Educación Artesanal Rural. 2d. ed. (revised) 1966.

Corte y Costura, Proyecto I, Aprenda a Coser. 1962.

Corte y Costura, Proyecto II, Mejoro Mis Nociones de Costura. 1962.

242

Corte y Costura, Proyecto III, La Niña Bien Vestida, 1962.

Corte y Costura, Proyecto IV, Costo para mi Familia. 1962.

Cursos para Clubes 5-V de Niñas. 1966.

Día de Logros de los Clubes Agrícolas 5-V, Palo Negro y San Francisco de Asís, Estado Aragua. 27 Abril 1956.

El Día de Logros de los Clubes Juveniles 5-V en Palo Negro y San Francisco de Asís. 1957.

Diario de un Delegado a la Primera Convención Nacional de Clubes 5-V de Venezuela. Maracay 11 al 17 de Agosto 1957.

Documento Constitutivo y Estatutos de la Asociación Civil Pro-Clubes 5-V, 2d. ed. (revised) 1961.

Ellis, Wayne. Venezuela Viewed Through the Eyes of an IFYE. 1959.

Faidley, Paul. Report of My IFYE Experiences in Venezuela. 1959.

Fruticultura, Proyecto I, Semilleros y Viveros Frutales. 1962.

Fruticultura—Proyecto II, Huertos Frutales Caseros. 1963.

González M., J. Ricardo. Las Explotaciones Agropecuarias de Montana Vistas por IFYE Venezolano. 1959.

Herrera Aldaña, Bernardo. Asociación Civil Pro-Clubes 5-V Proyecto de Crédito para la Explotación de Cerdos. 1966.

Ideas para la Celebración del Día de Logros. 1959.

Industrias Caseras—Proyecto II, Artesanía Criolla. 1963.

Itinerario para los IFYE's de 1966.

Johnson, E. The Bolivar-Dollar Exchange. 1965.

Libro de Actas para los Clubes Juveniles 5-V. 4th ed. (revised) 1962.

Lowe, Richard. Seis Meses como IFYE en Venezuela 1962.

Mejoramiento del Hogar, Proyecto I, Aprendo a Manejar el Equipo de Carpintería. 1962.

Mejoramiento del Hogar, Proyecto III, Mejoro y Equipo la Cocina. 1962.

Mejoramiento del Hogar, Proyecto IV, Mi Dormitorio Confortable y Alegre. 1962.

Moreno B., N. El Programa IFYE en mi Vocación Agrícola. 1966.

Organization, Function and Activities of the "Asociación Civil Pro-Clubes 5-V en Venezuela." 1963.

Paolini, Luis R. Festivales Sabatinos de Reforestación. 1962.

Primer Día de Exito de los Clubes 5-V, El Pilar (Sucre) 1965.

Programa del Día de Logros. Clubes Agrícolas 5-V Palo Negro, 16 Mayo 1957, San Francisco de Asís 17 Mayo 1957.

Proyecto Piloto de Créditos para Clubes 5-V, 25 Marzo 1960.

Qué es la Asociación Civil Pro-Clubes 5-V? 2d. ed. 1962.

Registro de Proyectos. 1962.

Rodríguez Brito, J. La Colectividad y los Clubes 5-V. 1959.

Sabe Ud. lo que es un Club Juvenil 5-V?

Threadgould, T. Los Seis Meses más Interesantes de mi Vida. (Also in English) 1966.

Tovar, Evelio. Los Clubes Juveniles 5-V y la Conservación de Recursos Naturales Renovables. 1962.

——————. Consideraciones Acerca de los Clubes Juveniles 5-V. 1964.

——————. Consideraciones Acerca de los Clubes de la Juventud Rural. 1966.

——————. El Día de Logros de los clubes 5-V de Tucupita. 1962.

——————. Informe que Presenta la Asociación Civil Pro-Clubes 5-V de Venezuela. II° Reunión del Comité

Técnico para la Juventud Rural. 1963.

——————. *Primer Campamento Nacional de Clubes 5-V y Tercer Intercambio Educacional de Jóvenes Rurales.* 1966.

Uzcátegui, Edgard. *Mis Experiencias como IFYE Venezolano en los Estados Unidos.* 1962.

Wessellius, F. *The Chance of a Lifetime.* 1965.

Home Economics and Community Development Publications

Aprende a Coser. 1955.

Aprovecha un Cajón y una Lata Vacía para Hacer un Fregadero. 1957.

Bebe Agua Pura. 1956.

Campaña de Limpieza de un Pueblo. 1950.

Canastilla para el Bebé. 2d. ed. 1961.

El Centro Comunal de Ciudad Ojeda. 1957.

Centro Comunal—Desarrollo de la Comunidad. 1959.

La Cocina, Taller del Ama de Casa. 1957.

Como Construir Muebles Baratos en su Casa. 1950.

Conservación de Frutas. 3d. ed. 1964.

Construye este Gabinete para tu Cocina. 1957.

Curso Nacional de Educación para el Hogar Rural. 1959.

Dabrowski, Denise y Elda Marquina. *Contabilidad Hogareña.* 1962.

——————, ——————. *Doña Limpieza a su Orden.* 2d. ed. 1963.

——————, ——————. *Gabinetes y Armarios en la Cocina.* 2d. ed. 1965.

——————, ——————. *El Hogar Rural.* 1960.

Dormitorio Confortable, Sueño Reparador. 1957.

Es Fácil Mantener tu Cocina Limpia. 1957.

Estatutos del Centro Comunal de Ciudad Ojeda. 1957.

de González, I. y E. Riera. *El Centro Comunal—Su Organización y Objetivos.* 1964.

Informe Sobre Actividades del Centro Comunal de Ciudad Ojeda. 1957.

Instituto Agrario Nacional. *Mejoramiento Rural-Servicio Social.* Programa a Desarrollarse en la Colonia Las Manoas. 1959.

Limpieza, Primer Paso Hacia la Salud y la Felicidad. 2d. ed. (revised) 1957.

Macías, Josefina. *Preparación de Alimentos.* 1964.

Manual de Referencia sobre Temas Tratados en Cursillos de Economía del Hogar. 1954.

Marquina, Elda. *La Organización de la Comunidad por Medio de los Centros Comunales.* 4th ed. (revised) 1960.

——————. *Proyecto de Desarrollo Comunal del Barrio El Dique.* 1960.

—————— y Denise Dabrowski. *El Centro Comunal.* 1961.

——————, ——————. *El Equipo de Carpintería al Servicio del Ama de Casa.* 4th ed. 1967.

——————, ——————. *Salud con Frutas.* 1961.

——————, ——————. *Usted Puede Contribuir a Solucionar los Problemas de su Comunidad.* 1960.

Ministerio de Agricultura y Cría. *Las Agentes Demostradoras del Hogar Campesino.* 1957.

Objetivos y Deberes de la Demostradora dentro del Programa de Crédito Supervisado. 1965.

de Pérez, María Luisa. *Manual de Corte y Costura.* 1958.

Produce Huevos para el Mercado. 1957.

244

Programa del Centro Comunal de Ciudad Ojeda. 1957.

Programa a Desarrollarse en el Centro Comunal de Ciudad Ojeda. 1957.

Programa Inaugural del Centro Comunal de Ciudad Ojeda. 1957.

Prosdocimi, Ludmilla. *Análisis de la Necesidad de Organizar una Escuela de Ciencias del Hogar a Nivel Universitario. 1960.*

Salud con Hortalizas. 1956.

Siembra Maíz Híbrido. 1957.

Su Salud Depende de su Alimentación. 2d. ed. 1962.

Taylor, Sue E. *Primera Cartilla sobre Economía del Hogar. 1950.*

Yo Tomo Leche Diariamente. 2d. ed. 1961.

Progress Reports of CBR

Actividades del CBR, 1954-56. (Supplement in English)

Anteproyecto de Programa y Presupuesto para el Año Fiscal 1960-61. 1960.

Dos Años de Labor: 1952-53 y 1953-54. (supplement in English)

Gondelles, Ricardo. *El Programa de Estudios y Proyectos Especiales del Consejo de Bienestar Rural. 1966.*

Hacia una Vida Mejor. 1958. (Also in English)

Informe Anual del CBR. 1950. (Also in English)

Informe Anual del CBR. 1952.

Informe del Consejo de Bienestar Rural Correspondiente a 1965.

Informe sobre el Consejo de Bienestar Rural y las Actividades que ha Desarrollado en Venezuela desde 1948 a 1959.

Informes Mensuales del CBR, enero-diciembre, 1952.

Publicaciones del Consejo de Bienestar Rural 1948-1967.

Relación de las Publicaciones del Consejo de Bienestar Rural de 1948 a 1960.

Resumen de Actividades del Consejo de Bienestar Rural en 1964.

Manuals, Guides, Instructions and Other Publications Related to Supervised Credit

Acuerdo de Préstamo de la Alianza para el Progreso. 3d. ed. 1965.

El Análisis de la Explotación Agrícola. Programa de Crédito Supervisado. 1965.

Convenio de Asistencia Técnica Celebrado entre el BAP, el CBR y la USAID en Venezuela. 1963.

Costos de Producción del Departamento de Estudios Económicos y Financieros del Banco Agrícola y Pecuario. 1965.

Costos de Producción por Hectárea. 1965.

Costos de Producción por Hectárea de Algunos Productos Agrícolas del Estado Bolívar. 1965.

Crédito Agrícola y Programa de Reforma Agraria. Iª Reunión de Dirigentes de Crédito Agrícola de América Latina. 1966.

Créditos de Mecanización Menor. 1962.

El Crédito Supervisado—Ponencia Presentada por el Consejo de Bienestar Rural a la Reunión Especial de Expertos en Asunción, Paraguay. 1965.

El Crédito Supervisado como Contribución al Desarrollo de la Reforma Agraria en Venezuela. V Convención Nacional de Ingenieros Agrónomos. 1964.

El Cultivo del Ajo. Programa de Crédito Supervisado. 3d. ed. 1965.

El Cultivo de la Cebolla. Programa de Crédito Supervisado. 3d. ed. 1965.

245

Informe Acerca de los Asentamientos Campesinos del Estado Anzoátegui. 1964.

Informe Acerca de los Asentamientos Campesinos del Estado Aragua. 1963.

Informe Acerca de los Asentamientos Campesinos del Estado Barinas. 1965.

Informe Acerca de los Asentamientos Campesinos del Estado Bolívar. 1964.

Informe Acerca de los Asentamientos Campesinos del Estado Carabobo. 2d. ed. 1964.

Informe Acerca de los Asentamientos Campesinos del Distrito Federal. 1963.

Informe Acerca de los Asentamientos Campesinos del Estado Falcón. 1965.

Informe Acerca de los Asentamientos Campesinos del Estado Guárico. 1965.

Informe Acerca de los Asentamientos Campesinos del Estada Lara. 1963.

Informe Acerca de los Asentamientos Campesinos del Estado Mérida. 1964.

Informe Acerca de los Asentamientos Campesinos del Estado Miranda. 1963.

Informe Acerca de los Asentamientos Campesinos del Estado Monagas. 1964.

Informe Acerca de los Asentamientos Campesinos del Estado Portuguesa. 1963.

Informe Acerca de los Asentamientos Campesinos del Estado Sucre. 1964.

Informe Acerca de los Asentamientos Campesinos del Estado Táchira. 1963.

Informe Acerca de los Asentamientos Campesinos del Estado Trujillo. 1963.

Informe Acerca de los Asentamientos Campesinos del Estado Yaracuy. 1963.

Informe Acerca de los Asentamientos Campesinos de la Zona Noroeste del Estado Zulia. 1963.

Herrera Aldaña, Bernardo. *Construcción de Vaqueras y Manejo de Potreros.* Programa de Crédito Supervisado. 2d. ed. 1965.

————. *Indicaciones sobre la Explotación de la Cabra Lechera.* Programa de Crédito Supervisado. 2d. ed. 1966.

————. *Proyecto de Crédito para Explotación de Cerdos.* 2d. ed. 1967.

————. *Proyecto de Crédito para la Explotación de Ponedoras.* 2d. ed. 1965.

Informe Mensual de Actividades. 2d. ed. 1964.

Manual de Campo para Créditos Supervisados. 1949. (Also in English)

Normas de Crédito Agrícola Preparadas para el BAP. 2d. ed. 1960.

Plan para el Hogar. 1963.

Problemas que Implica la Aplicación del Orden de Prioridad a las Solicitudes del Crédito Supervisado. 1964.

El Programa de Crédito Supervisado en el Táchira. 1965.

El Programa de Crédito Supervisado en el Zulia. 1965.

Proyecto de Concesión de Créditos para el Desarrollo del Programa de Mecanización Menor. 1963.

Resumen de los Informes Presentados por los Supervisores del Consejo de Bienestar Rural, acerca del Programa de Crédito Supervisado en el Estado Yaracuy. 1966.

Rondón, Fernando. *Las Características del Crédito Supervisado.* 3d. ed. 1965.

————. *El Programa de Crédito Supervisado del Consejo de Biene-*

star *Rural y sus Experiencias en Venezuela.* 1958. (Also in English)

_____, A. Fernández Yépez y Denise Dabrowski, *Programa de Crédito para el Mejoramiento de las Condiciones Económicas y Sociales de los Agricultores, Ganaderos y Pescadores del Estado Nueva Esparta.* 3d. ed. 1962.

Selección de Semillas de Maíz. Programa de Crédito Supervisado. 1965.

Supervisión y Control de Créditos. 2d. ed. 1964.

Zúñiga. José. L. *Análisis de los Datos Seleccionados de los Informes Mensuales de las Actividades del Programa de Crédito Supervisado.* 1965.

_____. *Anteproyecto de Instructivo para la Subrogación de Obligaciones en el Programa de Crédito Supervisado.* 1967.

_____. *Cursillos para Agrotécnicos de Crédito Supervisado del BAP.* 3d. ed. 1965.

_____. *Informe que Presenta la Comisión BAP-AID-CBR sobre el Desarrollo del Programa de Crédito Supervisado.* 1965.

_____. *Instrucciones para Llenar el Informe del Comité Ad Honorem y el del Agrotécnica.* 1967.

_____. *Instrucciones para Llenar el Informe de Progreso Familiar.* 2d. ed. 1964.

_____. *Instrucciones para Llenar el Informe de Supervisores de Grupo y el de Supervisores Zonales.* 1967.

_____. *Manual de Crédito Supervisado.* 3d. ed. 1964.

_____. *Manual de Crédito Supervisado del Banco Agrícola y Pecuario.* 1965.

_____. *Normas de Cobro.* 3d. ed. 1965.

_____. *Normas para la Planificación a Mediano y Largo Plazo en el Banco Agrícola y Pecuario.* 1967.

_____. *Supervisión y Control de Créditos.* 1967.

_____. *Trabajos para la II ª Convención del Banco Agrícola y Pecuario, Valencia 9-12 junio.* 1965.

Publications Related to Fruit Culture

Algunas Consideraciones Sobre la Siembra de Arboles Frutales. 1962.

Análisis Químico de Algunas Frutas de Importancia Comercial. 1962.

Araque, Ricardo. *Anteproyecto para un Plan Frutícola Nacional.* 1961.

_____. *Aspectos Económicos de la Fruticultura en Venezuela.* 1964.

_____. *Consideraciones Sobre la Necesidad de Desarrollar el Plan Frutícola en Escala Nacional.* 1961.

_____. *Cosecha y Mercadeo de Frutales.* 1966.

_____. *Posibilidades Frutícolas de la Isla de Margarita.* 1962.

_____. *Posibilidades Frutícolas de la Región Nororiental.* 1967.

_____. *Producción de Frutales en Venezuela.* VII° Reunión Latinoamericana de Fitotécnica (ALAF). 1967.

_____. *Producción de Frutas Tropicales en Venezuela.* 2d. ed. 1964.

_____. *Programa del Plan Frutícola de Yaracuy.* 2d. ed. 1965.

_____. *Recomendaciones Sobre el Cultivo de la Guanábana.* 2d. ed. 1965.

_____. *Situación Actual de Nuestra Fruticultura.* Segunda Asamblea Anual de la Asociación Nacional de Fruticultores, 3 a 5 de Mayo 1966.

_____. *Sugerencias para la Organización de un Servicio de Control de las Plagas de Frutales.* Semi-

247

nario de Entomología Agrícola.
1966.

―――――― y E. Stolk. Consideraciones Acerca del Desarrollo de la Fruticultura en Venezuela. 2d. ed. 1964.

―――――――, ―――――――. Estimación de Costos de Producción de los Principales Frutales que se Cultivan en Venezuela. 4th ed. 1966.

Bibliografía de Fruticultura. 1962.

Castillo, J. J. y C. Thomas. El Cultivo del Maracuyá. 3d. ed. 1967.

La Cooperativa Agrícola y de Consumo para la Siembra y Explotación de Parchita Maracuyá. 1962.

Costos Estimados para el Desarrollo de una Plantación de Cítricos hasta los Cuatro Años. 1962.

El Cultivo de Frutales como Medio de Conservación, Mejor Aprovechamiento y Valorización de los Suelos. 1962.

Documento Constitutivo del Fondo de Desarrollo Frutícola. 2d. ed. 1966.

Estimación de Costos para la Fundación de Una Hectárea Mecanizada de Cítricos. 1963.

Herrera Klindt, Bernardo. Recomendaciones para el Cultivo del Melón, Patilla, Pepino, Zanahoria y Berenjena. 1967.

Ochoa, J. M. Informe para el Plan Frutícola del Consejo de Bienestar Rural—Sistema de Riego para el Vivero de Pueblo Hondo, Estado Táchira. 1966.

Paolini, L. R. Realizaciones del Plan Frutícola de Los Andes. 1964.

Perspectivas de la Industria Frutícola en el Estado Zulia. 1964.

El Plan Frutícola Nacional Preparado para el Ministerio de Agricultura y Cría por el Consejo de Bienestar Rural. 3d. ed. 1966.

I Seminario Nacional de Fruticultura —Acta Final 1962.

Proyecto de Acuerdo para el Establecimiento de Normas de Colaboración entre el MAC, el BAP y el CBR para la Ejecución del Plan Frutícola Nacional. 2d. ed. 1966.

Proyecto de Documento Constitutivo del Fondo de Desarrollo Frutícola. 1964.

Manuals, Guides, Instructions and Other Miscellaneous Publications

Aprovechamiento de las Vertientes del Motatán y sus Aspectos más Relevantes. 1966.

Balances Hidrológicos y Aprovechamiento de las Aguas en la Vertiente del Cojedes. 1966.

Bases para la Formación de una Política Nacional de Recursos Naturales Renovables. 1962.

Calatrava, Alonso. "Generalidades Sobre el Seguro Agrícola." (Separata del Estudio: El Seguro Agrícola y su Institución en Venezuela.) 1963.

Christ, Harold y Antonio Pérez G. Método de Extensión Agrícola. 1953.

Consideraciones sobre la Ganadería Caprina en el Estado Lara y Recomendaciones para su Mejoramiento. 1964.

Croy, Otto C. Análisis del Progreso Logrado en la Extension Agrícola en Venezuela. 1959.

IV Convención Nacional de Peritos Agropecuarios, Resoluciones y Acuerdos. 1961.

Cuenca Turbio-Cojedes. Síntesis Preliminar de los Estudios Hidrológicos. 1965.

Demostraciones de Resultados de Maíz. 1961.

Desarrollo Agrícola y Reforma Agraria. Informe que el Ministerio de Agricultura y Cría presenta ante la VII Convención de Gobernadores. 1963.

Encuesta sobre las Condiciones Prevalecientes en el Asentamiento Campesino de La Caripucha, Estado Portuguesa. 1962.

Encuesta Nacional de Ingresos y Gastos Familiares en Venezuela. 2d. ed. 1964.

Encuesta Socioeconómica para el Programa de Adiestramiento Agropecuario Popular. 1966.

Espey, Lawrence V. *Manual para el Planeamiento de Carreteras de Penetración Agrícola.* 1952.

Estudios de Reconocimiento de Recursos Agrícolas y Forestales para la América Latina. 2d. ed. 1963. (also in English)

Explosives Handbook. 1950.

Farmer, Wilfred L. *Manual para Uso de los Instructores en los Centros de Entrenamiento Agrícola.* 1953.

——————— y Colaboradores. *Manual para el Adiestramiento en Maquinaria Agrícola.* 1960.

French, M. H. *Situación de los Pastos de la Ganadería Venezolana.* 1960.

La Función de Extensión Dentro del Desarrollo Nacional VII Convención Nacional de Peritos Agropecuarios. 1966.

Giménez Landínez, Victor M. *Objectives and Requirements of an Integral Agrarian Reform.* 1962.

Gondelles, Ricardo. *Plan Directivo del Programa de Ordenación de Cuencas Hidrográficas.* 2d. ed. 1964.

Heaton, Louis E. *Analyzing a Farm Business.* 1952.

Heilman, John. *Entreamiento de Tractoristas.* 1949.

——————— . *Manual de Operaciones Agrícolas.* 1960.

Herrera Aldaña, Bernardo. *Necesidad de Racionalizar la Explotación de Ganado Caprino como Defensa de los Recursos Naturales Renovables.* 1962.

Hidrógrafos Sintéticos de las Zonas Aridas Adyacentes a Barquisimento, Quebradas Ruezga y Mamón. 1966.

Instituto Agrario Nacional. *Organización del Departamento de Extensión Agrícola.* 1959.

Instrucciones para el Programa de Ensayo con Fertilizantes y Análisis de Suelos. 1952.

Investigaciones sobre la Economía Agrícola y su Aplicación a los Problemas del Campo Venezolano. 1952.

Jiménez, César. *Investigación de Mercados y Mercadeo en los Estados Lara y Yaracuy.* 1963.

——————— . *Investigación de Mercados y Mercadeo de Productos Agropecuarios en Aragua y Carabobo.* 1963.

——————— y Walter Güdel. *Factibilidad y Diseño de un Mercado Terminal de Productos Agropecuarios y Pesqueros en Maracaibo:* Informes I y II. 1964.

Labarthe, Enrique. *El Servicio de Extensión Agrícola en Venezuela.* 1957.

Law, Howard E. *Ensayos sobre el Uso de Abonos Químicos.* 1952.

León, Carlos. *Segundo Cursillo de Mecanización Menor para Personal de Tropas.* 1964.

Manejo de Tierras Agrícolas y Pastorales. 1966.

Marr, James C. *Conferencias sobre Riego y Avenamiento.* 1959.

Material Didáctico sobre Extensión Agrícola. 1956.

La Mecanización Menor en Función de Reforma Agraria. 1964.

Mecanización Menor, Recurso Básico de la Reforma Agraria. 1961.

249

Methodology for Economic Studies in the Cojedes and Motatán Watersheds of Venezuela. 1966.

Mondolfi, Edgardo. *Alimentación y Manejo de las Vacas Lecheras en los Potreros.* Primeras Jornadas Agropecuarias de la Sociedad Regional de Ganaderos de Occidente. 1965.

_____. *La Fauna Silvestre como Recurso Económico.* 1962.

Morrison, Frank B. *Productor de Leche, Aumente sus Ganancias con Silos de Trinchera.* 1954.

Nelson, Charles F. *Ensayo sobre el Cultivo del Sorgo Granífero en Barinas—Proyecto MONACA.* Translated by Antonio Pons. 1967.

Neubauer, L. W. *Estudios Recientes sobre Construcción con Adobe.* 1952.

Observaciones al Anteproyecto de la Ley de Mercadeo Agrícola. 1966.

Observaciones al Anteproyecto del Reglamento de la Ley de Reforma Agraria. 1966.

Observaciones sobre la Ejecución de la Reforma Agraria en Venezuela. 1964.

Observaciones sobre Manejo de Pastos en los Llanos de Venezuela. 1959.

Observaciones sobre Manejo de Pastos en los Llanos de Venezuela. 1960.

Pardo S., Antonio y Martín Rivero. *Manual para el Adiestramiento en Mecanización Menor.* 1963.

Pérez Garcia, Antonio. *La Organización que Necesita Tener el Servicio de Extensión Agrícola para Facilitar su Función Educativa.* 1959.

_____ y Otto C. Croy. *Observaciones sobre Problemas, Preocupaciones, Necesidades, Sugerencias.* 1959.

Perspectivas para una Etapa de Prosecución de Actividades. Proyecto "Venezuela 1" de Fondo Especial de la ONU (Ríos Cojedes Superior y Motatán.) 1966.

Planeamiento de Cuencas Hidrográficas. Guías 1-10. 1965-66.

Planificación del Programa de Extensión. 1959.

Preparemos una Publicación. 1956.

I Asamblea Nacional de Conservación de Recursos Naturales Renovables—Bases y Organización. 1961.

Primera Reunión Latinoamericano de Producción Animal. Maracay 1966.

Procedimientos para Estudios de Evotranspiración. 1964.

Programa del Centro de Entrenamiento en Agricultura Mecanizada del CBR en Yaracuy. 1954. (Also in English)

Programa Cooperativo de Investigaciones. 1963.

Programa Experimental de Forrajes para el Oriente de la Guayana. 1961.

Programa para la Preparación de Instructores de Talleres, Campo, Cría y Educación para el Hogar. 1966.

Programa de Trabajo para el Estado Nueva Esparta. 1964.

Programa de la Unidad Móvil de Adiestramiento Agropecuario Popular MAC - BAP - IAN - CBR - Fundación Creole. 1965.

Proposición para Efectuar un Estudio para la Evaluación del Desarrollo Agrícola en Venezuela a Solicitud de la Fundación Ford y Financiado por Ella. 1966.

Proposición para Establecer un Proyecto Piloto de Desarrollo Rural Integral en Dos Distritos del Estado Yaracuy. 1966.

Proyecto del Reglamento de la Ley de Reforma Agraria.

Proyecto de Trabajo para el Estudio sobre el Desarrollo Agrícola en Venezuela. 1966.

Relaciones Area, Frecuencia, Magnitud de Avenidas para los Ríos Sarare, Cojedes y Tirgua Utilizando el Método Grumbel-Powell. 1966.

Resoluciones y Acuerdos del Primer Seminario de Mejoramiento Profesional. 1964.

Rivero, Martín. *Cursos Teórico Prácticos sobre Mecanización Menor para Agentes de Extensión del MAC —Escuela Práctica de Agua Blanca.* 1962.

Rodríguez, J. *Proyecto Choro Soteldeño-Los Puertos.* 1967.

Seminario de Extensión Agrícola, 1959.

Seminario de Forrajes de las Primeras Jornadas Agronómicas. 1961.

Síntesis del Proyecto en Ejecución en los Ríos Turbio-Cojedes y Motatán. 1964.

Situación Económica de los Agricultores de Los Andes. 1966.

Studies in Rice Farming in Venezuela. 1963.

Study of the Supply and Demand of Twenty-Eight Agricultural Products in Venezuela, Progress Report No. 2. 1963.

Trujillo. B. "Vegetación." Separata del Volumen *Industria Animal y Vegetación* del Proyecto Venezuela 1 del Fondo Especial de la ONU (Rio Cojedes Superior y Motatan.) 1966.

Unidad Móvil de Divulgación del Programa de Adiestramiento Agropecuario Popular. 2d. ed. 1965.

Upper Cojedes and Motatán Watersheds—Notes on Water Pollution and Sewage Treatment.

Veihmeyer, Frank J. *Empleo de los Registros de Evaporación dados por los Atmómetros Blanco y Negro.* 1959.

—————————. *La Humedad de Suelo y su Aprovechamiento por las Plantas.* 1959.

5. Consejo Informativo de Educación Alimenticia (CIDEA); Instituto Nacional de Nutrición, Caracas, Venezuela—1948-1956.

CIDEA publications were designed to tell the Venezuelan people about better nutrition and health, with emphasis on graphic presentation. Titles numbered more than 50 and copies distributed probably exceeded 1,500,-000. Following is a general classification of the publications, with examples of titles.

(1) *Reports*
   Informe Anual, 1951-1952.
   Seis (6) Años de Progreso, 1948-1954.

(2) *Teachers' Guides or Manuals* (Part of a series prepared by the Instituto Nacional de Nutrición for use in the schools)
   El Mercado Libre. (Cuaderno 9). 1952.

   Lo Que Comemos en Casa. (Cuaderno 13). 1952.

(3) *Children's Stories* (With a health or nutrition theme)
   La Ratoncita Margarita
   Aventuras de Mediecito
   Titirifí, El Perrito de Circo
   Las Aventuras de Juancito Salud (series of ten comic books)

(4) *Pamphlets* (Explaining the relationship of good nutrition to health)
   Qué Es Alimentación?
   Tu Salud Depende de Una Alimentación Equilibrada
   No Le Tengas Miedo a Las Comidas Livianas
   Vida Larga Sana y Feliz

(5) *Pamphlets* (The advantages of different types of foods)
La Leche Alimenta Tanto Que Siempre Resulta Barata
Platos Criollos Sabrosos y Nutritivos
A Falta de Carne—Coma Huevos
Si No Hay Carne—Coma Pescado

(6) *Pamphlets* (one health subjects)
No Abra La Puerta a La Tuberculosis (Describes tuberculosis and its prevention)
Confesiones de Una Mosca (Flies as disease carriers)
Educación Higiénica del Niño (Simple rules for better health)
Anquilostomo (Hookworm and its control)

(7.) *Periodicals*
Annual pictorial kitchen calendars with recipes using local foods. Issued in 1952, 1953, 1954, 1955, 1956.
Monthly pamphlets of menus using local foods available at the time. Issued over a period of several years.

(8) *Testimonial Pamphlets* (On the importance of good nutrition)
La Vida de "Chico" Carrasquel (baseball hero)
Luis Sánchez "Diamante Negro" (Venezuelan bullfighter)
Carmen Guevara "Doña Bárbara" (lady automobile racing driver)

(9) *Leaflets* (Describing in simple terms protective and energy foods, vitamins and minerals)
Alimentos Protectores de Su Salud
Alimentos Constructores y Energéticos
Las Vitaminas y Los Minerales Son Imprescindibles Para Su Salud

6. Programa Interamericano de Información Popular (PIIP) San José, Costa Rica—1958-68

Adis Castro, Gonzalo, and Frederick B. Waisanen. *Attitudes Toward Mental Illness in a Socio-Economic Context.* San José, Costa Rica: Center for Psychological Research of the University of Costa Rica, 1965. (Also in Spanish)

——————, ——————. *Attitudes Toward Mental Illness: Some Socio-economic and Modernization Correlatives.* San José, Costa Rica, 1965.

——————, ——————. *Modernity and Tolerance in Relation to Attitudes Toward Mental Illness.* San José, Costa Rica: Center for Psychological Research of the University of Costa Rica, 1965. (Also in Spanish)

——————, ——————. *Place of Residence and Attitudes Toward Mental Illness.* San José, Costa Rica: Center for Psychological Research of the University of Costa Rica, 1965. (Also in Spanish)

Anderson, H. Calvert. *The ABC Communication Team.* (folder) Montevideo, Uruguay, 1966. (Also in Spanish)

——————. *Agricultural Communications in Latin America.* Paper prepared for delivery at the International Congress of Farm Writers, Montreal, Canada, June 21, 1967.

——————. *Agricultural Information in Southern Brazil: A Situation Study with Recommendations for Cooperative Training Programs.*

252

Montevideo, Uruguay, 1964. (Also in Portuguese)

—————. *Communications and Agrarian Reform.* Montevideo, Uruguay, 1964. (Also in Spanish)

—————. *Communications Training, A Chain Reaction.* Montevideo, Uruguay, 1965.

—————. *Creando Una Oficina de Información.* Montevideo, Uruguay, 1964.

—————. *Directorio de Servicios de Información: Argentina, Bolivia, Brasil, Paraguay, Perú y Uruguay.* Montevideo, Uruguay, 1963.

—————. *Establecimiento de Una Oficina Técnica de Información Agrícola.* La Paz, Bolivia: Ministerio de Agricultura, 1967.

—————. *Planificación y Presentación de Cursos Cortos de Comunicación.* Montevideo, Uruguay, 1966. (Also reprinted in English, 1967)

—————. (ed.) *Research in Action for the Economic Development of Uruguay.* Agricultural Research Center of the Ministry of Livestock and Agriculture of Uruguay. Translated by Yvonne Bourdette. Montevideo, Uruguay, 1967.

—————. *The Role of Communication in Agricultural Economic Development.* Montevideo, Uruguay, 1965.

————— y Carlos A. Prato Blume. *Manual de Operaciones para Una Oficina de Información Agrícola—* Partes I, II, III. Ministerio de Agricultura. Lima, Perú, 1964.

————— y Eduardo Pereira Brum. *Plan para Un Servicio de Información para el Centro de Investigaciones Agrícolas Alberto Boerger, La Estanzuela, Uruguay.* Montevideo, Uruguay, 1964.

Arce, Antonio M. *A Study of the Human and Institutional Resources in the Social Sciences and Communications Research in Selected Countries in Latin America.* San José, Costa Rica: Inter-American Institute of Agricultural Sciences, 1961. (Also in Spanish)

Arce, Eduardo Tironi. *Visión Panorámica de la Television Educativa.* Lima, Peru: Oficina Técnica de Información Agraria. Ministerio de Agricultura, 1965.

Bradt, H. Schuyler. *Agricultural Motion Picture Production and Distribution for Brazil.* Prepared for the U.S. International Cooperation Administration (a predecessor of the Agency for International Development), Rio de Janeiro, Brazil, 1959.

—————. *Investigación en Comunicaciones.* San José, Costa Rica, 1961.

—————. *Procedure for Setting up Rural Radio Programs.* Prepared for the U.S. International Cooperation Administration (a predecessor of the Agency for International Development), Minas Gerais, Brazil, 1959.

—————. *El Proceso de las Comunicaciones para Las Masas.* San José, Costa Rica, 1961.

—————. *Televisión para Programas de Información.* San José, Costa Rica, 1961.

Campañas Educativas. Producidas durante el Curso Básico de Adiestramiento en Comunicaciones. Montevideo, Uruguay, 1962.

Chile. Ministerio de Agricultura e Instituto Interamericano de Ciencias Agrícolas. *Seminario: El Papel de la Comunicación en el Desarrollo Económico.* Santiago, Miscelanea No. 11. Ed. Raúl E. Torres Ramos. 1965.

Comuniquémonos. Newsletter distributed bimonthly to communications specialists throughout Latin America, from Montevideo, Uruguay, 1964-67.

Costa Rica. Misión de Operaciones de los Estados Unidos. Administración de Cooperación Internacional y Instituto Interamericano de Ciencias Agrícolas. *Fotografía Educativa.* La edición y traducción de los artículos del inglés al español escritos por Mario M. Vázquez.

Deutschmann, Paul. *A Machine Simulation of Attitude Change in a Polarized Community.* San José, Costa Rica, 1962.

——————. *A Machine Simulation of Information Diffusion in a Small Community.* San José, Costa Rica, 1962.

——————. "The Mass Media in ai Underdeveloped Village," *Journalism Quarterly,* Vol. 40, No. 1— Winter 1963.

——————. *A Model for Machine Simulation of Information and Attitude Flow.* San José Costa Rica, 1962.

—————— and Orlando Fals-Borda. *Communication Among Colombian Peasants.* Monografías Sociológicas No. 14. Universidad Nacional de Colombia, 1962. (Also in Spanish)

——————, ——————. *Communication and Adoption Patterns in an Andean Village.* San José, Costa Rica: Universidad Nacional de Colombia, 1962.

——————, ——————. *Communication in an Andean Village.* Presented at the Convention of the Association for Education in Journalism, University of North Carolina, Chapel Hill, 1962. (Also in Spanish)

—————— and John T. McNelly. "Characteristics of Latin American Countries," *The American Behavioral Scientist,* Vol. 1, September 1964.

——————, ——————. *Reporte Preliminar sobre la Difusión y Adopción de Tecnicas Agrícolas en Saucio.* San José, Costa Rica, 1962.

——————, ——————. *El Uso de Los Medios de Comunicación Masiva en Dos Comunidades Latinoamericanas.* Presentado en el XIII Congreso Nacional de Sociología, Hermosillo, Sonora, México, 1962.

Deutschmann, Paul, and Alfredo Méndez. *Adoption of New Foods and Drugs in Cholena, A Preliminary Report.* San José, Costa Rica, 1962.

——————, ——————. *A Preliminary Report on Perception of Hot and Cold Foods in Two Villages.* San José, Costa Rica: Instituto de Nutrición de Centro América y Panamá, 1963.

——————, —————— and William Herzog. *Adoption of Drugs and Foods in Five Guatemalan Villages.* San José, Costa Rica: Instituto de Nutrición de Centro América y Panamá, 1967.

Díaz Bordenave, Juan, Antonio M. Arce and John T. McNelly. *Three Preliminary Bibliographies of Works Related to the Social Sciences in Latin America.* San José, Costa Rica, 1962. (English and Spanish in one publication)

—————— y Frederick B. Waisanen. *What is Communication Research?* San José, Costa Rica: Scientific Communication Service of the Inter-American Institute of Agricultural Sciences, 1965. (Also in Spanish)

Fonseca, Luiz, and William R. Lassey. *Comprehension and Meaning in Visual Communication among Illiterate, Low Literate and Higher Literate Individuals.* (preliminary report). San José, Costa Rica: Scientific Communication Service of the Inter-American Institute of Agricultural Sciences, 1964.

Impact Training. Montevideo, Uruguay, 1963.

Instituto Interamericano de Ciencias Agrícolas. *Como Escribir para Educar al Agricultor.* Resumen informativo del Curso Internacional de Comunicación Escrita. Montevideo, Uruguay, 1963.

——————. *Comunicación Escrita en Programas de Información Agrícola.* Montevideo, Uruguay, 1963.

——————. *Curso en Comunicaciones para Personal de Servicios de Información.* (Under contract between the Institute and the U.S. Agency for International Development.) Montevideo, Uruguay, 1962.

Instituto Nacional de Tecnología Agropecuario. *Estudio de la Prensa del Interior de la República Argentina.* Buenos Aires, Argentina, 1966. (Also profile in English)

Inter-American Institute of Agricultural Sciences. *Better Communicators: Report of Basic Course in Communications.* Montevideo, Uruguay, 1962. (Also in Spanish)

Manual de Comunicaciones. San José, Costa Rica, 1962.

McNelly, John T., and Paul Deutschmann. "Media Use and Socioeconomic Status in a Latin American Capital," *Gazette: International Journal of Communication Studies,* Vol. IX, No. 1, 1963.

——————. and Eugenio Fonseca. "Media Use and Political Interest at the University of Costa Rica," *Journal Quarterly,* Spring 1964.

——————. and Augusto Torres. *A Study of the Use of the Mass Media and Knowledge of Current Affairs as Related to Socioeconomic Status*

in San José, Costa Rica. Paper presented at the Convention of the Association for Education in Journalism, University of North Carolina, Chapel Hill, 1962.

——————. El Uso de Los Medios de Comunicación en Una Capital Latinoamericana. San José, Costa Rica, 1963.

Méndez, Alfredo, and Frederick B. Waisanen. *Some Correlates of Functional Literacy.* Instituto de Nutrición de Centro América y Panamá. Paper prepared for the Inter-American Congress of Psychology, Miami, 1964. (Also in Spanish)

Perú. Ministerio de Agricultura. Oficina Técnica de Información Agraria. *Manual de Operaciones.* Basado en *Manual de Operaciones para una Oficina de Información Agrícola* por H. Calvert Anderson (PIIP) y Carlos A. Prato Blume (Ministerio de Agricultura) Lima, Perú, 1964.

Rogers, Everett M. "Mass Media Exposure and Modernization among Colombian Peasants," *Public Opinion Quarterly,* Winter, 1965-66.

——————. and Johannes C. van Es. *Opinion Leadership in Traditional and Modern Colombian Communities.* East Lansing, Michigan: Michigan State University. 1964.

——————. and William Herzog. "Functional Literacy Among Colombian Peasants," *Economic Development and Cultural Change,* January 1966.

——————. and Wicky L. Meynen. "Communication Sources for 2, 4-D Weed Spray Among Colombian Peasants," *Rural Sociology,* June 1965.

——————. and Ralph E. Neill. *Achievement Motivation Among Colombian Indians.* East Lansing,

255

Michigan: Michigan State University, 1966.

Sánchez, Rodrigo. *Objectivos y Actividades del Programa Interamericano de Información Popular.* San José, Costa Rica, 1965.

————. *Situación de la Documentación y Comunicación en Centro América.* San José, Costa Rica, 1965.

Twelve Months' Report (1958-1959). San José, Costa Rica.

Uruguay. Ministerio de Ganadería y Agricultura. Centro Nacional de Extensión Agropecuaria. Centro de Investigaciones Agrícolas Alberto Boerger. *La Prensa del Interior del Uruguay.* Montevideo, Uruguay, 1966. (Also English supplement)

Waisanen, Frederick B. *Aspects of the Adoption Process.* San José, Costa Rica, 1963.

————. *Change Orientation and the Adoption Process.* San José, Costa Rica, 1964. (Also in Spanish)

————. *Communication Flow to Traditional Social Systems.* San José, Costa Rica, 1963.

————. *Security, Insecurity and the Process of Socio-economic Development.* San José, Costa Rica, 1963. (Also in Spanish)

————. *Social Science: Problems and Prospects.* San José, Costa Rica, 1963. (Also in Spanish)

————. *Some Perspectives for Research in Communication and Development.* San José, Costa Rica, 1965.

————. *Some Theoretical Convergencies in the Social Psychology of Alienation.* San José, Costa Rica, 1963.

————. "Stability, Alienation and Change," *Sociological Quarterly,* Vol. 4, No. 1, Winter 1963.

————. *A Symbolic Interactionistic Approach to Communication and Change.* San José, Costa Rica, 1963.

———— and Jerome T. Durlak. *The Impact of Communication on Rural Development: An Investigation in Costa Rica.* A final report submitted in accordance with UNESCO contract. East Lansing: Michigan State University, 1967.

7. Programa Interamericano para la Juventud Rural (PIJR) San José, Costa Rica 1960-68.

Announcement of PIJR Awards. (pamphlet) San José, Costa Rica, 1967. (Also in Spanish)

Boletín Informativo Trimestral Juventud Rural. San José, Costa Rica, 1967.

Boletín Informativo Trimestral Juventud Rural. San José, Costa Rica, 1966.

Costa Rica. Ministerio de Agricultura y Ganadería. Servicio de Extensión. *Programa Experimental de Premios, Estímulos e Intercambio.* San José, 1961.

Flamm, Gerald. *Your Publicity Program.* San José, Costa Rica, 1965. (Also in Spanish, revised 1967)

Ford Motor Company. *Juventud Rural.* (bulletins issued quarterly, also in English and Portuguese). Dearborn, Michigan, 1962, 1963, 1964.

————. *Rural Youth in the Americas.* San José, Costa Rica, 1965.

Guía Para Líderes Juveniles. Translation of "Guide for Junior Leaders," *National 4-H News.* San José, Costa Rica, 1967.

Informe del Cuarto Seminario Inter-americano de Líderes de Juventudes Rurales (IFYE). San José, Costa Rica, 1964.

Informe de la IV Reunión Nacional de Líderes Estatales de Clubes 4-S. Rio de Janeiro, Brazil, 1963.

Informe del Seminario Interamericano de Líderes de Juventudes Rurales (IFYE). San José, Costa Rica, 1962.

Informe del Seminario Interamericano de Líderes de Juventudes Rurales (IFYE). San José, Costa Rica, 1961.

Informe de la III Reunión Nacional de Líderes Estatales de Clubes 4-S. Rio de Janeiro, Brazil, 1962.

Informe del Tercer Seminario Inter-americano de Líderes de Juventudes Rurales (IFYE). San José, Costa Rica, 1963.

Instituto Interamericano de Ciencias Agrícolas. *Memoria del X Curso Internacional de Extensión Agrícola*. San José, Costa Rica, 1962.

——————. *Taller Educativo Inter-americano Sobre Programas de Juventudes Rurales*. Turrialba, Costa Rica, 1960.

Inter-American Institute of Agricultural Sciences. *Report of the Inter-American Rural Youth Program Advisory Meeting*. San José, Costa Rica, 1961. (Also in Spanish)

Jones, Earl. *A Study of Rural Youth Programs in The Americas (except United States and Canada)*. Ph.D. thesis submitted to Montana State College. Publication pre-prepared under provisions of contract between the Inter-American Institute of Agricultural Sciences and the U.S. Agency for International Development. Turrialba, Costa Rica, 1962.

——————. *Summary of a Study of Rural Youth Programs in the Amer-icas*. San José, Costa Rica, 1962. (Also in Spanish and Portuguese)

——————, Edgar Arias, Marina Chacón, y Virginia Solano. *Fundamentos del Trabajo con Juventudes Rurales*. San José, Costa Rica, 1962.

——————, Howard Law and Manuel Valverde. *Preliminary Report: Study of the Rural Youth Programs in the Americas*. Inter-American Institute of Agricultural Sciences. San José, Costa Rica, 1961. (Also in Spanish)

Make the Best Better. Report of the 1966 Inter-American Rural Youth Leaders' Conference, Rio de Janeiro, Brazil. San José, Costa Rica, 1966. (Also in Spanish and Portuguese)

Métodos de Enseñanza. Translation. San José, Costa Rica, 1967.

National Corn Production Contest in Venezuela. San José, Costa Rica, 1966. (English and Spanish in one publication)

National 4-H Club Foundation. *VI Seminario Interamericano de Líderes de Juventudes Rurales*. San José y Turrialba, Costa Rica, 1966.

Perú. Ministerio de Agricultura. Instituto de Reforma y Promoción Agraria. *II Intercambio Educacional de Juventudes Rurales y V Concurso Nacional de Clubes Agrícolas Juveniles Perú*. Lima, 1964.

Proceedings of the 1964 Inter-American Rural Youth Leaders' Conference. (Three Parts). San José, Costa Rica, 1964. (Also in Spanish and Portuguese)

Report of the First Inter-American Rural Youth Club Congress. Rio de Janeiro, Brazil, 1966. (Also in Spanish)

Report—First Inter-American Seminar for Executive Secretaries (Mana-

gers) *of National Support Entities in Colombia.* San José, Costa Rica, 1967. (Also in Spanish)
Report—Inter-American Rural Youth Club Congress in Panamá. San José, Costa Rica, 1967. (Also in Spanish)
Report of the Inter-American Rural Youth Technical Committee Meet- ing. San José, Costa Rica, 1962. (Also in Spanish)
Standard Oil Company (N.J.) *Artículos Sobre Juventudes Rurales Publicados en Extensión en las Américas.* San José, Costa Rica, 1967.
What is PIJR? (pamphlet) San José, Costa Rica, 1967. (Also in Spanish)

8. Programa Interamericano para el Desarrollo Rural (PIDR), San José, Costa Rica 1962-68.

Brazil. Estado de Minas Gerais. Secretário da Agricultura. *Colonization Plan: Land Reform Program of the State of Minas Gerais.* Belo Horizonte, 1961.

Brazilian National Research Council. *Coordinated Research Program in Campo Cerrado Areas of Brazil.* Translated by Walter Crawford and Lawrence Witt. Rio de Janeiro, 1966. (Also in Portuguese)

Crawford, Walter L. *Colonization in Paraguay.* (a confidential report) Asunción, 1964.

——————. *Producción y Crédito Agrícola en el Paraguay.* Asunción, 1963. (Also in English)

—————— and others. *Preliminary Report of the Planalto Pre-Survey Group.* Prepared under contract for the U.S. Agency for International Development. Rio de Janeiro, Brazil, 1963.

——————, ——————. *Survey of the Agricultural Potential of the Central Plateau of Brazil.* Prepared under contract for the U.S. Agency for International Development. Rio de Janeiro, Brazil, 1963. (Also in Portuguese)

Fundação Antunes. *Possibilidades de Desenvolvimento Rural Nos Municípios de Campos e São João da Barra.* (Preliminary Study). Rio de Janeiro, Brazil, 1965.

Heaton, Louis E., Walter L. Crawford and John R. Camp. *Rural Development in Latin America.* New York, 1963.

—————— and Victor PraSisto. *Agricultural Production Situation and Program Needs in Venezuela.* Caracas, 1963.

Montero, Emilio. *Colonization Plan of the State of Minas Gerais, Brazil: Size of Economic Unit in Jaíba, Minas Gerais.* Belo Horizonte, Minas Gerais: Inter-American Institute of Agricultural Sciences, 1962.

Tosi, Jr., Joseph A. *Reconnaissance Ecological and Forest Survey of the Jaíba Colonization Area, State of Minas Gerais, Brazil.* Belo Horizonte, Minas Gerais: Inter-American Institute of Agricultural Sciences, 1962.

APPENDIX IV

Rural Youth Clubs in the Hemisphere

	Ages	Members	Clubs	Founded
ARGENTINA				

4-A Clubs (Clubes 4-A)   10-21   8,000   386   1954

Acción—action, Adiestramiento—training, Amistad—friendship, Ayuda —help.

* Asociación Pro-Clubes 4-A (Association for 4-A Clubs)

4-M Rural Youth Clubs (Clubes Rurales Juveniles 4-M)
                    10-25

Mente—mind, Mano—hand, Misión—mission, Mérito—merit.

BOLIVIA

4-S Clubs (Clubes 4-S)   10-25   4,896   337   1947

Saber—knowledge, Sentir—feeling, Servir—service, Ser—to be.

* Fundación Pro-Clubes 4-S de Bolivia (Association for 4-S Clubs of Bolivia)

BRAZIL

4-S Clubs (Clubes 4-S)   10-21   21,478   997   1952

Saúde—health, Saber—knowledge, Sentir—feeling, Servir—service

* Comitê Nacional de Clubes 4-S (National 4-S Clubs Committee)

CHILE

4-C Rural Youth Clubs (Clubes Agrícolas Juveniles 4-C)
                    12-25   2,725   109   1952

Cabeza—head, Corazón—heart, Capacidad—ability, Cooperación—co-operation.

* Junta Nacional Pro-Desarrollo de la Juventud Agrícola de Chile (National Council for the Development of Rural Youth of Chile)

COLOMBIA

4-S Clubs (Clubes 4-S)   10-21   12,238   779   1954

Saber—knowledge, Sentimiento—feeling, Servicio—service, Salud—health.

* Asociación Nacional Pro-Clubes 4-S de Colombia (National Association for 4-S Clubs of Colombia)

---

* National Private Support Group

COSTA RICA
4-S Clubs (Clubes 4-S)   10-21   4,266   301   1949
Salud—health, Saber—knowledge, Sentimiento—feeling, Servicio—service.
* Fundación Nacional de Clubes 4-S (National 4-S Club Foundation)

DOMINICAN REPUBLIC
5-D Clubs (Clubes 5-D)   10-20   1,200   54   1962
Dios—God, Dignidad—dignity, Deber—duty, Derecho—human rights, Dominicano—Dominican.
* Comité Pro-Desarrollo de la Juventud 5-D (Committee for Development of 5-D Youth)

ECUADOR
4-F Clubs (Clubes 4-F)   10-20   3,198   120   1954
Fe—faith, Fecundidad—fruitfulness, Fortaleza—strength, Felicidad—happiness.
* Fundación Nacional 4-F (National 4-F Foundation)

EL SALVADOR
4-C Clubs (Clubes 4-C)   10-20   8,101   333   1957
Cabeza—head, Corazón—heart, Conocimiento—knowledge, Cooperación—cooperation.
* Comité Nacional de Clubes 4-C (National 4-C Clubs Committee)

GUATEMALA
4-S Agricultural Youth Clubs (Clubes Agrícolas Juveniles 4-S)
                 9-20   4,000   182   1957
Saber—knowledge, Salud—health, Sentir—feeling, Servir—service
* Consejo Nacional de Clubes 4-S (National 4-S Club Council)

GUYANA
4-H   10-21   3,000   58
Young Farmers' Club   16-35   300   13   1963

HAITI
4-C   10-21   5,095   392   1938
Cerveau—head, Coeur—heart, Corps—body, Cooperation—cooperation
* Comité National Haïtien de Jeunesse Rurale (National Youth Committee)

JAMAICA
4-H Clubs   10-21   25,698   609   1940
* Central Managing Committee of 4-H Clubs

MARTINIQUE
Catholic Rural Youth Movement (Mouvement Rural de la Jeunesse Catholique)   10-21   215   17   1939
* Mouvement Rural de la Jeunesse Catholique (Catholic Rural Youth Movement)

MEXICO

Rural Youth Clubs of Mexico (Clubes Juveniles Rurales de México)

10-18	9,380	432	1954

* Comité de Ayuda a la Juventud Rural, Asociación Pro Entendimiento Internacional (Rural Youth Assistance Committee, Association for International Understanding).

NICARAGUA

4-S Clubs (Clubes 4-S)

Junior—10-15
Senior—16-21   815   46   1957

Sentimiento—feeling, Salud—health, Saber—knowledge, Servicio—service.

*Comité Nacional 4-S (National 4-S Committee)

PANAMA

4-S Clubs (Clubes 4-S)   9-20   4,066   213   1953

Saber—knowledge, Sentimiento—feeling, Servicio—service, Salud—health.

* Patronato Nacional de los Clubes 4-S. (National Association of 4-S Clubs)

PARAGUAY

4-C Rural Youth Clubs (Clubes Agrarios Juveniles 4-C)

10-17
17-25   6,843   289   1953

Cabeza—head, Corazón—heart, Capacidad—ability, Cooperación—cooperation.

* Asociación Pro-Desarrollo de los Clubes Agrarios Juveniles 4-C del Paraguay (Association for the Development of 4-C Rural Youth Clubs of Paraguay.)

PERU

Agricultural Youth Clubs of Peru (Clubes Agrícolas Juveniles Perú)

9-21   12,913   724   1950

Caracter—character, Acción—action, Juicio—judgment, Patria—country.

* Asociación Nacional Clubes Agrícolas Juveniles Perú (National CAJP Association)

SURINAM

4-H   9-20   437   30   1957

URUGUAY

Agrarian Youth Movement (Movimiento de la Juventud Agraria)

8-25   7,000   123   1945

* Comisión Nacional de Apoyo al MJA (National Commission to Support the MJA)

	Ages	*Members*	*Clubs*	*Founded*
VENEZUELA				
5-V Clubs (Clubes 5-V)	8-18	13,252	740	1938

Valor—bravery, Vigor—strength, Verdad—truth, Vergüenza—conscience, Venezuela.

* Asociación Civil Pro-Clubes 5-V (Civil Association for 5-V Clubs)

	Ages	*Members*	*Clubs*	*Founded*
WEST INDIES				
Barbados—*4-H Clubs*	10-21	579	23	1963
* Barbados 4-H Council				
Grenada—*4-H Clubs*	10-21	750	38	1959
St. Kitts—*4-H Programme*	12-21	500	19	1960
St. Lucia—*Young Farmers Club*	15-30	50	1	1940
* St. Lucia National Youth Council				
St. Vincent—*4-H Club Movement*	10-21	570	13	1961
* 4-H Advisory Council.				

Source: National 4-H Club Foundation. *World Atlas of 4-H and Similar Rural Youth Educational Programs.* 2d. ed. Compiled and Edited by Theodore Hutchcroft. pp. 11-17. Washington, D.C., 1966.

APPENDIX V

Inter-American Rural Youth Committee

José Figueres Ferrer
Former President of Costa Rica
San José, Costa Rica

Orville L. Freeman
Secretary of Agriculture
Washington, D. C., U.S.A.

Arnaldo Gabaldón
Former Minister of Health and
Social Assistance
Caracas, Venezuela

Gabriel González Videla
Former President of Chile
Santiago, Chile

Juscelino Kubitschek
Former President of Brazil
Rio de Janeiro, Brazil

Galo Plazo Lasso
Secretary General of the Organiza-
tion of American States and Former
President of Ecuador
Washington, D. C., U.S.A.

Nelson A. Rockefeller
Governor of the State of New York
Albany, New York, U.S.A.

Armando Samper, Director General
Inter-American Institute of Agricul-
tural Sciences of the OAS
San José, Costa Rica

Joâo Gonçalves de Souza, Director
Department of Technical Coopera-
tion
Pan American Union
Washington, D. C., U.S.A.

Inter-American Rural Youth Technical Committee

Norberto A. R. Reichart, Under Secretary of Agriculture and Livestock
Secretariat of Agriculture and Livestock
Buenos Aires, Argentina

Joâo Napoleão de Andrade, President
Brazilian Rural Credit and
Assistance Association (ABCAR)
Rio de Janeiro, Brazil

Roberto Celis
San Salvador, El Salvador

Wilmer Gullette, President
Association for International Under-
standing
Mexico, D.F., Mexico

Nicolás de Mendiburu, Manager[1]
National Association of Rural
Youth Clubs of Peru
Lima, Peru

Francisco Esculies, President
Association for the Development of
4-C Rural Youth Clubs of Paraguay
Asunción, Paraguay

Alfredo L. Weiss, President
Agrarian Youth Movement
Montevideo, Uruguay

Kenneth H. Anderson
Associate Director
National 4-H Service Committee
Chicago, Illinois, U.S.A.

263

Edgar Mata Q.
　Regional Coordinator PIJR
　Maracay, Venezuela

Antonio Pérez-García
　FAO Extensionist
　United Nations
　Mexico, D.F., Mexico

Grant A. Shrum, Director
　National 4-H Club Foundation
　Washington, D. C., U.S.A.

Mylo S. Downey, Director[2]
　4-H and Youth Development
　Federal Extension Service
　U.S. Department of Agriculture
　Washington, D. C., U.S.A.

Dean Vaughn, Director
　4-H and Youth Development
　Federal Extension Service
　U.S. Department of Agriculture
　Washington, D. C., U.S.A.

─────────

[1] Deceased 1964.
[2] Until retirement 1967.

APPENDIX VI

CAR Organizations in Brazil

ABCAR	Associação Brasileira de Crédito e Assistência, Rural, Rio de Janeiro, Guanabara
ACAR	Associação de Crédito e Assistência Rural, Belo Horizonte, Minas Gerais
ACARES	Associação de Crédito e Assistência Rural do Espírito Santo, Vitória, Espírito Santo
ACARESC	Associação de Crédito e Assistência Rural do Estado de Santa Catarina, Florianópolis, Santa Catarina
ACAR-GOIÁS	Associação de Crédito e Assistência Rural do Estado de Goiás, Goiânia, Goiás
ACAR-MARANHÃO	Associação de Crédito e Assistência Rural do Estado do Maranhão, São Luiz, Maranhão
ACARMAT	Associação de Crédito e Assistência Rural do Estado de Mato Grosso, Cuiabá, Mato Grosso
ACARPA	Associação de Crédito e Assistência Rural do Paraná, Curitiba, Paraná
ACAR-RJ	Associação de Crédito e Assistência Rural do Estado do Rio de Janeiro, Niterói, Rio de Janeiro
ANCAR-ALAGOAS	Associação Nordestina de Crédito e Assistência Rural do Estado de Alagoas, Maceió, Alagoas
ANCARBA	Associação Nordestina de Crédito e Assistência Rural do Estado da Bahia, Salvador, Bahia
ANCAR-CEARÁ	Associação Nordestina de Crédito e Assistência Rural do Estado do Ceará, Fortaleza, Ceará
ANCAR-PARAÍBA	Associação Nordestina de Crédito e Assistência Rural do Estado da Paraíba, João Pessoa, Paraíba
ANCARPE	Associação Nordestina de Crédito e Assistência Rural do Estado de Pernambuco, Recife, Pernambuco
ANCAR-RN	Associação Nordestina de Crédito e Assistência Rural do Estado do Rio Grande do Norte, Natal, Rio Grande do Norte

| ANCARSE | Associação Nordestina de Crédito e Assistência Rural do Estado de Sergipe, Aracajú, Sergipe |
| ASCAR | Associação Sulina de Crédito e Assistência Rural, Pôrto Alegre, Rio Grande do Sul |

APPENDIX VII

Contributors to AIA
1946-1968

Chase Manhattan Bank Foundation
Creole Petroleum Corp.
Gerald R. Flamm
Ford Motor Co.
Hemisphere Films, Inc.
IBM do Brasil, Indústria, Máquinas e Serviços Ltda.
IBM World Trade Corp.
Indústria e Comércio de Minérios S.A.
International Basic Economy Corp.
International Minerals & Chemical Corp.
International Petroleum Company, Ltd.
Johnson Foundation
R. M. Laverty, Sr.
Lawrence H. Levy
Abby R. Mauzé
Mene Grande Oil Company, C.A.
Milbank Memorial Fund

Pan American-Grace Airways, Inc.
Pan American World Airways
Price Waterhouse & Co.
Price Waterhouse Peat & Co.
Rockefeller Brothers Fund
David Rockefeller
David Rockefeller, Jr.
John D. Rockefeller, Jr.
John D. Rockefeller 3rd
Laurance S. Rockefeller
Nelson A. Rockefeller
Rodman C. Rockefeller
Winthrop Rockefeller
Sears-Roebuck Foundation
Shell Caribbean Petroleum Company, Inc.
Socony-Vacuum Oil Company, Inc.
Sorg Printing Co.
Standard Oil Co. (New Jersey)
Mr. & Mrs. William J. Strawbridge, Jr.

NOTE: In addition to the contributors listed above, the following individuals, corporations and foundations made contributions to AIA for the IRI program during the period it was a division of AIA (1957-1963):

Contributors to AIA for IRI 1957-1963

Amaral, Machado & Cia, Ltda.
Anderson Clayton & Cia., Ltda.
Banco do Comércio e Indústria de São Paulo
Climax Molybdenum Co.
Companhia Industrial e Administrativa S. Francisco
Companhia Itaú de Fertilizantes
Companhia Paulista de Adubos

Companhia Rhodia Brasileira
Companhia de Superfosfatos e Produtos Químicos
Copas S.A.
Cotton Association
Elekeiroz Produtos Químicos
Esso Brasileira de Petroleo S.A.
Esteve Irmãos S.A. Comércio e Indústria

267

Fazenda Alvorada
Fazenda Santa Tereza
Fazenda Ubatuba
Filibra Produtas Quimicas Ltda.
Ford Foundation
Frigorifico Anglo S.A.
Gesso Nacional Tapuyo Ltda.
Indústrias Reunidas F. Matarazzo S.A.
Manah S.A. Comércio e Indústria
    Adubos e Rações
McFadden & Cia., Ltda.
Moinho Sta. Francisca S.A. Indústrias
    Gerais
Olin Mathieson Chemical Corp.
Pfizer Corporation do Brazil S.A.

Potash Export Association, Inc.
Produtos Guarany S.A.
Quimbrasil Química Industrial Brasi-
    leira S.A.
Refinações de Milho Brasil
Sanbra Sociedade Algodoeira do Nor-
    deste Brasileira S.A.
Sigurd W. Schindler
Sociedade Brasileira de Participações e
    Financiamento Sofibraz
Stauffer Chemical Co.
Sulphur Institute
United Nations Techinol
Volkart Irmãos Ltda.
James V. Zucchi

AIA Program Expenditures[1]
1946-1968

BRAZIL

Demonstration, training and experimental programs (1946-51)	63,557
ACAR, ABCAR and related activities (1948-63)	1,387,442
IRI program (1957-63)	2,029,820
	3,480,819

VENEZUELA

Inter-American Institute of Agricultural Sciences (1947-52)	189,861
Program planning (1949-53, 1954)	20,973
CIDEA (1948-56)	756,436
CBR (1948-68)	2,988,476
Vocational teacher training (1952-57)	311,484
Direct grants and miscellaneous projects (1948, '49, '51, '52, '55, '56)	107,525
IRI program (1951-53)	140,000
	4,514,755

INTER-AMERICAN PROGRAMS

Information Program (1959-68)	1,402,020
Rural Youth Program (1960-67)	1,015,983
Rural Development Program (1962-68)	640,548
	3,058,551

OTHER PROGRAMS

Indian Cooperative Union Ltd. (1951-57)	102,146
Grants to other non-profit organizations (1953-54)	63,000
Chile—"Plan Victoria" rural education (1962-66)	525,864
	691,010
	11,745,135

[1] Fixed assets not included.

Source: Price Waterhouse & Co. reports.

APPENDIX IX

Members of the Board of Directors and Officers 1968

DIRECTORS

LOUISE A. BOYER

BERENT FRIELE

WALLACE K. HARRISON

JOHN E. LOCKWOOD

LAWRENCE H. LEVY

ARTHUR T. PROUDFIT

NELSON A. ROCKEFELLER

RODMAN C. ROCKEFELLER

OFFICERS

President	WALLACE K. HARRISON
Senior Vice President	BERENT FRIELE
Executive Vice President	JOHN R. CAMP
Vice President	LOUISE A. BOYER
Treasurer	LAWRENCE H. LEVY
Comptroller and Assistant Treasurer	W. NEIL PIERCE
Secretary	FLOR P. BRENNAN
Assistant Secretary	JOHN FRENCH
Assistant Secretary	SONIA K. SHULTZ

270

INDEX

ABCAR, 35, 36, 56, 58-60, 147
ACAR, 35, 41, 49-51, 60
ACARESC, 55
ACARPA, 55
Acción Democrática, 85
achievement days (*see* rural youth club movement)
ADECO, 137
Adis Castro, Gonzalo, 139
Administrative Studies of the Forestry Service and the Extension Service of the Ministry of Agriculture, 94
Adventure of the Valiant Vitamin, 77
Agency for International Development, 26, 121, 164, 170, 171, 185
agrarian reform, 107, 108
Agrarian University, La Molina, Peru, 136
agreements (*see* AIA, operational techniques)
Agricultural and Forest Resources of the State of Barinas, 94
Agricultural and Forestry Survey of Guayana Area of Venezuela, 96
agricultural information program, Venezuela, 66, 99-105
Agricultural and Livestock Atlas of Venezuela, 94
Agricultural and Livestock Bank of Venezuela, 81, 97, 164, 192
agricultural production, Venezuela, 118, 119
Agricultural Research in Venezuela, 94
Agricultural Resources of the State of Yaracuy, 94
Agriculture in Brazil, 53, 165-167
Agriculture, Ministry of,
   Bolivia, 133
   Brazil, 17, 26, 30, 48, 170
   Paraguay, 176
   Peru, 132, 133
   Venezuela, 23, 87, 93, 97, 100, 103, 109, 115, 116, 142, 144
Agriculture, U.S. Department of, 25, 40, 175, 193

Agronomy, University School of, Maracay, 98
AIA, contributions by, 29, 41, 80, 115
   contributions to, 11, 188, 189
   evaluation, 123, 124
   evaluation of Venezuela program, 116-119
   operational techniques, 27-29
   purposes of, 10, 11
AIA Record, The, 15
AID (*see* Agency for International Development)
Aid to People's Film Project of Chinese Education Movement, 18
Allee, Ralph, 20, 21, 121, 122, 125, 126
Alliance for Progress, 107, 191, 192
Almeida, Rómulo de, 53
Amapá, territory of, 172
Amazon river, 172
Analysis of Governmental Policies Concerning the Prices and Marketing of the Milk Industry of Venezuela, 94
ANCAR, 53, 54, 56
ANCARBA, 54
ANCAR-Ceará, 54, 55
Anderson, H. Calvert, 126-128, 130-133, 137, 194
Andes, Development Corp. for, 96, 116
Andes, Venezuela, 85, 96, 115, 116
Andrade, Aurea Helena, 146, 147
Andrade, Carlos, 161
Andrade, Eduardo, 156
Andrade, João Napoleão de, 57-59
ants, leaf-cutting, 42
Antunes Foundation, 171, 172
Apodaca, Santiago D., 43, 145-148
Aragua, state of, 93, 96, 97, 105, 161
Aranha, Oswaldo, 31
Araujo, Antonio Martín, 71
Arce, Antonio M., 139
Argentina, 125, 133, 139
Arias, Edgar, 148, 162
Arkansas, 172
ASCAR, 55

271

274

278